You've got this.

This is the final stretch of your CPA Exam preparation – the Final Review. You've diligently studied these topics, and now it's crunch time. This Final Review has completely new content from the Becker CPA Exam Review and focuses on the key concepts on the CPA Exam. Remember, fortune favors the brave, but the CPA Exam favors the prepared.

Access Becker's Final Review

You can access Final Review under Additional Resources on each section home page when you log in to **cpa.becker.com** or when you use the mobile apps.

What's inside

Your Final Review is designed to mimic the actual CPA Exam, and has all-new task-based simulations and multiple-choice questions. If you need help at any point, remember that you still have access to the features of the CPA Exam Review, including:

- Access to 1-on-1 academic support from our experienced CPA instructors
- Unlimited practice tests to work on your weaknesses

You're not in it alone!

For tips, stories and advice, visit our blog at **becker.com/blog.** You can also collaborate with other Becker students studying REG on our Facebook study group at **facebook.com/groups/ BeckerREGStudyGroup/.**

Exam day tips

We want you to be prepared and confident when exam day rolls around. Here are some tips to keep in mind:

+ Arrive at least 30 minutes early on exam day.

+ Bring your NTS and two forms of identification.

+ Your cell phone is NOT allowed in the testing center, even during scheduled breaks.

+ No outside calculators are allowed. The testing software will have a built-in calculator for you to use.

+ Breathe. Relax. Ground yourself. You've got this.

S0-CPB-127

Becker™

ACADEMIC HELP
Click on Contact Academic Support from within the course software
at the top at cpa.becker.com

CUSTOMER SERVICE AND TECHNICAL SUPPORT
Call 1-877-CPA-EXAM (outside the U.S. +1-630-472-2213)
or contact us at www.becker.com/contact-us

This textbook contains information that was current at the time of printing.
Your course software will be updated on a regular basis as the content
that is tested on the CPA Exam evolves and as we improve our materials.
Note the version reference below and select your replacement textbook at
becker.com/cpa-replacements-upgrades to learn if a newer version of this
book is available to be ordered.

CPA Exam Review

Regulation Final Review

For Exams Scheduled
After June 30, 2022

V 4.2

COURSE DEVELOPMENT TEAM

Timothy F. Gearty, CPA, MBA, JD, CGMA . . . . Editor in Chief, Financial/Regulation (Tax) National Editor

Angeline S. Brown, CPA, CGMA. . . . . Sr. Director, Product Management

Michael Potenza, CPA, JD. . . . . Director, Curriculum

Lauren Chin, CPA . . . . Sr. Manager, Curriculum

Stephen Bergens, CPA. . . . . Manager, Accounting Curriculum

Nancy Gauldie, CPA . . . . Sr. Specialist, Curriculum

Bill Karalius, CPA. . . . . Sr. Specialist, Curriculum

Tom Cox, CPA, CMA . . . . Financial (GASB & NFP) National Editor

Steven J. Levin, JD . . . . Regulation (Law) National Editor

Danita De Jane . . . . Director, Course Development

Joe Antonio . . . . .Manager, Course Development

Shelly McCubbins, MBA. . . . . Project Manager, Course Development

CONTRIBUTING EDITORS

Teresa C. Anderson, CPA, CMA, MPA	Julie D. McGinty, CPA
Valerie Funk Anderson, CPA	Sandra McGuire, CPA, MBA
Heather Baiye, CPA, MBA	Stephanie Morris, CPA, MAcc
Katie Barnette, CPA	Michelle Moshe, CPA, DipIFR
Elliott G. Chester, CPA, CMA, CFE	Peter Olinto, JD, CPA
Courtney Chianello, CPA	Sandra Owen, JD, MBA, CPA
Cheryl Costello, CPA, CGMA	Michelle M. Pace, CPA
Jim DeSimpelare, CPA, MBA	Jennifer J. Rivers, CPA
Tara Z. Fisher, CPA	Josh Rosenberg, MBA, CPA, CFA, CFP
Melisa F. Galasso, CPA	Jonathan R. Rubin, CPA, MBA
R. Thomas Godwin, CPA, CGMA	Michael Rybak, CPA, CFA
Holly Hawk, CPA, CGMA	Jacob Shortt, CPA
Liliana Hickman-Riggs, CPA, CMA, CIA, CFE, CITP, CFF, CGMA, FCPA, MS	Denise M. Stefano, CPA, CGMA, MBA
	Elizabeth Lester Walsh, CPA, CITP
Patrice W. Johnson, CPA	

Permissions

Material from *Uniform CPA Examination Selected Questions and Unofficial Answers*, 1989–2022, copyright © by American Institute of Certified Public Accountants, Inc., is reprinted and/or adapted with permission.

Any knowing solicitation or disclosure of any questions or answers included on any CPA Examination is prohibited.

Regulation

Final Review Sections

Regulation Section I | *Ethics, Professional Responsibilities, and Federal Tax Procedures*

A   Ethics and Responsibilities in Tax Practice

B   Federal Tax Procedures

C   Legal Duties and Responsibilities

Regulation Section II | *Business Law*

A   Agency

B   Contracts

C   Debtor-Creditor Relationships

D   Federal Laws and Regulations

E   Business Structure

Regulation Section III | *Federal Taxation of Property Transactions*

A   Acquisition and Disposition of Assets

B   Cost Recovery

C   Gift Taxation

Regulation Section IV | *Federal Taxation of Individuals*

A   Filing Status and Dependents

B   Gross Income

C   Passive Activity Losses

D   Adjustments and Deductions to Arrive at Taxable Income

E   Tax Computations and Credits

Regulation Section V | *Federal Taxation of Entities*

A   Differences Between Book and Tax Income

B   C Corporations

C   S Corporations

D   Partnerships

E   Trusts

F   Tax-Exempt Organizations

Introduction

Final Review is a condensed review that reinforces your understanding of the most heavily tested concepts on the CPA Exam. It is designed to help focus your study time during those final days between your Becker CPA Exam Review course and your exam date.

This Book

Becker's Final Review is arranged based on the AICPA's blueprints. The blueprints outline the technical content to be tested on each of the four parts of the CPA Exam. The blueprints can be found in the back sections of Becker's main CPA textbooks.

The Software

The Final Review software uses an interactive eBook (IEB) format. Watch the introduction video in the Final Review software for a tour of the IEB features.

We recommend progressing through this course in the following order:

- Review the IEB content, including the video introduction to each topic and the lecture audio associated with each page of the IEB.
- Work the embedded multiple-choice questions for each topic as you progress through the content.
- Work the related multiple-choice questions in the question bank for each topic.
- Once you have completed all of the IEB sections, topics, and multiple-choice questions, do the practice Simulations in the software.

Becker Customer and Academic Support

You can access Becker's Customer and Academic Support from within the course software by clicking Contact Support at the top at:

cpa.becker.com

You can also access customer service and technical support by calling 1-877-CPA-EXAM (outside the U.S. +1-630-472-2213).

I

Ethics, Professional Responsibilities, and Federal Tax Procedures

A Ethics and Responsibilities in Tax Practice

B Federal Tax Procedures

C Legal Duties and Responsibilities

1 Treasury Department Circular 230

The publication addresses the practice before the IRS of "practitioners" with regard to the rules governing the authority to practice before the IRS, the duties and restrictions relating to practice before the IRS, the sanctions for violation of the regulations, and the rules applicable to disciplinary proceedings. Ethical considerations address the responsibilities of the practitioner with respect to preparing returns and representing clients before the IRS.

1.1 Duties and Restrictions of Tax Practitioners

A tax practitioner is responsible to the IRS and/or the client for the following:

- Refraining from willfully or recklessly signing a tax return or advising a client to take a tax position that the practitioner knows or should know lacks a reasonable basis or is a willful attempt to understate tax liability.

- Providing information requested unless the tax preparer believes in good faith and on reasonable grounds that the information is privileged.

- Avoiding delay of any matter before the IRS.

- Refraining from assisting anyone under disbarment or suspended from practice by the IRS.

- Adhering to the conflict of interest rules set forth by the IRS.

- Refraining from charging an unconscionable fee and only charge a contingent fee in certain allowable circumstances.

- Charging no more than the tax preparer's published written fee schedule, if one exists.

- Soliciting and advertising according to the parameters identified by the IRS.

- Adhering to "best practices" to provide clients with the highest quality representation.

- Refraining from endorsing or otherwise negotiating a client's refund check issued by the IRS.

- Refraining from notarizing a signature of any person in regard to any matter in which the tax preparer has an interest.

- Refraining from the unlicensed practice of law.

1.2 Standards With Respect to Tax Returns

1.2.1 Not Frivolous

A practitioner cannot advice a client to take a tax return position unless the position is not frivolous.

1.2.2 Reasonably Likely Penalties

The practitioner must inform the client of any penalties "reasonably likely" to apply with respect to a position taken on a tax return.

1.2.3 Practitioner's Reliance Upon Client-Furnished Information

Generally, a practitioner who signs the tax return or other document may rely "in good faith without verification" upon client-furnished information. The practitioner is not required to verify client-provided information; however, he must make reasonable inquiries if the client-furnished information appears to be questionable or incomplete.

1.2.4 Knowledge of Omission by a Client

The practitioner must advise the client promptly of any noncompliance, errors, or omissions in tax returns and other documents and the related consequences under the law.

1.2.5 Diligence as to Accuracy

The practitioner must exercise due diligence regarding (i) preparing returns and other documents; and (ii) determining the correctness of her/his representations to the IRS.

1.2.6 Return of Client Records

Generally, at the request of the client, the practitioner must return all client records.

1.3 Tax Advice

When a practitioner gives written advice regarding federal tax matters, the practitioner must base the advice on reasonable factual and legal assumptions, consider known relevant facts, use reasonable efforts to obtain relevant facts, not unreasonably rely on statements of the taxpayer or other persons, and refrain from taking into account that a return might not be audited.

1.4 Sanctions

The Secretary of the Treasury or her/his delegate, after conducting a proceeding, may censure (publicly reprimand), suspend, or disbar any practitioner from practice before the IRS if the practitioner (i) is shown to be incompetent or disreputable; (ii) fails to comply with Circular 230; or (iii) with intent to defraud, willingly and knowingly misleads or threatens a client or prospective client.

Question 1   MCQ-09715

Treasury Department Circular 230 provides rules regarding due diligence with respect to certain types of written advice regarding tax matters. These rules apply to which of the following types of written advice?

1. Covered opinions, as defined in the provisions.
2. Excluded opinions, as defined in the provisions.
3. Written advice relating to an entity or plan that has been used for the principal purpose of tax avoidance.
4. All written advice concerning one or more federal tax matters.

2 Internal Revenue Code and Regulations Related to Tax Return Preparers

Several sections of the Internal Revenue Code ("IRC") and related U.S. Treasury regulations govern the conduct of tax return preparers. Civil liabilities and penalties may be imposed on those who are guilty of misconduct.

2.1 Tax Return Preparer

A tax return preparer is any person who prepares, or employs other persons to prepare, a substantial portion of any federal tax return or claim for federal tax refund for compensation.

A tax return preparer does not include a person who:

- merely furnishes mechanical assistance (e.g., typing);
- prepares a return or claim for refund for an employer; or
- prepares a return or claim for refund as a fiduciary.

2.2 Conduct That Could Result in a Fine

- Preparing or signing a tax return when the practitioner does not have a valid tax preparer's ID;
- Understating a client's tax liability due to an unreasonable tax position;
- Understating a client's tax liability due to willful or reckless misconduct (negligent or intentional disregard of tax rules);
- Endorsing/negotiating a client's refund check;
- Failing to provide the client with a copy of his/her tax return;
- Failing to sign a tax return or refund claim;
- Failing to furnish the tax identification number of the tax return preparer;
- Failing to retain records properly;

- Failing to correct information returns;

- Failing to be diligent in determining a client's eligibility for the earned income credit;

- Aiding and abetting in the understatement of a client's tax liability; and

- Disclosing client supplied information without authority.

2.3 Preparer Responsibilities

A preparer must do the following:

1. Legally minimize the taxpayer's tax liability and abide by the tax code.

2. Make a reasonable attempt to obtain necessary information from the taxpayer and make inquiries if the information appears incorrect or incomplete. (Note, however, that the preparer is not responsible for verifying taxpayer-provided information.)

3. Recommend a tax return position only if the preparer has a good faith belief that position has a realistic possibility of being sustained if challenged.

4. Notify the taxpayer if the preparer becomes aware of a tax return error.

5. Upon becoming aware of a taxpayer's failure to file a return, inform the taxpayer on how to correct the situation.

6. Consider whether to continue a professional relationship if the taxpayer does not remedy the above situations (items 4 and 5); however, the preparer may not inform the IRS without the taxpayer's permission.

Question 2   MCQ-09712

A taxpayer presented her tax return preparer, Mr. Powell, with documentation supporting income she had earned as an independent contractor. Although Mr. Powell knew that the taxpayer's income should be reported on the taxpayer's Form 1040 (U.S. individual income tax return), he intentionally did not report the income on the taxpayer's tax return. Mr. Powell understated the taxpayer's liability because he believed keeping the tax liability low would help retain the taxpayer as a client. In this situation, Mr. Powell may be subject to which of the following penalties:

    1. Understatement of taxpayer's liability due to failure to follow substantial authority by the tax return preparer.

    2. Failure to file correct information returns by a tax return preparer.

    3. Wrongful disclosure or use of tax return information by the tax return preparer.

    4. Understatement of taxpayer's liability due to willful or reckless conduct of the tax return preparer.

---

1 The Internal Revenue Service Audit and Appeals Process

The federal income tax system of the United States is based on the self-assessment of taxes. All "persons" with taxable incomes exceeding certain amounts are required to file annual income tax returns and to remit taxes that are due in a timely manner.

1.1 Audit Process

The audit process is part of the enforcement system to ensure that this "voluntary" assessment and payment is actually occurring. A return may be examined (audited) for a variety of reasons, and the examination may take place in any one of several ways. After the audit, if there are any changes to the tax payable, the taxpayer either can agree with the changes and pay the additional tax or can disagree with the changes and appeal the decision. Interest on unpaid taxes may also be due.

1.2 Appeals Process

The Appeals Division is authorized to settle all tax disputes based on the hazards of litigation. Appeals within the IRS appeals process must come within the scope of the tax laws and cannot be on "moral, religious, political, constitutional, or similar grounds."

2 The Federal Judicial Process

When a taxpayer and the Internal Revenue Service cannot reach agreement on a tax matter using the administrative appeals process, the dispute must be settled in the Federal Court system. Either the IRS or the taxpayer can initiate the process. In the federal court system, the U.S. Tax Court, a U.S. District Court, and the U.S. Court of Federal Claims are considered trial courts. The U.S. Court of Appeals, the Federal Court of Appeals, and the U.S. Supreme Court are considered appellate courts (appellate courts do not hold trials). In most civil tax cases, the taxpayer has the burden of proof. In certain situations, however, the burden of proof shifts to the IRS.

For a taxpayer who chooses to litigate a tax position, which of the following courts should the taxpayer choose to start in if he does not want to pay the disputed tax in advance?

1. U.S. Supreme Court

2. U.S. District Court

3. U.S. Tax Court

4. U.S. Court of Federal Claims

3 Penalties Imposed on Taxpayers

The Internal Revenue Code contains many sections setting forth penalties, both civil and criminal, which the Internal Revenue Service can seek to impose to the taxpayer.

3.1 Common Penalties That Apply to Taxpayers

- Earned income credit penalty
- Penalty for failure to make estimated income tax payments
- Failure-to-file penalty
- Failure-to-pay penalty
- Negligence penalty with respect to an understatement of tax
- Penalty for substantial underpayment of tax
- Penalty for substantial valuation misstatement
- Fraud penalties

3.2 Defenses Available to Taxpayers

Generally, a taxpayer can avoid any penalty by showing that the taxpayer had reasonable cause to support the tax return position, acted in good faith, and did not have willful neglect. In addition to this, various defenses (based on the standards of compliance) are available to taxpayers.

3.2.1 A Position That Is Not Frivolous

A frivolous position is a position taken on the return that is patently improper, and it is not a defense to avoid any penalty. A position that is not frivolous is not patently improper, but arguable. Not having a frivolous position is not a sufficient basis to avoid penalties—even if the tax return discloses the tax position.

3.2.2   Reasonable Basis Standard

The reasonable basis standard is a position that has at least a 20 percent chance of succeeding, one that is arguable but fairly unlikely to prevail in court. This standard is not met if the taxpayer fails to make a reasonable attempt to determine the correctness of a position that seems too good to be true. This basis will avoid the negligence penalty with respect to an understatement of tax that is not substantial and the penalty for rules or regulations, even if the taxpayer does not disclose the tax return position for which the taxpayer has a reasonable basis. This basis will avoid the substantial underpayment penalty only if the taxpayer discloses the tax return position (except for tax shelters) for which the taxpayer has a reasonable basis.

3.2.3   Substantial Authority Standard

The substantial authority standard is a position that has more than a 40 percent chance of succeeding in court. This basis will avoid the substantial underpayment penalty even if the taxpayer does not disclose the tax return position (except for tax shelters) for which the taxpayer has substantial authority.

3.2.4   More-Likely-Than-Not Standard

The more-likely-than-not standard is a position that has more than a 50 percent chance of succeeding. With respect to certain nondisclosed tax shelters, this basis will avoid both the negligence penalty with respect to an understatement of tax that is not substantial and the substantial underpayment penalty.

Question 2   MCQ-09705

Irving R. Spayer has not filed federal income tax returns or paid any federal income taxes for the last several decades because he feels that the federal income tax is unconstitutional. Which of the following penalties might apply to him?

1. The failure-to-file penalty in the amount of 10 percent of the tax due for each year (or fraction thereof) the return is not filed.

2. The failure-to-pay penalty in the amount of one-half of one percent of the tax due for each month (or fraction thereof), up to a maximum of 25 percent of the unpaid tax.

3. The total of the failure-to-file penalty and the failure-to-pay penalty.

4. The failure to file penalty of $220 for each month or part thereof (up to a maximum of 12 months) the return is late.

---

1 Common Law Duties and Liability to Clients and Third Parties

1.1 Liability for Negligence

1.1.1 Liability to Clients for Negligence—Four Elements

- **Duty of Care:** The accountant must owe a duty of care to the party harmed.

- **Breach:** The accountant breaches by failing to use due care. Failure to use due care occurs when the accountant fails to act as a reasonably prudent accountant (usually a failure to follow GAAS or GAAP).

- **Damages:** There must be some type of harm suffered.

- **Causation:** The damages must be caused by the accountant's negligence.

1.1.2 Liability to Third Parties for Negligence—Privity Defense

- **Liability:** Accountants are usually not liable to third parties for negligence because there is no *privity of contract* (no direct relationship between the accountant and the third party). Privity is only a defense to a lawsuit for negligence. It is not a defense to fraud.

- **Exception:** An accountant is liable to third parties for negligence if the accountant had reason to know the third party would rely on the accountant's work. This is the *third-party beneficiary rule* or *intended user* rule.

- **Ultramares Rule (Minority View):** The accountant is liable to third parties for negligence only if there is privity of contract or the accountant knows the exact name of the third party who will be relying on the accountant's work.

1.2 Liability for Fraud

- **Actual Fraud:** Actual fraud has the same five elements covered in the section on contracts (**MAIDS**: **M**aterial misrepresentation of fact, **A**ctual reliance, **I**ntent to induce reliance, **D**amages, and **S**cienter).

- **Constructive Fraud or Gross Negligence:** Constructive fraud has the same elements of actual fraud, but scienter is replaced by a lower standard—reckless disregard for the truth.

Question 1   MCQ-09540

Rhodes Corp. desired to acquire the common stock of Harris Corp. and engaged Johnson & Co., CPAs, to audit the financial statements of Harris Corp. Johnson failed to discover a significant liability in performing the audit. In a common law action against Johnson, Rhodes at a minimum must prove:

1. Gross negligence on the part of Johnson.
2. Negligence on the part of Johnson.
3. Fraud on the part of Johnson.
4. Johnson knew that the liability existed.

Question 2   MCQ-09572

If a stockholder sues a CPA for common law fraud based on false statements audited by the CPA, which of the following, if present, would be the CPA's best defense?

1. The stockholder lacks privity to sue.
2. The false statements were immaterial.
3. The CPA did not financially benefit from the alleged fraud.
4. The contributory negligence of the client.

2 Confidential Client Information

Confidential client information generally cannot be revealed to others without the client's consent.

- If subpoenaed, the accountant must testify, unless the given state recognizes accountant-client privilege.
- Confidential information must be revealed to the state CPA society's voluntary quality control review board.
- Working papers belong to the accountant, not the client, but the same rules of confidentiality apply.

Question 3

MCQ-09492

The accountant-client privilege:

1. May not be waived by the client.

2. Does not prohibit an accountant from disclosing confidential client information without the consent of the client to a voluntary quality control review board.

3. Is as widely recognized as the attorney-client privilege.

4. Only applies to written documents.

II | Business Law

Notes

1 Formation and Termination

1.1 Formation

An agent is anyone authorized to act for another. Minors can be agents.

1.1.1 Requirements for an Agency

An agency requires assent, but does not require consideration or a writing. Only agencies for sale of land or agencies impossible to complete in one year require a writing in most states.

1.1.2 Power of Attorney

Power of attorney is a written authorization of agency.

- The principal, not the agent, is the only party required to sign the power of attorney.
- The agent need not be an attorney at law.
- A power of attorney usually limits the agent's authority to specific tasks.

1.2 Termination

1.2.1 Terminable at Will

Most agencies are terminable at will, but if either party breaches a contract by terminating it, he is liable for damages.

1.2.2 Termination by Law

The following terminate an agency immediately:

- Death or insanity of either party (although in many states, death of the principal will not terminate the agent's authority until the agent has knowledge of the death).
- Bankruptcy of the principal, but not bankruptcy of the agent.
- Failure of the agent to have a required license.
- Destruction of the subject matter of the agency.

1.2.3 Notice

If an agent resigns or is terminated by the principal, to terminate apparent authority, the principal must give actual notice to persons with whom the agent has dealt and constructive notice (e.g., by advertisement in the newspaper) to all others.

1.2.4 Agency Coupled With an Interest

Agency coupled with an interest is not terminable by the principal.

- An agent has interest in the subject matter of the agency (such as a security interest or a buyer of stock who was appointed the seller's agent to vote the stock).

- Death or insanity of the principal does not end this agency.

Question 1   MCQ-09559

Owner sells his stock in ABC Corporation to Buyer and appoints Buyer as his agent to vote the stock at a shareholders' meeting that will be held the following week. The agency appointment provides that it is irrevocable. Which of the following statements is true?

1. Owner can revoke the appointment anytime before the meeting despite the language stating that the agency is irrevocable.

2. Buyer's appointment will be revoked by operation of law if Owner dies before the shareholders' meeting.

3. The agency cannot be terminated by either Owner or Buyer because it is coupled with an interest.

4. The agency may be terminated only by Buyer.

---

2 Authority of Agents and Principals

2.1 Actual Authority

Actual authority may be either express or implied. Express authority is the power that the principal specifically tells the agent that the agent has. Implied authority is the power that the agent reasonably believes the agent has based on the communications and past dealings between the principal and agent (e.g., authority to do whatever is reasonably necessary to do assigned tasks; authority to do what the principal has allowed the agent to do in the past).

2.2 Apparent Authority

Apparent authority arises from the principal's communications or actions toward third parties, which make it appear to the third parties that the agent is authorized.

- The law looks to see if it was reasonable for the third party to believe the agent was authorized.

- Secret instructions given to the agent have no effect on apparent authority unless the third party was aware of the instruction.

2.3   Agency by Estoppel

Where no actual agency relationship exists, if a person intentionally or carelessly causes a third party to believe another person is his or her agent and the third party detrimentally and justifiably relies on this belief, the person will be estopped (legally barred) from denying the other person acted as his or her authorized agent and so will be bound.

Question 2   MCQ-09479

Terrence has been Pauline's agent in the liquor business for 10 years and has made numerous contracts on Pauline's behalf. Under which of the following situations could Terrence continue to have the power to bind Pauline?

1. Terrence lost his license to sell liquor in that state.
2. The death of Pauline with Terrence's knowledge.
3. The bankruptcy of Pauline with Terrence's knowledge.
4. The firing of Terrence by Pauline.

---

3   Duties and Liabilities of Agents and Principals

3.1   Duties of the Principal and Agent

- Unless otherwise agreed, the principal owes the agent the *duty to reimburse* the agent for expenses while acting on the principal's behalf, the *duty to compensate* the agent, and the *duty to indemnify* the agent for losses incurred while acting on the principal's behalf.

- Unless otherwise agreed, the agent owes the principal the *duty of due care*, the *duty to inform* the principal of all relevant facts, the *duty to account* for money spent or received, the fiduciary *duty of loyalty*, and the *duty of obedience*.

3.2   Liability for Contracts

3.2.1   Liability of the Principal

- The principal is liable for all authorized contracts made by the agent (whether authority was express, implied, or apparent and whether the principal was disclosed, unidentified/partially disclosed, or undisclosed).

- The principal is not liable for unauthorized contracts unless the principal ratifies the contract.

3.2.2 Ratification

- The principal must know all relevant facts to ratify the contract.

- If the principal accepts the benefits of the contract knowing all of its material terms, the principal has impliedly ratified.

- In most states, the principal cannot ratify unless the agent indicated to the third party when making the contract that he was doing so on behalf of the principal.

- Once the principal ratifies the contract, the third party cannot withdraw from the contract.

3.2.3 Liability of the Agent

- The agent is liable (in warranty) for all unauthorized contracts.

- The agent is not liable for authorized contracts unless she was acting for an undisclosed or partially disclosed principal.

3.3 Undisclosed or Unidentified/Partially Disclosed Principal

- If the agent had authority, both the principal and the agent are liable in an undisclosed and unidentified/partially disclosed principal case.

- The third party cannot withdraw from the contract because of an undisclosed or unidentified/partially disclosed principal unless the nondisclosure was fraudulent.

3.3.1 Unidentified/Partially Disclosed Principal

The agent reveals to the third party that there is a principal, but does not disclose the principal's identity.

3.3.2 Undisclosed Principal

The agent never reveals to the third party that there is a principal involved. An agent for an undisclosed principal can only have actual authority, not apparent authority.

3.4 Liability for Torts—Respondeat Superior

- The principal is liable for all torts of employees committed while the employee was acting in the scope of employment (i.e., doing something in connection with the job).

- The principal generally is not liable for the torts of independent contractors.

- The difference between an employee and an independent contractor is that the principal controls the manner in which work is performed as to an employee but not as to an independent contractor.

- The principal is liable even if the employee disobeyed instructions.

- The agent is also liable for torts the agent commits, even if the agent was following the principal's orders.

Question 3
MCQ-09495

Able, on behalf of Pix Corp., entered into a contract with Sky Corp., by which Sky agreed to sell computer equipment to Pix. Able disclosed to Sky that she was acting on behalf of Pix. However, Able had exceeded her actual authority by entering into the contract with Sky.

If Pix wishes to ratify the contract with Sky, which of the following statements is correct?

1. Pix must notify Sky that Pix intends to ratify the contract.
2. Able must have acted reasonably and in Pix's best interest.
3. Able must be a general agent of Pix.
4. Pix must have knowledge of all material facts relating to the contract at the time it is ratified.

Question 4
MCQ-09590

Phil asks his employee Ed to take a company truck to deliver some lumber to a customer, Carl. After delivering the lumber, Ed drives 10 miles beyond the customer's house to visit his mother at her house. While pulling the truck into his mother's driveway, Ed negligently strikes a pedestrian, Vic. If Vic sues Phil for his injuries, will Vic likely recover?

1. Yes, because Ed was Phil's employee.
2. Yes, because Ed was driving Phil's truck.
3. No, because Ed was negligent.
4. No, because the collision did not occur within the scope of Ed's employment.

1 Formation

A contract is a promise or set of promises that the law will enforce.

1.1 Offer

1.1.1 Making an Offer

- An offer must be seriously intended, communicated, and definite in its terms.

- Advertisements and price quotes generally are not offers, but rather are invitations to deal.

1.1.2 Termination of Offers

- An offeror can revoke an offer. Revocation is effective when received. Most offers can be revoked any time prior to acceptance except option contracts, merchant's firm offers under the Sales Article, and offers for unilateral contracts where there has been a substantial beginning in performance.

- An offeree can terminate an offer through a rejection. The offeree can reject expressly (e.g., by saying "no") or through making a counteroffer, which is considered to be both a rejection of the original offer and an offer (of which the original offeror is now the offeree who may accept or reject). A rejection is effective when received.

- An offer can also be terminated by operation of law. For example, destruction of the subject matter, death or incompetency of either party, or illegality all would end an offer immediately.

- An offer will end at its stated time, and if no time is stated, it ends after a reasonable time.

1.2 Acceptance

An acceptance must be communicated, but it need not be in writing. An offer can only be accepted by the party to whom it was made; an offer is not assignable unless the offer is an option contract (i.e., consideration was given to keep the offer open).

1.2.1 Common Law vs. Sales Article

- At common law (e.g., contracts for land or services), an offeree must assent to every term in the offer without change or addition; otherwise the offeree makes a counteroffer (i.e., the mirror image rule).

- On the other hand, new or different terms in an acceptance of a contract under the Sales Article generally do not affect the validity of the acceptance and do not prevent formation of a contract.

1.2.2 Mailbox Rule

- An acceptance is valid when sent if properly addressed and stamped and the offeree uses either the expressed means of communication or any reasonable means of communication if the means was not expressed.

- If an offer states the acceptance must be received to be effective, then it must be received (i.e., one may opt-out of the mailbox rule this way).

1.3 Consideration

Consideration must have legal value and must be mutually bargained for.

1.3.1 Legal Value

- Legal value is doing something you are legally free not to do or refraining from doing something that you are allowed to do. It need not have monetary value or be of value equal to what it is exchanged for.

- There is no consideration given when you are already contractually obligated to perform. Past consideration is not valid consideration. Thus, to modify an existing common law contract, both parties must give additional consideration.

1.3.2 Mutually Bargained For

"Mutually bargained for" means consideration was given in exchange for the other party's consideration.

1.3.3 When Consideration Is Not Required

No consideration is needed to modify a contract under the UCC Sales Article, to make enforceable a promise to pay a debt barred by the statute of limitations, or where there is foreseeable and reasonable detrimental reliance.

1.4 Defenses to Formation

1.4.1 Fraud

Actual fraud has five elements—**MAIDS**:

M = **M**isrepresentation of **M**aterial fact or deliberate concealment (opinions do not count unless made by an expert).

A = **A**ctual and reasonable reliance: The victim actually and reasonably relied on the misrepresentation.

I = **I**ntent to induce reliance: The misrepresentation was made with the intention that it be relied upon.

D = **D**amages: The defrauder is liable to anyone suffering harm.

S = **S**cienter: An intent to deceive, done knowingly or intentionally.

1.4.2 Innocent Misrepresentation (Comparison)

Innocent misrepresentation involves the same elements as actual fraud, except there is no scienter requirement.

1.4.3 Fraud in the Execution and Fraud in the Inducement

- **Fraud in the Execution:** The victim never knew a contract was being made. It makes a contract void.

- **Fraud in the Inducement:** Occurs when the victim knows a contract is being made, but terms are misrepresented. This makes a contract *voidable* (the defrauded party can disaffirm or rescind).

1.4.4 Duress

Duress is forcing someone into a contract by threat of violence or criminal action. The duress must actually induce the victim to make the contract.

1.4.5 Mistake

- **General Rule:** A mutual mistake allows the adversely affected party to avoid the contract. A unilateral mistake usually is not a defense.

- **Exception:** *Unilateral mistakes of material fact* make a contract voidable if the other party *knew or should have known a mistake* was being made.

1.4.6 Illegality—Contract Generally Void

If the consideration or the subject matter of a contract is illegal or becomes illegal after the contract is made, the contract generally is *void* unless the illegality is merely because a party failed to have a license that is required for revenue-raising purposes.

1.4.7 Minority

- Minors can disaffirm *anytime* while a *minor* or within a *reasonable* time thereafter.

- Minors cannot disaffirm contracts for necessities.

- Minors can ratify only after becoming an adult. They must ratify the entire contract, not just part.

1.4.8 Incompetency and Intoxication

Legally incompetent persons are not bound by their contracts. Intoxicated persons can disaffirm only if they were incapable of understanding what they were doing when the contract was made.

Question 1 MCQ-09456

The president of Deal Corporation wrote to Boyd, offering to sell the Deal factory for $300,000. The offer was sent by Deal on June 5 and was received by Boyd on June 9. The offer stated it would remain open until December 20. The offer:

   1. Constitutes an enforceable option.

   2. May be revoked by Deal any time prior to Boyd's acceptance.

   3. Is a firm offer under the UCC but will be irrevocable for only three months.

   4. Is a firm offer under the UCC because it is in writing.

---

2 Performance

2.1 Statute of Limitations

Statutes of limitations provide that lawsuits must be commenced within a certain period of time (for contracts, four to six years is typical). Generally, if the statute of limitations period has expired on a contract, it is unenforceable. Actions for breach usually are measured from the time of the breach rather than from the time the contract was made.

2.2 Statute of Frauds

2.2.1 Contracts Requiring Some Type of Writing

Six types of contracts require some type of writing—**MYLEGS**:

M = **M**arriage: Contracts where *marriage is the consideration.*

Y = **Y**ear: Contracts *impossible to perform within one year.*

L = **L**and: Contracts involving an *interest in real estate.*

E = **E**xecutor: Contracts by an executor promising *to be personally liable* for the debt of an estate.

G = **G**oods: Contracts for the *sale of goods for $500 or more.*

S = **S**uretyship: Contracts to *act as a surety* (promise to pay the debt of another).

2.2.2 Type of Writing Needed to Satisfy the Statute of Frauds

■ The "contract" itself need not be in writing; any type of writing that states the material terms is sufficient.

■ The writing need only be signed by one party, but the contract can only be enforced against the one who signed.

■ The terms can be stated in more than one document.

2.3 Parol Evidence Rule

■ Prior oral or written statements and contemporaneous oral statements generally cannot be admitted into evidence at trial in an attempt to vary the terms of a fully integrated (i.e., seemingly complete) written contract.

■ You may always introduce evidence of the following:

  • Subsequent modifications

  • Explanations of ambiguities

  • Fraud, duress, or mistake

3 Discharge and Remedies

3.1 Discharge

3.1.1 Discharge by Performance or Prevention of Performance

Performance or tender of performance discharges a party. If a party hinders another party's performance, the hindrance constitutes a waiver of the condition of performance.

3.1.2 A Material Breach by One Party Discharges or Releases the Other

- **Exception:** At common law, if one party has substantially performed but commits a minor breach, no discharge occurs. The breaching party may recover under the contract, but damages are subtracted for the minor breach.

- **Anticipatory Repudiation:** An anticipatory repudiation occurs when one party, prior to the time of performance, states they won't perform. The nonrepudiating party may cancel the contract, sue immediately, or wait until the time of performance and then sue.

3.1.3 Discharge by Agreement

- **Accord and Satisfaction:** An accord is an agreement to substitute one contract for another, and satisfaction is the execution of the accord. Accord and satisfaction discharge the original duty. Until the accord is satisfied, a party may sue under the original contract or the accord.

- **Novation:** In a novation, the parties agree to replace one party in a contract with a new party. It is the same deal, but with new parties. The creditor releases the old party and looks only to the new party for performance.

3.1.4 Discharge by Operation of Law

■ **Impossibility of Performance:** Will release all parties to a contract. Examples of impossibility of performance are death of party in a personal service contract or destruction of the subject matter prior to performance.

3.2 Remedies

3.2.1 Compensatory Damages

An award of money to compensate for all foreseeable harm done.

3.2.2 Specific Performance

■ Specific performance is a court order that the breaching party "specifically perform" contract duties. It is only used with unique property and never with personal service contracts.

■ Courts will not award both money damages and specific performance.

3.2.3 Liquidated Damages

■ The parties agree in advance what damages will be if there is a breach (e.g., forfeiture of a down payment).

■ Liquidated damages must be a reasonable estimate of the actual harm likely to be caused by a breach, and not a penalty.

Question 2   MCQ-09612

Lark, CPA, entered into a signed contract with Bale Corp. to perform management advisory services for Bale. If Lark repudiates the contract prior to the date performance is to begin and Bale Corp. had not yet performed, which of the following is *not* correct?

1. Bale could successfully maintain an action for breach of contract prior to the date performance is due to begin.

2. Bale can obtain a judgment for the monetary damages it incurred as a result of the repudiation.

3. Bale could successfully maintain an action for breach of contract after the date performance was due to begin.

4. Bale can obtain a judgment ordering Lark to perform.

---

4 Sales Contracts

4.1 Formation of a Sales Contract

The Sales Article (UCC Article 2) governs sales of goods: moveable personal property. It doesn't govern contracts involving personal services, real estate, or intangible personal property.

4.1.1 Acceptance Need Not Mirror Offer

Under the Sales Article, an acceptance generally will be valid even if it includes terms different from or in addition to the terms stated in the offer.

4.1.2 Can Accept by Prompt Shipment

The seller can accept an order for goods by prompt shipment. If the seller ships nonconforming goods, the seller has both accepted and breached the contract, unless the seller notifies the buyer that the nonconforming goods were sent only as an accommodation.

4.1.3 Merchants

A merchant is one who ordinarily sells goods of the type being sold or who has special knowledge regarding the goods being sold or practices involved. Special rules apply to merchants.

4.1.4 Good Faith

All parties in a sales contract must act in good faith.

4.1.5 Can Modify a Sales Contract Without Additional Consideration

Contracts for the sale of goods can be modified without new consideration, as long as the modification is sought in good faith. To modify the price to $500 or more, a writing is required.

4.2 Merchant's Firm Offer Rule

- A merchant's firm offer is irrevocable without consideration.
- The offer must be for the sale of goods, made by a merchant, be in writing, and guarantee that it will be held open.
- The offer is irrevocable for the time stated, but the maximum period is three months. If no time is stated, it is irrevocable for a reasonable time.

4.3 Duties of Seller and Buyer

4.3.1 Seller's Basic Duties

- Unless otherwise agreed, the basic duties of a seller are to hold conforming goods for the buyer and give reasonable notice to enable the buyer to take delivery. If no place of delivery is stated, the place is the seller's place of business or, if none, the seller's home.

- The seller must make a perfect tender—no defects are allowed. If the goods are nonconforming in any way, the buyer may reject by notifying the seller within a reasonable time and following the seller's reasonable instructions.

- The buyer may reject all, some, or none of the goods.

4.3.2 Buyer's Basic Duties

Unless otherwise agreed, the buyer's basic duties are to accept conforming goods and pay for them at delivery.

4.4 Sales Statute of Frauds Exceptions

Generally, to be enforceable, contracts for the sale of goods for $500 or more must be evidenced by a writing signed by the party being sued (and include the quantity, unless it is an output or requirements contract). However, no writing is required with respect to: (i) specially manufactured goods or (ii) where a merchant sends another merchant a written confirmation of a contract that is sufficient to bind the sender and the recipient does not object within 10 days (confirmatory memo rule).

4.5 Rules for Risk of Loss (ROL)

Risk of loss (that is, whether the buyer or seller will bear a loss if the goods are damaged or destroyed) is determined by the delivery terms rather than by when title passes. However, title typically passes on delivery unless the parties agree otherwise.

4.5.1 Identification and Agreement

- For ROL and title to pass, the goods must first be identified as the ones that will fulfill the contract (set aside or designated as such).

- Once identified, the most important factor is the agreement between the parties.

- If the parties have not agreed, ROL is determined by the rules below.

4.5.2 Contracts Involving Transportation by Common Carrier

If transportation is by a common carrier, it is either a shipment contract or destination contract.

- **Shipment Contracts:** ROL and title pass to the buyer when the seller delivers the goods to a carrier.

- **Destination Contracts:** These are FOB contracts for a place other than the seller's location. ROL and title pass when goods reach the destination and the seller tenders delivery.

4.5.3 Contracts With No Common Carrier

- **Merchant Sellers:** ROL passes only when the buyer takes physical possession of the goods.

- **Nonmerchants:** ROL passes to the buyer upon the seller's tender of delivery.

4.5.4 Nonconforming Goods

ROL is always on the seller, regardless of the shipping terms.

4.5.5 Terms Affecting ROL

- **FOB:** "Free on board"; fixes the place where title and ROL will pass.

- **Sale on Approval:** ROL passes only after the buyer approves.

- **Sale or Return:** ROL passes on delivery, but the buyer has the right to return the goods.

4.6 Warranties—Express and Implied

4.6.1 Express Warranties

- Express warranties arise from a seller's statements of fact, description, sample, or model. The goods must conform to the statement of fact, description, sample, or model.

- The express warranty must have been part of the basis of the bargain.

- Once made, an express warranty generally cannot be disclaimed.

4.6.2 Three Types of Implied Warranties

Implied warranties require no written or oral words, and all implied warranties can be disclaimed.

- **Merchantability**

  Merchant sellers impliedly promise goods are fit and safe for normal uses. Such warranties may be disclaimed orally by an "as is" sale or by telling the buyer there is no warranty of merchantability. If a disclaimer is in writing, it must be conspicuous.

- **Title**

  All sellers impliedly promise good title and no unstated liens or attachments (encumbrances). Merchant sellers also promise no patent or trademark violations (infringements). To disclaim title requires very specific language (e.g., "as is," "with all faults," and the like are insufficient to disclaim the warranty of title). Can also be disclaimed by circumstances, such as a judicial sale where title is not guaranteed.

- **Fitness for a Particular Purpose**

  If the buyer tells the seller of a particular purpose for which the goods are needed and relies on the seller to provide goods fit for that purpose, and the seller knows of this reliance, there is a warranty that the goods will be fit for that purpose. Can be made by any seller—merchant or nonmerchant. Most disclaimers require a writing, except for an "as is" sale, which can be oral.

4.7 Remedies of Buyer and Seller

▪ If one party has reasonable grounds to believe the other party will not perform when required, the unsure party may make written demand for assurances of performance. Failure to give assurance within a reasonable time is an anticipatory repudiation (below).

▪ In the case of an anticipatory repudiation (that is, an indication by one of the parties that he or she will not perform), the nonbreaching party may: (i) sue immediately, (ii) cancel the contract, (iii) demand assurances, or (iv) await performance and sue later if the party does not perform.

▪ Punitive damages are not available, and neither party may recover avoidable damages (that is, both parties have a duty to take reasonable steps to mitigate damages).

4.8 Remedies of the Buyer Upon Seller's Breach

▪ Buyer is entitled to a perfect tender and may seek a remedy for any nonconformity.

▪ The buyer can *rescind* (cancel) *and sue* for money damages.

▪ The buyer can *cover* (buy suitable goods elsewhere) and charge the seller for the difference between the contract price and the cost of cover (or the difference between the market price and the contract price), plus incidental and consequential damages.

▪ The buyer can *recover goods* from an insolvent seller if the goods are identified as the ones under the contract.

▪ *Specific performance* is available if the goods are unique or the buyer otherwise cannot cover.

4.9 Remedies of the Seller Upon the Buyer's Breach—Unaccepted Goods

▪ The seller can *stop delivery* for any breach.

▪ If the buyer is insolvent the seller can *stop delivery and demand cash*.

▪ The seller can *resell and sue for money damages*. The seller can get the full contract price if the goods cannot be resold or if the goods were destroyed after ROL passed to the buyer.

▪ A *liquidated damage clause* is enforceable if it is reasonable and not a penalty.

4.10 Entrusting

If the owner of goods entrusts them to a merchant who deals in goods of the kind sold, and the merchant sells them in the ordinary course of business to a bona fide purchaser for value, the purchaser gets good title even though the merchant did not have good title.

Question 3
MCQ-09505

Greed Co. telephoned Stieb Co. and ordered 30 tables at $100 each. Greed agreed to pay 15% immediately and the balance within 30 days after receipt of the entire shipment. Greed forwarded a check for $450 and Stieb shipped 15 tables the next day, intending to ship the balance by the end of the week. Greed decided that the contract was a bad bargain and repudiated it. Stieb sued Greed. Which of the following will allow Stieb to enforce the contract in its entirety despite the statute of frauds?

1. Stieb shipped 15 tables.

2. Greed paid 15% down.

3. The contract is *not* within the requirements of the statute of frauds.

4. Greed admitted in court that it made the contract in question.

Question 4
MCQ-09489

Kirk Corp. sold Nix an Ajax freezer, Model 24, for $890. The contract required delivery to be made by June 23. On June 12, Kirk delivered an Ajax freezer, Model 52 to Nix. Nix immediately notified Kirk that the wrong freezer had been delivered and indicated that the delivery of a correct freezer would not be acceptable. Kirk wishes to deliver an Ajax freezer, Model 24, on June 23. Which of the following statements is correct?

1. Kirk may deliver the freezer on June 23 without further notice to Nix.

2. Kirk may deliver the freezer on June 23 if it first reasonably notifies Nix of its intent to do so.

3. Nix must accept the nonconforming freezer but may recover damages.

4. Nix always may reject the nonconforming freezer and refuse delivery of a conforming freezer on June 23.

1 Suretyship

1.1 The Relationship

1.1.1 Surety Defined

A surety is a third party who promises to pay a creditor if a debtor does not pay. The Statute of Frauds requires a writing signed by the surety for the surety's promise to be enforceable.

1.1.2 Gratuitous Surety

A gratuitous surety is not compensated for his or her promise to the creditor.

- Consideration is present if the gratuitous suretyship is created when the creditor-debtor relationship is created, because the consideration flowing to the debtor also serves as consideration for the surety's promise.

- A suretyship promise made *after* the creditor-debtor relationship has been created will not bind the gratuitous surety, due to lack of consideration.

- Any variation of the surety's risk by the creditor will release a gratuitous surety.

1.1.3 Compensated Surety

A compensated surety is paid for his or her promise to the creditor.

- A compensated surety's compensation serves as consideration for his or her promise, so the promise is binding even if made after the creditor-debtor relationship is created.

- Only a material variation of the compensated surety's risk by the creditor will release a compensated surety.

1.2 Creditors' Rights Upon Debtor Default

A creditor may do any of the following, in any order, upon the debtor's default. The creditor cannot be compelled by the surety to take any specific action.

- The creditor may immediately demand payment from the debtor.

- The creditor may immediately demand payment from the surety.

- The creditor may immediately go after collateral, if there is any.

- Exception: A surety who signs as a "guarantor of collectibility" promises to pay the creditor only after the creditor exhausts all remedies against the debtor. Additionally, the creditor must give notice of default to the guarantor.

1.3 Rights of a Surety

1.3.1 Subrogation

Once a surety pays the creditor in full, the surety acquires all of the creditors' rights (e.g., if the creditor was a secured creditor, the surety would have the rights of a secured creditor to the collateral).

1.3.2 Reimbursement (Also Called Indemnification)

The surety has the right to recover (i.e., to be reimbursed) from the debtor any money the surety had to pay the creditor due to the debtor's default.

1.3.3 Exoneration

Exoneration is the right of a surety to obtain a court order prior to default demanding that the debtor pay.

1.4 Cosureties and the Right of Contribution

1.4.1 Cosureties

Cosureties are two or more sureties of the same debt, even if unaware of each other.

1.4.2 Contribution

Once one cosurety pays the creditor, she may obtain a pro rata contribution from the other cosureties.

- The right of contribution is only available for cosureties.
- The proportional liability of each cosurety is determined by this formula:

$$\frac{\text{Amount guaranteed by individual cosurety}}{\text{Amount guaranteed by all cosureties}} \times \text{Amount paid} = \text{Amount owed by cosurety}$$

- If a cosurety's obligation is discharged in bankruptcy, the surety's agreed share should not be considered in determining the pro rata share of the remaining cosureties. The cosurety is eliminated from the calculation. Nothing can be collected from debts discharged in bankruptcy.

1.4.3 Defenses of a Surety Against a Creditor

- **Lack of a Writing and Lack of Consideration:** These are valid defenses for a surety.
- **Performance or Tender of Performance by Debtor:** This is a valid defense.
- **Fraud by the Creditor:** This is a valid defense.

  Fraud by the debtor to induce the surety to enter the relationship is not a valid defense for the surety against the creditor unless the creditor was aware of the fraud.

1.4.4 Personal Defenses of the Debtor

The surety may not use defenses that are personal to the debtor.

- Examples of personal defenses include bankruptcy of the debtor, the debtor's infancy or the debtor's insanity.
- The surety may use infancy, insanity, or bankruptcy as a defense if the surety was an infant, insane, or bankrupt.

1.4.5 Extension of Time

The creditor and debtor agree to extend the debtor's time of payment.

- Any extension of time discharges a gratuitous surety.
- A compensated surety is discharged only if the extension of time materially increased the surety's risk.
- If the creditor does not agree to extend time, but rather merely delays in collection, the surety is not discharged.

1.4.6 Release of Collateral by the Creditor

Release of collateral by the creditor discharges the surety to the extent of the monetary value of the collateral.

1.4.7 Release of a Cosurety

A release of a cosurety without the consent of the other cosureties releases the remaining cosureties by the amount of contribution they could have collected from the released cosurety.

Question 1   MCQ-09587

Which of the following rights may a surety not assert against his or her principal?

   1. Exoneration.
   2. Contribution.
   3. Subrogation.
   4. Reimbursement.

1.5 Creditors' Rights Outside of Suretyship

1.5.1 Creditors' Composition

A creditor's composition is an agreement between the debtor and at least two creditors that the debtor pays the creditors less than their full claims in full satisfaction of their claims. It results in the debtor being discharged in full for the debts owed the participating creditors.

1.5.2 Assignment for the Benefit of Creditors

In an assignment for the benefit of creditors, the debtor transfers some or all of his or her property to a trustee, who disposes of the property and uses the proceeds to satisfy the debtor's debts. The debtor is not discharged from unpaid debts by this procedure since creditors do not agree to any discharge.

1.5.3 Prejudgment Attachment

Before final judgment in a suit on a debt is rendered, if the creditor has reason to believe that the debtor will not pay, the creditor can ask the court to provisionally attach a piece of the debtor's property. The court then issues a writ of attachment (to the local sheriff) and the property is then seized so that if the creditor prevails, she will be assured of recovering on the judgment through sale of the property.

1.5.4 Judicial Lien

■ If a debtor is adjudged to owe a creditor money and the judgment has gone unsatisfied, the creditor can request the court to impose a lien on specific property owned and possessed by the debtor.

■ After the court imposes the lien, it will issue a writ (e.g., a writ of attachment), usually to the local sheriff, to seize property belonging to the debtor, sell it, and turn over the proceeds to the creditor.

1.5.5 Garnishment

Where a debtor is adjudged to owe a creditor money and the debtor has property in the hands of a third party (e.g., money the debtor is owed by his employer, money in a bank account, debts owed to the debtor), a writ of garnishment may be sought. The writ orders the person holding the property to turn it over to the creditor or be held personally liable for the value of the property not turned over.

1.5.6 Mechanic's Liens and Artisan's Liens

Under common law, a mechanic or artisan who works on property and either improves it or repairs it automatically has a lien on the property—for the price of the repairs—for as long as the property is in the lienor's possession. These liens are possessory—they dissolve as soon as the lienor lets the owner have the property back.

1.5.7 Materialman's Lien

Materialman's liens often are imposed in favor of contractors who perform work on, or provide supplies for, real property improvements. The unpaid materialman must file a notice with the local recorder of deeds in order to preserve his or her lien.

1.6 Fraudulent Conveyances

A fraudulent conveyance occurs when a debtor transfers property with the intent to hinder, delay, or defraud any of her creditors. A fraudulent conveyance is void or voidable and will be set aside in a proper proceeding.

1.7 Fair Debt Collection Practices Act (FDCPA)

The Federal Fair Debt Collection Practices Act (FDCPA) curbs abuses by collection agencies in collecting consumer debts. The act does not apply to a creditor attempting to collect its own debts; just to services that collect consumer debts for others.

1.7.1 Prohibited Acts

The act severely restricts collection agencies' ability to call third parties, such as relatives of the debtor, to indirectly pressure the debtor. A collection agency can contact third persons to discover a debtor's whereabouts, but may not disclose that it is a collection agency or that the debtor owes a debt.

2 Bankruptcy

2.1 Types of Bankruptcy

The types of bankruptcy tested are Chapter 7 (voluntary and involuntary); Chapter 13—individual debt adjustment; Chapter 11—reorganization (voluntary and involuntary); and Chapter 15—ancillary and cross-border cases.

2.1.1 Chapter 7—Liquidation

- The debtor's estate is liquidated and distributed to creditors.
- Most of the debtor's debts are discharged. The debtor gets a "fresh start."
- A trustee is appointed to handle the liquidation.

2.1.2 Chapter 13—Individual Debt Adjustment

- The debtor repays all or a portion of his debts over a three- to five-year period.
- A Chapter 13 trustee oversees the handling of the Chapter 13 proceeding.

2.1.3 Chapter 11—Reorganization

- Restructures the debtor's debts so the business can continue.
- No liquidation occurs and a trustee is not usually required.

2.1.4 Chapter 15—Ancillary and Cross-Border Cases

- Promotes uniform and coordinated legal regime for cross-border insolvency cases.
- A foreign representative may file for recognition of foreign proceeding or participate in a U.S. case.

2.2 Dismissal or Conversion of a Chapter 7 Case

A Chapter 7 case by an *individual consumer* debtor may be dismissed (or with the debtor's consent converted to a case under Chapter 13) upon a finding that granting relief under Chapter 7 would constitute abuse because the debtor has sufficient income to pay the debtor or because the debtor acted in bad faith.

2.3 Specific Provisions of Chapter 7 Liquidations

2.3.1 Chapter 7 Voluntary

- The debtor voluntarily files for liquidation. A trustee is appointed to handle the liquidation.

- A debtor can file even if solvent, and spouses may file jointly.

- Debts will not be discharged under a Chapter 7 case until the debtor completes a government-approved financial management education program.

2.3.2 Chapter 7 Involuntary

- Creditors file to force liquidation. A trustee is appointed to handle the liquidation.

- With 12 or more creditors—three or more creditors must file who are owed $18,600 or more in aggregate in unsecured claims.

- With fewer than 12 creditors—one or more are required to file who are owed $18,600 or more in unsecured claims.

- If the debtor contests the involuntary proceeding, the order for relief is entered after a hearing has determined insolvency. The test for insolvency is not generally paying debts when due.

- Farmers and charities are exempt from Chapter 7 filings.

Note

Bankruptcy Code dollar amounts are adjusted for inflation every three years.

2.4 Specific Provisions of Chapter 11 Reorganizations

- The debtor submits a plan to restructure debts for the purpose of allowing the debtor's business to continue. The debtor has exclusive rights to submit the plan for 120 days. No liquidation occurs.

- The plan divides creditors into classes. Each class has an opportunity to accept the plan. The plan can be approved if as few as one class accepts the plan if a court finds it fair and equitable.

- Chapter 11 can be voluntary or involuntary. If involuntary, the same number of creditors and dollar requirements apply as with Chapter 7.

- A trustee is not usually required.

- Upon the court's final decree, the debtor pays off debts according to the plan.

2.5 Property Included in Debtor's Estate in Chapter 7 Liquidation

▨ The debtor's nonexempt property as of the filing date goes to the trustee to pay creditors. This includes proceeds of that property gained after the filing. Social Security and disability benefits are exempt. Certain things necessary to live (up to a certain amount) are also exempt.

▨ The debtor keeps most property acquired after the filing. Exceptions include property acquired within 180 days after the filing by divorce, inheritance, or insurance; this goes to the trustee to pay creditors.

▨ The trustee is free to accept or reject a lease.

2.6 Preferential Payments (Voidable Preferences)

Preferential payments are property transfers by the debtor before filing for bankruptcy that the trustee may set aside. The trustee may disaffirm voidable preferences if five tests are met.

1. **Transfer**

   The debtor must have transferred property to the creditor that benefited the creditor.

2. **Antecedent**

   The transfer must have been for an antecedent debt (an existing debt).

   - A new debt is not an antecedent debt (a contemporaneous exchange for new value).

   - Domestic support obligations (e.g., alimony, child support) are not counted as antecedent debts and cannot be disaffirmed.

   - Payments on secured debts (up to the value of the security) and current bills in the ordinary course of business are exempted.

   - Payments on consumer debts of up to $600 or less are exempted.

3. **Ninety Days**

   - The transfer must have occurred within ninety days prior to the filing.

   - The time limit may be up to one year prior to the filing if the creditor was an insider (e.g., relative of an individual debtor, officer of a corporate debtor).

4. **Insolvent**

   The transfer was made while the debtor was insolvent (presumed during 90-day period before filing).

5. **More**

   The creditor received more than he or she would have received in bankruptcy.

2.7 Priority of Debts in Chapter 7 Liquidation—11 Categories

Upon liquidation, debts are paid in the order of their priority. If there are insufficient funds to pay all debts within a given category, each debt within that category receives a pro rata share.

1st Secured creditors are paid up to the value of their collateral (category 11 for any deficiency).

2nd Domestic support obligations (alimony, child support, maintenance, etc.).

3rd Administrative costs of the bankruptcy proceedings.

4th Gap creditors (debts incurred after the filing, but before the order for relief is entered in an involuntary petition case).

5th Wages unpaid, but only if earned within 180 days of filing. The maximum priority is $15,150.

6th Employee benefits unpaid, but only if earned within 180 days of filing. The maximum priority is $15,150 per employee reduced by employee's wage claim.

7th Grain producers' and fishermen's claims against storage/processing facilities. The maximum priority is $7,475 per claimant.

8th Consumer deposits for goods and services paid for, but not received. The maximum priority is $3,350 per claimant.

9th Taxes unpaid, including federal state and local taxes.

10th Personal injury claims arising from intoxicated driving.

11th All other debts.

2.8 Discharge of Debtor in Chapter 7 Liquidation

Upon completion of a Chapter 7 proceeding, most of the debtor's debts are discharged. Only individuals can receive a discharge. Corporations and partnerships are dissolved.

2.8.1 Denial of Discharge

Certain actions by the debtor will preclude any discharge. Such actions include:

- Receiving a previous discharge within eight years of filing.

- Unjustifiably failing to keep adequate books and records.

- Fraudulent transfer or concealment of property within a year before or anytime after filing the petition.

2.8.2 Debts Excepted From Discharge

Even if a discharge is granted, certain debts are not dischargeable (**WAFTED**). These include:

- Debts from causing **w**illful and malicious injury to others.

- Debts concerning **a**limony and child support.

- Debts resulting from **f**raud.

- **T**axes owed within three years of filing.

- **E**ducational loans.

- **D**ebts not reported by the debtor in the schedule of debts filed with the court and the creditor had no notice of the bankruptcy.

Question 2   MCQ-09576

Which of the following is a reason to deny a debtor a discharge in bankruptcy?

1. Debtor owes debts arising from willful and malicious injury to others.

2. Debtor owes his home state and the federal government tax payments from the past two years.

3. Debtor received a discharge in bankruptcy five years ago.

4. Debtor owes debts arising from fraud.

---

3 Secured Transactions

3.1 Three Definitions

- **Secured Transaction:** Simply a debt that is secured by personal property (i.e., if the debt is not paid, the creditor has rights to take or sell the specified personal property—the collateral).

- **Purchase Money Security Interest Creditor:** A creditor who advances money or credit to enable a debtor to obtain property and retains a security interest in that property.

- **After-Acquired Property Clause:** A clause giving a creditor a security interest in the property acquired by a debtor after the security agreement is executed.

3.2 Requirements for Attachment

Attachment marks when a creditor's security interest is effective against the debtor. Generally, a security interest will attach to an item of collateral if the parties agree that the security interest will attach. The agreement can be in writing (including electronic documents) or it can be oral if the secured party takes possession of the collateral (which is called a pledge).

Note

Filing is related to perfection, not attachment.

3.3 Ways to Perfect

Perfection sets the secured party's rights against third parties who also have an interest in the collateral. The following are different methods of perfection:

- The creditor can perfect by possession or control. Basically, a secured party (or other purchaser) has control of an item of investment property when the secured party has taken whatever steps are necessary to be able to have the investment property sold without further action from the owner. This is the only way to perfect if the collateral is stocks, bonds, or negotiable instruments.

- The creditor can perfect by filing a financing statement that gives constructive notice to all third parties of the security interest. The financing statement must give the names and addresses of the debtor and creditor and an indication of the type of collateral covered by the financing statement (such as "the debtor's inventory and equipment").

- The creditor can perfect by attachment, an automatic but very limited type of perfection. Generally, this only occurs with a PMSI creditor in consumer goods and with small-scale assignments of accounts.

- There are also a few temporary periods of perfection (e.g., when the debtor moves to a new state).

3.4 Creditors' Rights Upon Debtor's Default

If a debtor defaults on a secured obligation, the creditor has three possible remedies:

3.4.1 Peacefully Repossess and Sell or Lease

- If the debtor defaults, the creditor can peacefully repossess (or have the sheriff repossess) and sell or lease (whatever is commercially reasonable) the collateral. The item may be sold at a public or private sale. The creditor must give proper notice to debtor and junior security interest holders prior to sale. The debtor can redeem prior to sale by paying all creditors in full.

- After the sale, the debtor is liable for any deficiency and is entitled to any surplus.

- A good faith purchaser for value at a sale takes free of the security interest and subordinate liens.

3.4.2 Keep the Collateral

- The creditor may peacefully repossess and keep the collateral after default, but must cancel the entire debt in consumer cases. The creditor must notify the debtor and other creditors in writing. If anyone objects, the creditor must sell the collateral.

- If the debtor has paid 60 percent or more of the price of consumer goods, the creditor must sell unless the debtor waives this right after defaulting.

3.4.3 Sue the Debtor for Debt

The creditor may forgo repossession and sue the debtor for the debt and reduce the claim to a judgment.

1 Worker Classification

1.1 Employee vs. Independent Contractor

For government regulation questions, know whether you are dealing with an employee or an independent contractor. Businesses must consider:

- Whether the business has the right to control the manner or method of performing the work (employee) or not (independent contractor).
- Whether the worker has his or her own tools (indicative of independent contractor) or the business supplies them (indicative of employee).
- Whether the worker is paid by the job (indicative of independent contractor) or is salaried or is paid hourly (indicative of employee).
- Whether the job is of limited duration (indicative of independent contractor) or is continuous (indicative of employee).
- Whether the worker receives benefits (indicative of employee).

2 Federal Insurance Contributions Act (FICA)

FICA provides workers and their dependents with benefits in case of death, disability, or retirement.

2.1 Participation and Funding

- All employees must participate as well as self-employed persons earning more than $400 profit in a year.
- FICA is funded by taxing income.

2.2 Employer Responsibility/Deductibility

Employers are responsible for collecting and submitting the tax and must match the tax imposed on employees. The employer's match is a deductible business expense.

2.3 The Tax

For 2022, employees must pay 6.2 percent of their taxable wages up to $147,000 as FICA and 1.45 percent of their full, gross wages for Medicare.

There is an additional 0.9 percent Medicare surcharge for income exceeding $200,000 for single persons and $250,000 for married persons filing jointly.

2.4 Self-Employed Persons

Self-employed persons pay both the employer's and employee's tax but may deduct the employer's tax as a business expense.

3 Unemployment Compensation

The Federal Unemployment Tax Act (FUTA) provides federal guidelines for collecting a tax to fund unemployment benefits under an insurance system run by each state.

3.1 Participation

All employers who have quarterly payrolls of at least $1,500, or who employ at least one person for 20 weeks in a year, must participate.

3.2 Funding and Deductibility

- Employers must pay into the federal system 6 percent of the first $7,000 of compensation for each employee annually.

- Employers can get a credit of up to 5.4 percent of the first $7,000 for each employee for sums paid to state unemployment tax systems.

- The employer's payment is a deductible business expense.

3.3 Benefits

Amounts vary among states and are payable when employees lose their job and it is not their fault.

4 Workers' Compensation

Workers' compensation is a state-run system that pays workers for injuries sustained while on the job.

- Employers are strictly liable regardless of fault.

- Most employers must participate.

4.1 Funding and Deductibility

- The employer pays by purchasing insurance from the state or a private carrier.

- The payment is a deductible business expense.

4.2 Benefits

Benefits are paid for injuries and diseases resulting from employment. Benefits may include money for loss of income, medical services, burial costs, survivor benefits, and the like.

5 Affordable Care Act

The purpose of the Affordable Care Act (ACA) is to improve access to health care in the United States by providing workers with access to affordable health care coverage. Both employers and employees are required to participate (although there is no penalty for an employee who chooses not to).

5.1 Funding

Both the employer and the employee contribute to the purchase of affordable coverage.

5.2 Employer Responsibility

Employers with 50 or more full-time employees are called applicable large employers, or ALEs. They must provide full-time employees the opportunity to purchase affordable minimum essential health care coverage for themselves and their dependents under an eligible employer-sponsored health care plan.

- An employee who works for an employer on average at least 30 hours a week, or 130 hours of service a month, is a full-time employee.

- Coverage is considered affordable if the employee's contribution to the plan does not exceed 9.5 percent of the employee's household income for the taxable year.

- A dependent is an employee's child who has not reached the age of 26.

- Employers who do not comply with the ACA will pay a penalty for failure to do so.

5.3 Penalties for Failure to Comply

An ALE that does not offer minimum essential coverage to at least 95 percent of its full-time employees may owe a penalty.

Question 1 MCQ-14506

Which of the following statements is correct regarding the taxes payable under the Federal Unemployment Tax Act (FUTA)?

1. Half of the liability is the responsibility of the employer and half is the responsibility of the employee.

2. Self-employed persons do not participate.

3. Employer payments into FUTA are not deductible as an ordinary business expense.

4. Employers who meet a minimum quarterly payroll and who employ at least one person for 20 weeks in a year must participate.

Question 2   MCQ-14507

Which one of the following statements concerning workers' compensation laws is generally correct?

1. Employers pay for workers' compensation by purchasing insurance from the state or from a private carrier.

2. Workers' compensation programs are federally run programs designed to enable employees to recover for injuries incurred while on the job.

3. Workers' compensation insurance premiums are deductible by the employee on the employee's individual tax return.

4. An employee can collect workers' compensation even if the employee was negligent, grossly negligent, or intoxicated.

1 Sole Proprietorship

1.1 Advantages

- One person owns and manages all affairs. The sole proprietor is free to transfer the business.

- It is easy to form and there is no need to file with the state.

- Unlike a corporation, the business is not taxed as a separate entity.

1.2 Disadvantages

- The sole proprietor is personally liable for debts of the business.

- A sole proprietorship ends with the death of the sole proprietor.

2 General Partnership

2.1 Formation of a Partnership

- A partnership is an association of two or more persons to carry on as *co-owners a business for profit.*

- A joint venture is similar, but involves an agreement to engage in a more limited undertaking. A joint venture is treated like a partnership in all respects.

- *No filing* is necessary for formation. The partnership is formed simply by the agreement of all partners to form a business; the agreement need not be "to form a partnership." The agreement can be oral unless the partners agree *in advance* that the partnership is to last for more than one year.

- Any partner breaching the agreement is liable to the partnership and to fellow partners.

- A partnership is a *legal entity* separate from its owners for most purposes *except for federal income tax* purposes and for obligations (partners are personally liable for the obligations of the partnership).

2.2 Liability of Partners

- All partners in a general partnership have *unlimited liability* for obligations of the partnership.

- They are jointly and severally liable for all partnership *torts* and for all partnership *debts*. If the partners vote to admit a new partner, the new partner is not liable for debts and obligations that existed before the new partner came to the partnership beyond any partnership contribution the new partner made.

2.3   Partners Are Agents of the Partnership and Agents of Each Other

- A partner can impose contract or tort liability on the partnership and fellow partners when acting with actual or apparent authority.

- An act of a partner apparently carrying on the business of the partnership in the ordinary course of business will bind the partnership through apparent authority.

- A partner has no apparent authority to make fundamental changes in the partnership, to admit liability in a lawsuit, or to submit a claim to arbitration.

- A partner owes the same duties all agents do (i.e., the duty of **d**ue care, the duty to **i**nform of all relevant facts, the duty to **a**ccount for money spent or received, the fiduciary duty of **l**oyalty, and the duty of **o**bedience [**DIAL-O**]).

- A partner acting without actual authority or breaching any duties is liable to other partners and the partnership.

2.4   Partners' Rights

- All partners have an *equal right to manage* unless otherwise agreed.

- Most decisions require only a majority vote.

- Exception: The following require *unanimous consent*:

  - Admitting new partners;

  - Transferring partnership property to others;

  - Admitting liability in a lawsuit or submitting a claim to arbitration; and

  - Making a fundamental change in the partnership (e.g., sell goodwill or change a written partnership agreement).

- Each partner has an *equal right to profits* unless otherwise agreed.

  - If division of profits is specified but not losses, then losses will *follow profits*.

  - Partners have no right to compensation unless otherwise agreed.

- Partners have the *right to be reimbursed* for loans made to the partnership and the *right to be indemnified* for liability incurred when properly acting on behalf of the partnership.

- All partners have the right to full information about the partnership (e.g., the right to inspect and copy books and records and the right to tax information).

2.5   Partnership Property

- Partners *own an interest in the business*; they *do not own partnership property*.

- Each partner has the right to use partnership property for partnership purposes, but not for other purposes.

- *Personal creditors of a partner cannot attach* partnership property.

- Partnership property is *not subject to a partner's liability for alimony.*

- If a partner dies, partnership property goes to the surviving partners, not to the deceased partner's heirs.

2.6 Assigning a Partnership Interest

- Any partner can assign or sell her/his/its partnership interest. Consent of fellow partners is not needed.

- The assignment does not dissolve the partnership. The assignor remains a partner and is still liable for all partnership debts.

- The only right the assignee receives is the right to the assignor's share of profits or surplus.

  - The assignee does not become a partner without the consent of all other partners.

  - The assignee is not liable for the assignor's share of losses.

  - The assignee has no right to participate in management, inspect books, etc.

2.7 Dissociation and Dissolution

2.7.1 Dissociation

Dissociation occurs when a partner ceases to be associated with the partnership business. It does not necessarily end the partnership business (it is just the term used to describe a partner's leaving the partnership).

- Dissociation may be voluntary (by the partner giving notice of withdrawal), or due to death, bankruptcy, expulsion, or some other event stated in the partnership agreement.

- The dissociated partner may be held liable for new debts of the partnership (for up to two years) as well, absent notice of the dissociation to third parties.

- Any partner has a right to withdraw from a partnership at will (one without a stated termination point) at any time.

- After dissociation, the dissociated partner's right to participate in management ceases, but the partner remains liable for partnership obligations and will continue to have apparent authority to bind the partnership until third parties are given notice of the dissociation.

2.7.2 Dissolution

Dissolution is the term that signifies that the partnership business is being terminated. Upon dissolution, partners must cease taking on new business and wind up the partnership's existing business. The following events cause a dissolution:

- The non-wrongful dissociation of a partner in a partnership at will.

- Bankruptcy of the partnership.

- In a partnership for a definite term or a particular undertaking, within 90 days after a partner's death or bankruptcy, a majority of the remaining partners vote to wind up the partnership.

2.8 Distribution Upon Dissolution

▪ Upon dissolution, creditors are paid first. This includes partners who are creditors.

▪ After creditors are paid, partners are credited or charged an amount equal to their capital contribution plus profits or minus losses. If this results in a partner having a negative balance, the partner will have to pay that amount into the partnership.

Question 1	MCQ-09103

Milton is a general partner in the Omni Company general partnership. Milton:

1. Has no apparent authority if the partnership agreement is contained in a formal and detailed signed writing.

2. Cannot be sued individually for a tort he has committed until the partnership has been sued and a judgment returned unsatisfied.

3. Can bind the partnership by renewing an existing lease that the remaining partners had decided to terminate.

4. Can bind the partnership by submitting a written admission of liability in a lawsuit brought against the partnership.

Question 2	MCQ-09143

Ted Fein, a partner in the ABC Partnership, wishes to withdraw from the partnership and sell his interest to Gold. All of the other partners in ABC have agreed to admit Gold as a partner and to hold Fein harmless for the past, present and future liabilities of ABC. A provision in the original partnership agreement states that the partnership will continue upon the death or withdrawal of one or more of the partners. The agreement to hold Fein harmless for all past, present and future liabilities of ABC will:

1. Prevent partnership creditors from holding Fein personally liable only as to those liabilities of ABC existing at the time of Fein's withdrawal.

2. Prevent partnership creditors from holding Fein personally liable for the past, present and future liabilities of ABC.

3. Not affect the rights of partnership creditors to hold Fein personally liable for those liabilities of ABC existing at the time of his withdrawal.

4. Permit Fein to recover from the other partners only amounts he has paid in excess of his proportionate share.

3 Limited Partnership

3.1 Formation of a Limited Partnership

- A limited partnership is a partnership of two or more parties formed in compliance with a state statute for the purpose of providing limited liability for limited partners.

- The certificate of limited partnership must be filed with the state.

- There must be at least one general partner and one limited partner. A general partner may also be a limited partner in the same partnership at the same time.

3.2 Liability in a Limited Partnership

- General partners have unlimited personal liability, as in a general partnership.

- Limited partners have no liability beyond their promised or paid capital investment, even if they take part in management of the business.

3.3 Operation of a Limited Partnership

- General partners have the same rights and powers as a partner in a general partnership.

- Limited partners are just investors and, absent an agreement otherwise, have no right to manage or control beyond the voting provided for above.

- Unless otherwise agreed, profits and losses are shared according to capital contributions, not equally.

- Admission or removal of a general partner or limited partner requires unanimous consent of all of the general partners and all of the limited partners.

- Limited and general partners may be secured or unsecured creditors of the limited partnership.

- Both general and limited partners have the right to full information about the business, specifically including the right to inspect books and records.

- A limited partnership is dissolved upon the death, withdrawal or bankruptcy of a general partner. Changes in limited partners do not cause dissolution.

- General or limited partners may assign their limited partnership interest without the consent of others.

  - As in a general partnership, the assignee does not become a substituted general or limited partner.

  - The only right the assignee gets is the right to the assignor's share of profits.

Question 3   MCQ-09153

Unless otherwise provided in the limited partnership agreement, which of the following statements is correct?

1. A limited partnership can be formed with limited liability for all partners.

2. Upon the death of a limited partner, the partnership will be dissolved.

3. A person may own a limited partnership interest in the same partnership in which he is a general partner.

4. Upon assignment of a limited partnership interest, the assignee will become a substituted limited partner if the consent of two-thirds of all partners is obtained.

---

4 Limited Liability Partnership (LLP)

4.1 Definition

A limited liability partnership is similar to a partnership with two major differences, filing and liability.

4.2 Filing

An LLP must file a registration statement with the state. The statement must include the name of the LLP and a clear indication that the entity is an LLP.

4.3 Liability

- A general partner in an LLP is liable for his or her own negligence or wrongful acts and for the negligence and wrongful acts of anyone acting under the partner's direct control or supervision.

- A partner is not liable for the negligence of other partners or for those not under his or her direct control.

- LLP partners are also not personally liable for LLP contracts.

5 Limited Liability Company (LLC)

5.1 Formation of a Limited Liability Company

- The *articles of organization* of the LLC must be filed with the state. The *operating agreement* (the agreement between the LLC members) is not filed with the state.
- The articles of organization must contain the name of the LLC, the name and address of its registered agent, and the names of the persons who will be managing the company.
- Virtually every state permits an LLC composed of only a single member.

5.2 Liability in a Limited Liability Company

- LLC members have *no liability beyond their capital investment*, but are liable for any capital contribution not made.
- LLC members are liable for their own negligence.

5.3 Operation of a Limited Liability Company

- An LLC member may *assign his or her right to profits*.
  - The assignee does not become an LLC member without the consent of other LLC members.
  - The assignment does not dissolve the LLC.
- In most states, profits and losses are shared proportionally based on contributions, but under the Uniform Limited Liability Company Act (followed by only a few states but sometimes specifically tested on the exam), *profits and losses are shared equally*.
- Unless otherwise agreed, all LLC members have the *right to participate in management*. However, the articles of organization may provide that the LLC will be managed by managers selected by the members.
- Unless the LLC elects otherwise with the IRS, an LLC having two or more members is *taxed like a partnership* for federal income tax purposes.
- LLC members have the *right to full information* about the business, specifically including the right to inspect books and records.
- An LLC is dissolved upon the death, withdrawal, or bankruptcy of a member, unless the remaining members vote to continue the business.

Question 4   MCQ-09104

In general, which of the following statements is correct with respect to a limited liability company (LLC)?

    1. The operating agreement must be filed with the state.

    2. Unless otherwise agreed, an LLC is taxed like a corporation.

    3. An LLC must have at least two members.

    4. An LLC can be formed with limited liability for all members.

---

6 Corporation

6.1   Formation of a Corporation

6.1.1   Promoters

Promoters procure capital commitments and other agreements before the corporation is formed.

■ They are liable for preincorporation contracts and remain liable unless a novation is executed.

■ If the corporation accepts (or ratifies) the promoter's contract, the corporation is also liable.

6.1.2   Articles of Incorporation

The articles of incorporation must be filed by incorporators with the state. The articles must contain the corporation's name, the name and address of its registered agent, the name of its incorporators, and the number of shares authorized to be issued.

6.1.3   Bylaws

Bylaws govern the corporation's internal management and are not filed. The directors or incorporators usually adopt bylaws at the first business meeting.

6.2   Financing the Corporation—Financed by Debt Securities, Equity Securities, and Retained Earnings

6.2.1   Debt Securities

Debt securities are bonds and represent a debtor-creditor relationship. Unsecured bonds are called debentures.

6.2.2   Equity Shares

Equity shares evidence ownership of the corporation and are commonly called shares or stock. At least one class of common stock must have voting power.

6.2.3 Preferred Stock

Preferred stock has special rights over other stock, usually as to dividends and/or liquidation distributions.

- Preferred stockholders must be paid before any dividends are paid to common stockholders.

- Cumulative preferred stock has dividend carryovers to future years if the dividends are not paid in any given year.

6.3 Stockholders' Rights and Liabilities

- Stockholders have *no liability beyond their investment*.

- The corporate entity may be disregarded and stockholders held personally liable (called "piercing the corporate veil") if the corporation was formed to perpetrate fraud, if the corporation was undercapitalized at the time of formation, or if the shareholders commingle personal and corporate funds.

- Stockholders may inspect books and records at reasonable times unless the stockholders have an improper motive.

- The *preemptive right* is the right of a stockholder to buy newly issued stock being offered to the public in order to maintain his pre-issuance percentage ownership of the corporation. Preemptive rights are only available if the articles so provide.

- If, in bad faith, the directors refuse to vindicate or enforce rights of the corporation, stockholders may bring derivative suits to do so.

6.4 Stockholder Management Rights

- Stockholders have two main management rights: the right to elect (and remove) members of the board of directors and the right to vote on fundamental changes in the corporation.

- There are four main fundamental changes in the corporation that stockholders can vote on—**DAMS**:

  D = **D**issolution

  A = **A**mending the articles of incorporation

  M = **M**ergers, consolidations, and compulsory share exchanges

  S = **S**ale of substantially all the corporation's assets outside the ordinary course of business, but not buying all of the assets of another corporation

6.5 Stockholder Right of Appraisal or Dissenters' Rights

The right of appraisal (sometimes called dissenters' rights) is the right of the stockholder to be bought out by the corporation at fair market value after a corporation's fundamental change (i.e., **DAMS**) for which the stockholder did not vote to approve.

6.6 Approval Steps for Fundamental Changes to the Corporation

- The first step is passage of a resolution by a *majority* of the board of directors approving the change.

- Mergers (except short-form mergers) and consolidations must be approved by a majority of both boards of directors.

- The resolution is then submitted to the stockholders for approval.

  - They must receive a copy of the resolution and notice of the time, date, and place where the vote is to occur.

  - A *majority* of the stockholders must approve. Mergers and consolidations must be approved by a majority of the stockholders of both corporations.

- Articles (e.g., of merger, of amendment, etc.) must also be filed with the state.

6.7 Dividends

- Dividends are declared by the board of directors.

  - There is no inherent right of stockholders to receive dividends.

  - Directors are personally liable for wrongfully declaring dividends but have a defense of reasonable reliance.

- Once declared and communicated to stockholders, cash dividends are a debt and cannot be revoked. Once a dividend is declared, stockholders become unsecured creditors of the corporation.

- Stock dividends (i.e., dividends paid in the form of company stock instead of cash) do not reduce the assets of the corporation or increase a stockholder's percentage of ownership or wealth. Thus, they have no effect on earnings and profits for federal income tax purposes.

6.8 Directors and Officers

- The board of directors handles overall management and sets corporate policy; individually, directors have no power and are not agents of the corporation.

- Officers handle day-to-day affairs and are selected and removed by the board. Officers are agents of the corporation and owe the same duties all agents do (**DIAL-O**).

- The business judgment rule provides that directors and officers are not liable for their actions if they acted reasonably and in good faith.

  - Both officers and directors are liable if they were grossly negligent.

  - Directors may usually rely on reports of officers and other agents.

▨ Both officers and directors owe a fiduciary duty of loyalty to the corporation.

- They must act solely in the best interest of the corporation.

- They can have a conflict of interest in a transaction, and the transaction can be approved if fair to the corporation or the details are fully disclosed to the disinterested directors or shareholders, who then approve the transaction.

▨ Directors and officers generally may be indemnified by the corporation for losses in a lawsuit if they were acting in a corporate capacity.

Question 5	MCQ-09124

Trinket Corp. is being sued by its distributor, International, for nonpayment of debts. Which of the following would be a reason that would justify a recovery from Trinket's sole shareholder personally?

1. Trinket Corp. is overcapitalized.

2. The shareholder's personal assets are materially commingled with Trinket's assets.

3. Trinket's articles of incorporation allow for more than one class of stock.

4. The shareholder incorporated the business as a shield from personal liability.

III Federal Taxation of Property Transactions

A Acquisition and Disposition of Assets

B Cost Recovery

C Gift Taxation

1 Capital Gains and Losses

Gains/losses on property held by the taxpayer (e.g., a personal vehicle, stocks and securities, real property not used in a trade or business, partnership interests, and other investment assets) are reported on Schedule D. The net gain or loss is calculated on Schedule D and reported as a single amount on Form 1040.

1.1 Gains and Losses From Dispositions

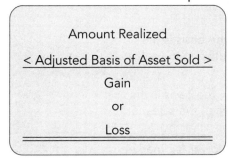

Amount Realized

< Adjusted Basis of Asset Sold >

Gain

or

Loss

- Amount realized includes cash, property (FMV), services provided (FMV), and relief from liability.

- Adjusted basis generally is the amount paid for the asset (cost) increased for any improvements and decreased for any depreciation (allowed or allowable).

1.1.1 Individual Taxpayers

- For individual taxpayers, gains/losses are long-term or short-term. Short-term gains and losses are for assets held for one year or less, and they are taxed using the same rates as ordinary income. Long-term gains and losses relate to assets held more than one year and are subject to a preferential tax rate of 0, 15, or 20 percent depending on the taxpayer's taxable income. Although most taxpayers are subject to a 15 percent preferential tax rate, a 0 percent preferential tax rate applies to taxpayers with a low taxable income, which in 2022 is $83,350 or less for MFJ taxpayers; $55,800 for head of household; and $41,675 or less for single taxpayers. A 20 percent preferential tax rate applies to taxpayers with a high taxable income, which in 2022 is more than $517,200 for MFJ taxpayers; $488,500 for head of household; and $459,750 for single taxpayers.

- Deduction of net long-term or short-term losses against ordinary income is limited to $3,000 ($1,500 if married filing separately) for individual taxpayers. Excess losses are carried forward indefinitely.

A   Acquisition and Disposition of Assets

1.1.2   C Corporation Taxpayers

▨ There is no distinction between short-term and long-term for C corporations, and there are no preferential tax rates. A net capital gain is taxed at the ordinary C corporation tax rate (21 percent).

▨ A net capital loss can be carried back three years (oldest year first) and forward five years to offset net capital gains. If a net capital loss is carried back to offset a net capital gain in a previous year, the taxpayer gets a refund for the income tax paid on the net capital gain.

1.2   Gift Property

Gifted assets are cash or property received as a gift. Generally, the gifted asset retains the donor's rollover cost basis at the date of gift. Gains and losses on the disposition of gift property are calculated as indicated above. However, if the property's FMV is lower than its basis on the gift date, the basis is determined by the ultimate sales price of the asset.

▨ If the sales price is higher than the rollover cost basis, the basis is the donor's basis, and the gain is equal to the difference between the sales price and rollover cost basis (minimizes gain).

▨ If the sales price is less than the lower fair market value, the basis is the lower FMV, and the loss is equal to the difference between the sales price and the lower fair market value (minimizes loss).

▨ If the sales price is between rollover cost basis and the lower fair market value, the basis equals the sales price, and no gain or loss is recognized.

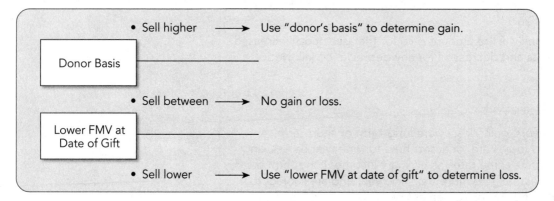

1.3   Inherited Property

▨ The basis of inherited property is generally the FMV at the date of death, unless the executor of the estate elects measurement on the alternate (lower) valuation date (six months after date of death).

▨ Inherited property is automatically classified as long-term property.

1.4   Gains/Losses Excluded, Deferred, or Disallowed

Certain gains and losses are excluded, deferred, or disallowed under the following circumstances.

1.4.1 Homeowner's Exclusion

Up to $500,000 (MFJ), or $250,000 (all other taxpayers) gain on personal residence sale is excluded from gross income.

For full exclusion, the taxpayer must have owned and used the property as the principal residence for two or more years during the five-year period ending on the date of the sale or exchange of the property. Either spouse can meet the ownership requirement, but both spouses must meet the use requirement (an exception exists for certain surviving spouses).

1.4.2 Involuntary Conversions

Gains realized on involuntary conversions of property (e.g., destruction, theft, or condemnation) are nontaxable to the extent that amounts are reinvested within two years (personal property) or three years (business property) after the close of the taxable year in which any part of the gain was realized.

The basis of the new asset is the same as the basis of the old asset, unless gain is recognized. If gain is recognized, the basis of the replacement property is its cost less the gain not recognized.

1.4.3 Divorce Property Settlements

Lump-sum payments and property settlements are nontaxable events. The recipient spouse's basis is the carryover basis, and there is no allowable alimony adjustment.

1.4.4 Exchange of Like-Kind Business or Investment Real Property

Real property used in a trade/business or held for investment exchanged for other real property used in a trade/business or held for investment qualifies for like-kind exchange treatment. No gain or loss is recognized unless boot is received (cash, relief from liability, or nonqualifying property). Gain recognized is the lower of realized gain or boot received. The basis of property received is the fair market value of the property reduced by any gain deferred (or increased by any loss deferred).

1.4.5 Installment Sale

An installment sale provides for deferral of gain until the time when payments are received. When a payment is received, gain is recognized in proportion to the gross profit percentage calculated on the original sale.

1.4.6 Treasury and Capital Stock Transactions

The issuing corporation does not recognize a gain or a loss on sales or repurchases of its own stock or on the reissuance of treasury stock.

1.5 Disallowed Losses

Certain losses are disallowed, meaning they are not deductible.

1.5.1 Wash Sales

A loss is disallowed when a security is sold at a loss and is repurchased within 30 days before or after the sale date. Gains are taxed.

1.5.2   Related Party Losses

Losses resulting from related party sales (brother/sister, husband/wife, lineal descendants—not in-laws) are disallowed. Gains are taxed.

The purchasing relative's basis rules are the same as the gift tax rules.

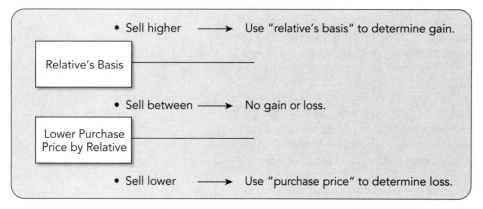

1.5.3   Personal Losses

Losses on disposition of nonbusiness assets (e.g., sale of a personal vehicle) are disallowed. Gains are taxed.

Question 1   MCQ-09566

On February 1 of the current year, Duffy learned that he was bequeathed 1,000 shares of common stock under his father's will. Duffy's father had paid $12,500 for the stock 20 years ago. Fair market value of the stock on February 1 of the current year, the date of his father's death, was $14,000 and had increased to $15,500 six months later. The executor of the estate elected the alternative valuation date for estate tax purposes. Duffy sold the stock for $14,500 on June 1 of the current year, the date that the executor distributed the stock to him. How much income should Duffy include in his current year individual income tax return for the inheritance of the 1,000 shares of stock which he received from his father's estate?

1. $5,500
2. $4,000
3. $2,500
4. $0

Question 2   MCQ-09529

Conner purchased 300 shares of Zinco stock for $30,000 in Year 1. On May 23, Year 6, Conner sold all the stock to his daughter Alice for $20,000, its then fair market value. Conner realized no other gain or loss during Year 6. On July 26, Year 6, Alice sold the 300 shares of Zinco for $25,000.

What was Alice's recognized gain or loss on her sale?

1. $0
2. $5,000 long-term gain.
3. $5,000 short-term loss.
4. $5,000 long-term loss.

2 Section 1231, 1245, and 1250 Assets

2.1 Section 1231 Assets Defined

Section 1231 assets are depreciable personal property, depreciable real property, and land used in a taxpayer's trade or business for longer than one year.

2.2 Section 1231 Tax Treatment (Capital Gains/Ordinary Losses)

2.2.1 Section 1231

Under Section 1231, taxpayers combine all their Section 1231 gains and losses for the tax year. If there is a net 1231 gain, it is long-term capital gain. If there is a net 1231 loss, it is an ordinary loss. This treatment often allows for net Section 1231 gains to be taxed at lower rates (for individuals, estates, and trusts) and for net Section 1231 losses to offset ordinary income.

2.2.2 Section 1231 Five-Year Lookback

If there is a net Section 1231 gain for the year, the taxpayer must first "look back" to see if there were any net Section 1231 losses treated as ordinary losses in the previous five years (oldest year first). If so, the taxpayer must "pay back," or recapture, this ordinary benefit by treating the net Section 1231 gain as ordinary income to the extent of any unrecaptured prior net Section 1231 losses.

2.3 Section 1245 Depreciation Recapture (Section 1231 Personal Property)

- If Section 1231 personal property is sold at a gain, the gain is treated as ordinary income to the extent of prior depreciation taken. Depreciation is an ordinary deduction, so the taxpayer must pay back, or recapture, the ordinary benefit.

- Any gain in excess of the asset's accumulated depreciation is a Section 1231 gain, which is netted with other Section 1231 gains and losses for the year.

2.4 Section 1250 or Section 291 Depreciation Recapture (Section 1231 Real Property)

For Section 1231 depreciable real property sold at a gain, depreciation recapture, or payback of prior ordinary benefit, is more limited.

2.4.1 Individual Taxpayers (Section 1250 Depreciation Recapture)

Section 1250 depreciation recapture for Section 1231 depreciable real property is the excess of any accelerated depreciation taken over straight-line. MACRS depreciation for real property placed in service after 1986 is straight-line, so this only applies to real property placed in service before 1987. The lesser of the gain or depreciation recapture amount for the real property is taxed at a maximum rate of 25 percent. The depreciation recapture only applies if there is a net Section 1231 gain for the year.

2.4.2 C Corporations (Section 291 Depreciation Recapture)

For C corporations, Section 291 depreciation recapture applies to Section 1231 depreciable real property sold at a gain. Under Section 291, the amount of the gain treated as ordinary is 20 percent of the lesser of the gain or accumulated depreciation taken on the property.

Any remaining gain is a Section 1231 gain, which is netted with other Section 1231 gains and losses for the year.

Flowchart of Gain or Loss From Section 1231 and 1245/1250 Assets

Sale or exchange of depreciable property, or land, used in trade or business and held for **more** than **one** year.

Gain

Loss

If **personal** property, Section **1245** determines the character of the gain.

If depreciable **real** property, and taxpayer is an individual, Section **1250** determines the character of the gain.

If depreciable **real** property, and taxpayer is a C corporation, Section **291** determines the character of the gain.

Gain = **Ordinary income** to the extent of **100%** of accumulated depreciation on the asset.

An amount equal to the lesser of (1) the recognized gain on the sale of the Section 1250 asset; or (2) accumulated depreciation on the asset, taxed at a maximum rate of 25 percent.

Gain = **Ordinary income** to the extent of **20 percent** of the lesser of the recognized gain or accumulated depreciation on the asset.

The remaining gain is treated as a Section 1231 gain.

The losses are to be netted with Section 1231 gains.

Compare

If the result is a net 1231 gain, then treat as ordinary to the extent of unrecaptured 1231 losses in the previous five years. The rest is treated as **long-term capital gain**.

If the result is a net 1231 **loss**, then treat as a Section 1231 **(ordinary) loss**.

Question 3   MCQ-09499

Bolton Company sold machinery for $45,000 on December 23, Year 7. The machinery had been acquired on April 1, Year 5 for $49,000 and its adjusted basis at the time of the sale was $14,200. The Section 1231 gain, Section 1245 depreciation recapture gain, and Section 1231 loss from this transaction are:

	Section 1231 Gain	Section 1245 Gain	Section 1231 Loss
1.	$0	$45,000	$0
2.	$0	$49,000	$14,200
3.	$0	$30,800	$0
4.	$0	$34,800	$0

1 MACRS

The MACRS method is typically applied to depreciable assets placed in service after 1986. Questions on the CPA Exam generally focus on the half-year, mid-month, and mid-quarter conventions.

1.1 Salvage Value

Salvage value is ignored for tax purposes.

1.2 Personal Property

- Generally, the half-year convention applies for MACRS depreciation (one-half year of depreciation is taken in the years of acquisition and disposition).
- The mid-quarter convention applies when more than 40 percent of depreciable personal property is placed in service in the fourth quarter of the year.
- Cost recovery (depreciation expense) is calculated using 200 percent double-declining balance for 3-, 5-, 7-, and 10-year property, switching to straight-line when greater.
- Qualified improvement property has a 15-year recovery period, using 150 percent declining balance and the half-year convention.

1.3 Real Property

- Residential real property is depreciated using the straight-line method over 27.5 years.
- Nonresidential real property is depreciated using the straight-line method over 39 years.
- The mid-month convention applies (one-half month of depreciation is taken in the month of acquisition and disposition).

2 Section 179 Expense Deduction

A taxpayer can elect to expense up to $1,080,000 (2022) of personal property acquired during the year. The maximum deduction is reduced dollar for dollar by the amount of personal property placed in service during the taxable year that exceeds $2,700,000 (2022). The Section 179 expense deduction is not allowed if a net loss exists or if the deduction would create a net loss.

3 Bonus Depreciation

A taxpayer can take 100 percent bonus depreciation for personal property with a recovery period of 20 years or less (including 15-year qualified improvements). Bonus depreciation is taken after Section 179 expense and before regular MACRS depreciation.

Question 1   MCQ-09639

Michael Sima, a sole proprietor craftsman, purchased an amount of equipment in the current year that exceeded the maximum Section 179 expense allowance by $20,000. Sima's total purchases of personal property placed in service in the current year did not exceed the Section 179 phase-out threshold. All of the personal property (including the equipment) was purchased in November of the current year. Sima elected the maximum Section 179 allowed for the year and elected out of bonus depreciation. The Section 179 expense election did not create or increase a net loss on Sima's Schedule C for the current year. Which method may Sima use to depreciate the remaining equipment in the current year?

1. Sima may not depreciate any additional equipment other than the Section 179 maximum in the current year and must carry forward the excess amount to use in the following taxable year.

2. MACRS half-year convention for personal property.

3. MACRS mid-quarter convention for personal property.

4. Straight-line, mid-month convention for real property.

---

1 Annual, Inflation-Adjusted Exclusion

In determining the amount of gifts made in a calendar year, the donor may exclude the first $16,000 (2022) of gifts made to each donee. This annual exclusion is not available for a gift of a future interest (i.e., a gift that can only be enjoyed by the donee at some future date), even if the donee does receive a current ownership interest in the gift. A gift by either spouse may be treated as made one-half by each. This gift splitting creates an exclusion of $32,000 per donee (2022).

2 Unlimited Exclusion

- Payments made directly to an educational institution.
- Payments made directly to a health care provider for medical care.
- Charitable gifts.
- Marital deduction (must be a terminable interest).

3 Gifts—Present vs. Future Interest

3.1 Definition

The postponement of the right to use, possess, or enjoy the property distinguishes a future interest from a present interest.

- A present interest qualifies for the annual exclusion of $16,000 (2022).
- A future interest (or a present interest without ascertainable value) does not qualify for the annual exclusion.

3.2 Future Interest Gifts

- Reversions (gifting assets and later getting the property back).
- Remainders (distributed at some future time).
- Trust income interests, where accumulation of income by a trustee is mandatory and accumulations are distributed at some future time at the discretion of the trustee.

3.3 Present Interest Gifts

- Outright gifts of cash or property.
- Trust income interests where annual or more frequent distribution is mandatory.
- Life estates (ownership of the right to use property presently but not ownership of the property itself).
- Estates for a term certain.
- Bonds or notes (even though interest is not payable until maturity).
- Unrestricted transfers of life insurance policies.

4 Gifts—Complete vs. Incomplete Gifts

Complete gifts are subject to gift tax and qualify for the annual exclusion. Incomplete gifts are not subject to gift tax.

4.1 Complete Gifts—A Gift Is Considered Complete

- Even though the donee is not yet born, provided his identity can later be ascertained.
- Despite the possibility that the property may revert to the donor at some future time.

4.2 Incomplete Gifts—Not Considered Complete

- **Conditional Gifts**

  If a gift is subject to conditions precedent and will not be complete until the conditions have been met (e.g., a recipient will not get the gift unless he graduates from a four-year accredited college), the gift is incomplete.

- **Revocable Gifts**

  If the donor reserves the right to revoke the gift or change the beneficiaries, the gift is considered incomplete. The gift is complete when those rights terminate by reason other than the donor's death.

Question 1   MCQ-09502

Which of the following requires filing a gift tax return if the transfer exceeds the available annual gift tax exclusion?

1. Medical expenses paid directly to a physician on behalf of an individual unrelated to the donor.

2. Tuition paid directly to an accredited university on behalf of an individual unrelated to the donor.

3. Payments for college books, supplies, and dormitory fees on behalf of an individual unrelated to the donor.

4. Campaign expenses paid to a political organization.

Notes

IV | Federal Taxation of Individuals

1 Filing Status

Filing status is determined as of the end of the year (i.e., December 31).

1.1 Single

- This status applies to individuals who are single or legally separated and living apart.

- Any taxpayer who does not qualify for one of the other filing classes must use the single status by default.

1.2 Married Filing Jointly

- In order to file a joint return, the parties must be married at the end of the year, living together in a recognized common law marriage, or married and living apart (but not legally separated or divorced).

- This status is available even if one spouse dies during the year.

1.3 Qualifying Widow(er)/Surviving Spouse

- A qualifying widow(er), also known as a surviving spouse, may use married filing joint (MFJ) tax rates and standard deduction for two years after the year in which a spouse dies.

- The taxpayer must maintain principal residence for a dependent child for the whole year.

1.4 Head of Household

- Must be not married, legally separated, or living apart from a spouse for the last six months of the tax year.

- Must not be a qualifying widow(er).

- Must not be a nonresident alien.

- Must maintain a household that for more than half the year is the principal residence of a "qualifying person": an unmarried son or daughter (not required to be a dependent, but must live with the taxpayer), father or mother (must be dependent but not required to live with the taxpayer), or other dependent relative (must live with the taxpayer).

2 Dependents

Certain tax benefits, such as an advantageous filing status or certain tax credits, require either a qualifying child or qualifying relative. Each category has requirements.

2.1   Dependency Definitions

Dependency requirements are as follows:

Qualifying Child	Qualifying Relative
Close Relative: Son, daughter, stepchild, brother, sister, stepbrother/sister, or a descendant of these. Also includes adopted and foster children.	**S**upport: Taxpayer must provide > 50%. To claim someone as a dependent in multiple support situations, one must provide > 10%.
Age Limit: In general, child must be < 19 (or 24 if a full-time student) and younger than the taxpayer.	**U**nder specific amount of taxable gross income ($4,400 for 2022).
Residency: Same principal abode for > ½ tax year. If a foster child, must be for the whole year.	**P**recludes dependent filing a joint tax return.
Eliminate Gross Income Test: Does not apply.	**O**nly U.S. citizens or residents of U.S., Canada, or Mexico.
Support Test: Qualifying child may not contribute more than one-half of their own support.	**R**elative or **T**axpayer lives with individual for whole year.

Question 1 MCQ-09545

Jeff and Rhonda are married and have two children, Max and Jen. Max is 20, attends college in the Los Angeles area full-time and works as a stunt double for a television show while he is in school. Max earns $15,000 per year as a stunt double and lives at home when school is not in session. Jeff and Rhonda pay for Max's tuition and all his living expenses. Jen, who lives at home, is 18 years old and makes $18,000 per year working full-time as an office administrator. Jeff and Rhonda pay for 65 percent of Jen's living expenses. In addition, Rhonda's mother, Joanne (a widow), resides with the family, earns $3,000 per year in taxable interest and dividends from her investments, and receives $9,000 per year in nontaxable Social Security benefits. Jeff and Rhonda receive no rent from Joanne and provide all the support she needs for the year. All those mentioned are U.S. citizens. How many people qualify as dependents for Jeff and Rhonda's income tax return?

   1. Two

   2. Three

   3. Four

   4. Five

Question 2 MCQ-09739

Bob provides more than half of his mother's support. His mother earns $6,000 per year as a hairdresser. She lives in an apartment across town. Bob is unmarried and has no children. What is Bob's most advantageous filing status?

   1. Single

   2. Head of household

   3. Qualifying single

   4. Supporting single

1 Inclusions and Exclusions

All income is taxable income unless specifically excluded by the Internal Revenue Code. Taxable items are included in income at the fair market value (FMV) of the asset received, and the tax basis of the asset is the FMV. Nontaxable items are excluded from income, and the tax basis of the asset received is the net book value (NBV), or basis, in the hands of the person giving the asset to the taxpayer.

General Rule			
Event		Amount Included in Income	Basis in Property Received
1. Taxable	=	FMV	FMV
2. Nontaxable	=	None	NBV

2 Characterization of Income

2.1 Wages

Cash or FMV of property received as compensation for services is included in income.

- Partially taxable fringe benefits include items like life insurance premiums. Cost of $50,000 coverage is excluded from income; cost of excess coverage is included.

- Nontaxable fringe benefits are excluded from income (e.g., any employer-paid portion of medical/health insurance premiums).

2.2 Interest (Schedule B)

- **Taxable Interest:** Interest on corporate and federal bonds (not qualified Series EE savings bonds), bank accounts, and late tax refund payments.

- **Tax-Exempt Interest:** State and local bonds and qualified Series EE savings bonds (qualified when acquired after 1989, the taxpayer is over age 24, and they are used for higher education expenses of the taxpayer, spouse, or dependents).

2.3   Dividends (Schedule B)

▪ Amounts received that represent a portion of a corporation's earnings and profits are taxable income. Property dividends are taxable income at the property's FMV.

▪ Amounts that do not represent a portion of a corporation's earnings and profits are first credited as a return of capital to the extent of the individual's basis in the stock. Any excess amounts are then taxable as a capital gain.

▪ Dividends on stock held more than 60 days in the 120-day period beginning 60 days before the ex-dividend date are subject to a 15 percent tax rate for most taxpayers (0 percent for taxpayers with low taxable income and 20 percent for taxpayers with high taxable income).

2.4   State and Local Tax Refunds

State and local tax refunds are taxable if the taxpayer received a benefit from the itemized deduction of those taxes on a prior return (called the "tax benefit rule").

2.5   Alimony

Alimony received from a divorce or separation agreement executed on or before December 31, 2018 is taxable income to the recipient and an adjustment from gross income for the payor.

▪ Payments must be in cash, be required by divorce decree, and be made "periodically" (e.g., monthly). Lump-sum property settlements are not alimony.

▪ Child support is *not* alimony. Child support must be paid first. If total payments do not cover all child support and alimony, they are first applied to child support and then to alimony.

2.6   Business Income (Schedule C)

Self-employed individuals report all business income and expenses allocable to business activities on Schedule C. A single amount is then transferred from Schedule C and reported on the face of Form 1040.

2.6.1   Business Gross Income

Business gross income includes cash or fair market value of property received as compensation.

2.6.2   Business Expenses

Business expenses include cost of goods sold, business licenses, salaries and commissions paid to others (not to sole proprietor), depreciation, business meals (deduction limited to 50 percent), rent, insurance, travel, supplies, etc. For 2021 and 2022, food and beverage provided by a restaurant is 100 percent deductible.

2.6.3   Net Income

Schedule C net business income is subject to both income tax and self-employment taxes on the taxpayer's Form 1040 individual income tax return.

2.6.4 Net Loss

A Schedule C net loss is deductible against other Form 1040 income. Net operating losses (NOLs) arising in 2018, 2019, and 2020 tax years can be carried back five years (oldest year first) and carried forward indefinitely to offset taxable income in other years. NOLs arising in 2021 and beyond cannot be carried back but can be carried forward indefinitely. Post-2017 NOLs carried forward to post-2020 tax years can only offset 80% of taxable income after deducting any pre-2018 NOL carryforwards.

2.7 Individual Retirement Account (IRA) Distributions

Taxable distributions from IRAs are ordinary income to the taxpayer. For traditional IRAs, distributions must start by April 1 of the year following the year in which the taxpayer reaches age 72.

2.7.1 Types of IRA Distributions

The extent to which a distribution is taxable depends on the type of IRA distribution and whether it is a distribution of earnings or principal (contributions made).

■ **Deductible Traditional IRA Distribution:**

- Distribution of contributions for which a deduction was taken when made are taxable.

- Earnings are taxable when distributed.

■ **Nondeductible Traditional IRA Distribution:**

- Distribution of contributions for which a deduction was not taken when made are nontaxable.

- Earnings are taxable when distributed.

- A distribution from a nondeductible traditional IRA is allocated between principal (contributions) and earnings pro rata based on relative amounts in the IRA account at the time of the distribution.

■ **Nonqualified Roth IRA Distribution:**

- Roth IRA contributions are not deductible, so distribution of contributions made are nontaxable.

- Earnings are taxable when distributed.

- Distributions from Roth IRAs are considered to first come from principal (contributions), then earnings.

■ **Qualified Roth IRA Distribution:**

- Both distribution of principal (contributions) and earnings are nontaxable.

- To be a "qualified" distribution, the Roth IRA must have been open for at least five years, and the taxpayer must be age 59 ½ or older, disabled, a first-time homebuyer using it to purchase a home (maximum $10,000), or a beneficiary receiving it after the owner's death.

2.7.2 10 Percent Additional Penalty (Before Age 59 1/2)

The taxpayer must pay an additional 10 percent penalty tax on taxable distributions taken before age 59 ½ unless the premature distribution was used to pay for:

- **H**ome (first-time homebuyer, $10,000 maximum)
- **I**nsurance, medical (if unemployed)
- **M**edical expenses (in excess of percentage of AGI floor)
- **D**isability (permanent, not temporary)
- **E**ducation expenses
- **A**doption or birth of child ($5,000 maximum)
- **D**eath

2.8 Miscellaneous Taxable Income Items

- Prizes and awards.
- For gambling and winnings, losses are deductible as an itemized deduction, but only to the extent of winnings.
- Unemployment compensation.

2.9 Partially Taxable Items of Income

- Social Security income (depending upon income levels).
- For scholarships and fellowships, amounts not used for qualified expenditures and those paid to a non-degree-seeking student are taxable. Graduate teaching assistant tuition reductions are taxable if it is the only form of compensation.

2.10 Nontaxable Items

- Life insurance proceeds
- Gifts and inheritances
- Medicare benefits
- Workers' compensation
- Personal physical injury awards

Question 1   MCQ-09481

Kyle and Kaylie were divorced in February 2018. The divorce decree required that Kyle give Kaylie $20,000 in exchange for keeping the house they both owned. In addition, beginning in March, Kyle is to pay Kaylie $3,000 per month under the divorce decree, which includes $2,000 per month for support for their two children, Kevin and Kelly. During 2018, Kyle paid Kaylie a total of $45,000. How much is taxable to Kaylie for 2018?

1. $5,000
2. $20,000
3. $25,000
4. $45,000

Question 2   MCQ-09450

Jeffrey Dean, a Master's Degree candidate at North State Central University, was awarded a $15,000 scholarship from North State Central in the current year. During the current year, he paid the following expenses:

Tuition	$12,000
Books	1,000
Fees	500
Room & Board	1,500

In addition, he received $6,000 for teaching two undergraduate accounting courses. What amount must be included in Dean's gross income?

1. $0
2. $6,000
3. $7,500
4. $21,000

3 Employee Stock Options

3.1 Nonqualified Options

3.1.1 Employee Taxation

A nonqualified option is generally taxed when granted if the option has a readily ascertainable value. Otherwise, the option is taxed when exercised.

3.1.2 Employer Taxation

Generally, an employer may deduct the value of the stock option as a business expense in the same year that the employee is required to recognize the option as ordinary income.

3.2 Incentive Stock Options (ISO) and Employee Stock Purchase Plans (ESPP)

ISOs and ESPPs are types of qualified options. An ISO is a right to purchase the stock at a discount. An ESPP allows employees to purchase stock at a discount.

3.2.1 Employee Taxation

If certain conditions are met, there is no taxation when ISOs and ESPPs are granted or exercised. A gain or loss is recognized on the subsequent sale of the stock.

3.2.2 Employer Taxation

Generally, an employer does not receive a tax deduction for an ISO or an ESPP because it is not considered compensation income to the employee.

1 Passive Activities

Passive activities are activities in which a taxpayer does not materially participate (limited partnership interests, rental real estate, other flow-through entities in which the taxpayer is not an active participant). All supplemental income and/or loss items such as rental real estate, royalties, and certain K-1 income/loss items from partnerships, S corporations, and trusts are reported on Schedule E.

2 Rental Income

Rental income is computed as:

> Gross Rental Income
>
> Prepaid Rental Income
>
> Rent Cancellation Payment
>
> Improvement in lieu of Rent
>
> < Rental Expenses >
>
> _____
>
> Net Rental Income   OR   Net Rental Loss

3 Losses From Passive Activities

Net passive activity losses (PALs) generally may not be deducted from other income. They are carried forward until offset by passive activity income or until the activity is disposed of (100 percent deductible in the year of disposition), unless limited by the excess business loss limitation.

3.1 "Mom and Pop" Exception

Taxpayers may deduct up to $25,000 (per year) of net rental real estate passive losses if they actively participate or manage the rental property and own more than 10 percent of the activity. The $25,000 is reduced by 50 percent of the excess of AGI over $100,000 and eliminated when AGI exceeds $150,000.

C Passive Activity Losses

Question 1   MCQ-09738

Sam rents his second home. During the current year, he reported a
$40,000 net loss from the rental. Assume Sam actively participates
in the rental activity and no phase-out limitations apply. What is the
greatest amount of the rental loss that Sam can deduct against ordinary
income in the current year?

1. $0
2. $5,000
3. $25,000
4. $40,000

1 Adjustments to Gross Income

Adjustments are subtracted from gross income to arrive at adjusted gross income.

1.1 Alimony Paid

Alimony paid pursuant to a divorce or separation agreement executed on or before December 31, 2018 is an adjustment to gross income and alimony received is income.

1.2 Retirement Plan Contributions

1.2.1 Maximum Contribution Amount

The maximum amount a taxpayer can contribute to an IRA is the lesser of earned income or $6,000 (2022).

- Taxpayers age 50 or older can contribute an additional $1,000.

- A married taxpayer can use a spouse's earned income to make a contribution.

- Earned income includes salary and wages, self-employment income, taxable alimony, and taxable non-tuition fellowship and stipends received by graduate and postdoctoral students.

1.2.2 Deduction for Contributions to Traditional IRAs

The amount a taxpayer can deduct depends on the taxpayer's AGI and whether the taxpayer (or spouse) is a participant in another qualified retirement plan:

- If a taxpayer is a participant in another plan, the deduction starts to phase out when AGI is $68,000 and is fully phased out when AGI is $78,000 ($109,000–$129,000 AGI for MFJ) (2022).

- If a taxpayer is not a participant in another plan but his or her spouse is, the deduction starts to phase out when the couple's AGI is $204,000 and is fully phased out when AGI is $214,000 (2022).

- If a taxpayer (and spouse, if any) is not a participant in another plan, there is no AGI phase-out for the deduction.

Traditional IRA Income Phase-Out Ranges for Married Individuals			
	Spouse 1 has earned income		If Spouse 2 has no earned income
2022 Modified AGI Phase-out	In ESRP?	Can IRA be deducted?	Can IRA be deducted?
N/A	No	Yes	Yes
<$109,000	Yes	Yes	Yes
$109,000–$129,000	Yes	Yes*	Yes
$129,001–$203,999	Yes	No	Yes
$204,000–$214,000	Yes	No	Yes**
>$214,000***	Yes	No	No

Note: If Spouse 2 has earned income, follow the same rules as Spouse 1.

ESRP = Employer Sponsored Retirement Plan

*The IRA deduction for the *working* spouse is phased out.

**The IRA deduction for the *nonworking* spouse is phased out.

***At modified AGI of more than $214,000, neither the working spouse nor the nonworking spouse can deduct their traditional IRA.

1.2.3 Nondeductible Contributions

■ **Traditional Nondeductible IRAs:** For 2022, maximum contribution is lesser of $6,000, individual's earned income, or the amount not contributed to other IRAs.

■ **Roth IRAs:** The maximum contribution amounts are the same. For 2022, eligibility to contribute to a Roth IRA starts to phase out when AGI is $129,000 and is fully phased out when AGI is $144,000 ($204,000–$214,000 AGI for MFJ, $0–$10,000 for MFS) (2022).

IRA Summary			
	Deductible Traditional IRA	Nondeductible Traditional IRA	Roth IRA
Maximum contribution (2022):	$6,000 combined annual maximum contribution with $1,000 additional "catch up" contribution for age 50 and older		
Above-the-line deduction for contribution:	Yes	No	No
Withdrawals:			
• Contributions	Taxable	Nontaxable	Nontaxable
• Earnings	Taxable	Taxable	Nontaxable (if qualified distribution), taxable (if nonqualified distribution)

1.2.4 Self-Employed Retirement Plans

The maximum amount that a self-employed taxpayer can contribute to a self-employed (S/E) retirement plan in 2022 depends on the type of plan.

- **SEP IRA**

  Lesser of 20 percent of S/E net income reduced by deduction for one-half of S/E tax, or $61,000 ($67,500 for taxpayers age 50 and older)

- **SIMPLE IRA**

  Lesser of 100 percent of S/E net income reduced by deduction for one-half of S/E tax, or $14,000 ($17,000 for taxpayers age 50 and older)

- **Solo 401(k)**

  Lesser of 20 percent of S/E net income reduced by deduction for one-half of S/E tax, or $61,000 ($67,500 if the taxpayer is age 50 or older)

1.3 Student Loan Interest

Deduction is limited to $2,500. For 2022, AGI phase-out amounts are $70,000–$85,000 (S or HH) and $145,000–$175,000 (MFJ).

1.4 Educator Expenses

A deduction of up to $300 is allowed as an adjustment for qualified teaching/classroom expenses for elementary and secondary school teachers.

1.5 Moving Expenses

Moving expense deductions are only allowed for members of the armed forces (or spouses and dependents) on active duty who move pursuant to a military order and incident to a permanent change of station.

1.6 Health Savings Accounts (HSA)

Health savings accounts allow employees with high-deductible insurance plans to make pretax contributions to an HSA to cover health care costs.

- For 2022, the maximum contribution is $3,650 for self-only coverage and $7,300 for family coverage.
- Funds grow tax-free, and there is no time limit for spending.
- Withdrawals used to pay qualified medical expenses are excluded from gross income.

1.7 Other Adjustments

- Interest penalty on early withdrawal of funds.
- Self-employed health insurance premiums (100 percent deductible).
- One-half of self-employment tax.

Question 1

Darwood and Samantha Stevens were divorced in January 2018. In accordance with the divorce decree, Darwood transferred title in their home to Samantha in 2018. The home, which had a fair market value of $300,000 was subject to a $100,000 mortgage that had more than 20 years to run. Monthly mortgage payments amount to $2,000. Under the terms of the settlement, Darwood is obligated to make the mortgage payments on the home for the full remaining 20-year term of the indebtedness, regardless of how long Samantha lives. Darwood made 12 mortgage payments in 2022. What amount is deductible by Darwood as alimony on his 2022 tax return?

1. $0
2. $24,000
3. $200,000
4. $224,000

2 Deductions From Adjusted Gross Income (AGI)

Taxpayers may generally choose between using the standard deduction and itemizing deductions. (This usually depends upon which produces the better tax result; however, if the taxpayer is MFS and his or her spouse itemizes deductions, the taxpayer must also itemize deductions).

2.1   Standard Deductions

	2022
Single (or MFS)	$12,950
Head of Household	$19,400
MFJ (or surviving spouse)	$25,900

For 2022, the additional standard deduction for taxpayers who are elderly (age 65 or older) and/or blind is $1,750 for unmarried taxpayers and $1,400 for MFJ taxpayers.

2.2 Itemized Deductions (Schedule A)

2.2.1 Medical Expenses

Medically necessary items (e.g., prescriptions, doctors, medical and accident insurance, and required surgery) are deductible on Schedule A, subject to 7.5 percent of AGI floor. Nondeductible expenses include elective/cosmetic surgery, life insurance, vitamins, etc.

Qualified Medical Expenses
< Insurance Reimbursement >
Qualified Medical Expenses "Paid"
< 7.5% of AGI >
Deductible Medical Expenses

2.2.2 State, Local, and Foreign Taxes

Real estate taxes, income taxes, and personal property taxes paid during the year are deductible up to an aggregate amount of $10,000. Federal taxes are not deductible.

2.2.3 Sales Tax

Sales taxes paid can be deducted instead of state and local income taxes (whichever is higher). The deduction is based on an IRS table or the actual substantiated sales tax.

2.2.4 Home Mortgage Interest

Qualified residence interest on a first or second home is deductible (both acquisition indebtedness and home equity indebtedness are included).

- **Acquisition:** Interest on up to $750,000 ($375,000 MFS) borrowed to construct, acquire, and improve a home.

- **Home Equity:** As part of the overall limit on total debt of $750,000, interest from a home equity line used to construct or substantially improve the residence may be deducted.

2.2.5 Investment Interest

The deduction is limited to net (taxable) investment income. Interest incurred for tax-free investments is nondeductible.

2.2.6 Charitable Contributions

The maximum deduction for contributions to public charities is 60 percent of AGI for cash contributions, 50 percent for contributions of ordinary income property, and 30 percent for contributions of long-term capital gain property. Contributions must be to qualified charities (i.e., gifts to individuals and political contributions are not deductible).

■ Deduction for long-term capital gain property contributions is FMV, and deduction for ordinary income property contributions is the lesser of FMV or adjusted basis.

■ Excess contributions can be carried forward for up to five years.

■ Contribution of services is nondeductible, but the out-of-pocket expenses are deductible.

2.2.7 Casualty Losses

Applicable to nonbusiness property located in a federally declared disaster area.

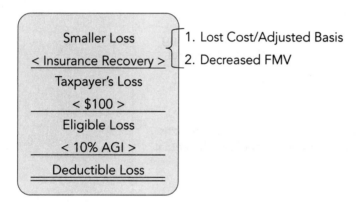

Smaller Loss	1. Lost Cost/Adjusted Basis
< Insurance Recovery >	2. Decreased FMV
Taxpayer's Loss	
< $100 >	
Eligible Loss	
< 10% AGI >	
Deductible Loss	

2.2.8 Gambling Losses

Gambling losses are deductible as an itemized deduction to the extent of gambling winnings.

2.3 Qualified Business Income Deduction

The Section 199A qualified business income (QBI) deduction is a deduction of up to 20 percent of qualified business income for eligible flow-through entities. The deduction is taken "below the line" or from adjusted gross income.

2.3.1 Definitions

1. **Qualified Business Income (QBI):** Ordinary business income less ordinary business deductions earned from a sole proprietorship, S corporation, limited liability company, or partnership connected to business conducted within the United States. QBI is reduced by any related self-employment (S/E) deductions, including the deductions for one-half of S/E tax, S/E retirement plan contributions, and S/E health insurance.

2. **Qualified Property:** Any tangible, depreciable property that is held by the business at the end of the year and is used at any point during the year in the production of QBI.

3. **Qualified Trade or Business (QTB):** Any business other than a specified service trade or business (SSTB).

4. **Specified Service Trade or Business (SSTB):** An SSTB is a trade or business involving direct services in certain fields (such as health, law, accounting, actuarial science, performing arts, consulting, athletics, financial services, and brokerage), and any trade in which the principal asset is the reputation or skill of one or more of its employees or owners. Engineering and architectural services are specifically excluded from the definition of SSTB.

2.3.2   Calculating the Deduction

The basic deduction:

> 20% × Qualified business income (QBI)

2.3.3   W-2 Wage and Property Limitation

When applicable, the QBI deduction is limited to the greater of:

- 50 percent of W-2 wages for the business; or
- 25 percent of W-2 wages for the business plus 2.5 percent of unadjusted basis of qualified property.

2.3.4   Limitations Based on Taxable Income Level

When applicable, the QBI deduction is limited to the greater of:

- 2022 Taxable Income (before QBI deduction) at or below $170,050 ($340,100 MFJ):
  - If QTB or SSTB → Full 20 percent QBI deduction, W-2 wage and property limit does not apply
- 2022 Taxable Income (before QBI deduction) above $220,050 ($440,100 MFJ):
  - If QTB → Full W-2 wage and property limitation applies
    If SSTB → No QBI deduction allowed
- 2022 Taxable Income (before QBI deduction) from $170,050 to $220,050 ($340,100 to $440,100 MFJ):
  - If QTB → Phase-in of W-2 wage and property limitation (if limitation is less than 20 percent of QBI)
  - If SSTB → QBI, W-2 wages, and qualified property amounts are reduced, then phase-in of W-2 wage and property limitation using reduced amounts

2.3.5 Overall Taxable Income Limitation

Once the tentative QBI deduction is calculated, an overall limitation based on the taxpayer's taxable income in excess of net capital gain must be considered. The Section 199A QBI deduction is the lesser of:

1. Combined QBI deduction for all qualifying businesses; or

2. 20 percent of the taxpayer's taxable income (before the QBI deduction) in excess of net capital gain (net LTCG over net STCL and qualified dividend income).

Question 2   MCQ-09482

In the current year, Wells paid the following expenses:

Premiums on an insurance policy against loss of earnings due to sickness or accident.	$3,000
Physical therapy after spinal surgery.	2,000
Premium on an insurance policy that covers reimbursement for the cost of prescription drugs.	500

In the current year, Wells recovered $1,500 of the $2,000 that she paid for physical therapy through insurance reimbursement from a group medical policy paid for by her employer. Disregarding the adjusted gross income percentage threshold, what amount could be claimed on Wells' current year income tax return for medical expenses?

1. $4,000
2. $3,500
3. $1,000
4. $500

---

1 Tax Computation

> Tax = Taxable income × Tax rate*
>
> *The rate is generally given on the exam.

2 Tax Credits

Tax credits reduce the calculated gross tax.

2.1 Child and Dependent Care Credit

■ **Maximum Expenses:** $3,000 (one dependent); $6,000 (two or more).

■ **Requirements:** Taxpayers must maintain a household, work, and incur eligible expenses for care of a dependent qualifying child under age 13, any disabled dependent, or a spouse.

■ **Eligible Expenses:** These include a babysitter and day care, but *not* school.

■ **Calculation of Credit:** Eligible expenses multiplied by 20–35 percent (specific credit percentage depends on AGI).

2.2 Child Tax Credit

■ Credit of $2,000 for each qualifying child under age 17 (2022).

■ Phased out for higher-income taxpayers. Credit reduced by $50 for each $1,000 (or portion thereof) by which AGI exceeds $400,000 for MFJ or $200,000 for all other taxpayers.

■ Partially refundable (i.e., can reduce tax due below zero and result in a refund).

■ Non-child dependent credit of $500 for each dependent who is not a qualifying child under age 17. The non-child dependent credit is subject to the same AGI phase-outs and is not refundable.

2.3 Credit for the Elderly or Permanently Disabled

Credit is equal to 15 percent of eligible income to individuals 65 years or older or less than 65 but permanently disabled.

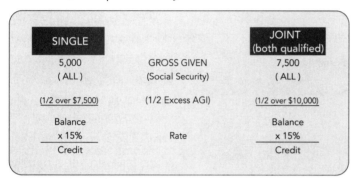

SINGLE	GROSS GIVEN	JOINT (both qualified)
5,000 (ALL)	(Social Security)	7,500 (ALL)
(1/2 over $7,500)	(1/2 Excess AGI)	(1/2 over $10,000)
Balance x 15%	Rate	Balance x 15%
Credit		Credit

2.4 Higher Education Credits

2.4.1 American Opportunity Credit

Individuals are eligible during the first four years of college. The credit is a maximum of $2,500 (100 percent of the first $2,000, plus 25 percent of the next $2,000 of qualified expenses). The American opportunity credit is partially refundable.

2.4.2 Lifetime Learning Credit

This credit is available for an unlimited number of years. It is equal to 20 percent of qualified expenses of up to $10,000.

2.4.3 Phase-outs

Both higher education credits are phased out for higher-income taxpayers. Phase-out begins with modified AGI of $80,000 ($160,000 MFJ) and is fully phased out at $90,000 ($180,000 MFJ).

2.5 Retirement Plan Contribution Credit

Up to $1,000 for traditional or Roth IRA contributions by lower-income taxpayers.

2.6 Earned Income Credit

The earned income credit is a *refundable* credit for low-income taxpayers.

■ The taxpayer must live in the U.S. for more than half the taxable year and meet certain low-income thresholds and other requirements.

■ The maximum basic earned income credit is between 7.65 and 45 percent of earned income, depending upon filing status and the number of dependents (note that having zero dependents does not preclude claiming the earned income credit).

■ The earned income credit cannot be claimed if the taxpayer has investment income in excess of $10,300 (2022).

2.7   Foreign Tax Credit

The credit is limited to the *lesser* of:

■ Foreign taxes paid; or:

$$\frac{\text{Taxable income from all foreign operations}}{\text{Total taxable income from U.S. and foreign sources}} \times \text{U.S. tax}$$

■ Any excess credit is either carried back one year and/or carried forward 10 years.

Question 1	MCQ-09578

Which of the following credits is considered "refundable"?

   1. Child and dependent care credit.

   2. Retirement plan contribution credit.

   3. Child tax credit.

   4. Credit for elderly or permanently disabled.

3   Estimated Tax

A taxpayer is required to make estimated quarterly tax payments if both of the following conditions are met:

1. $1,000 or more remaining tax liability (after withholding is applied).

2. Withholding (and estimated tax payments) is less than the lesser of:

   • 90 percent of current year tax; or

   • 100 percent of prior year tax [110 percent when the taxpayer's AGI is in excess of $150,000].

4   Extensions of Time to File

When a taxpayer files a timely Form 4868 (by the original due date of the return—usually April 15), the taxpayer will receive an automatic six-month extension of time to file (but not time to pay) his or her income tax return.

V | Federal Taxation of Entities

Notes

1 Book Income vs. Taxable Income

The following chart gives an overview of the differences between financial and tax accounting for corporations.

Corporation Tax Summary	GAAP: Financial Statements	IRC: Tax Return	Temp.	Perm.	None
Gross Income					
Gross sales	Income	Income			✓
Installment sales	Income	Income when received	✓		
Rents and royalties in advance	Income when earned	Income when received	✓		
State tax refund	Income	Income			✓
Dividends: equity method 100/65/50% exclusion	Income is subsidiary's earnings No exclusion	Income is dividends-received Excluded forever	✓	✓	
Items Not Includable in "Taxable Income"					
State and municipal bond interest	Income	Not taxable income		✓	
Life insurance proceeds	Income	Generally not taxable income		✓	
Gain/loss on treasury stock	Not reported	Not reported			✓
Ordinary Expenses					
Cost of goods sold	Currently expensed	Uniform capitalization rules			✓
Officers' compensation (top)	Expense	$1,000,000 limit			✓
Bad debt	Allowance (estimated)	Direct write-off	✓		
Estimated liability for contingency (e.g., warranty)	Expense (accrue estimated)	No deduction until paid	✓		
Interest expense: business loan	Expense	Deduct (up to limit)	✓		✓
Tax-free investment	Expense	Not deductible		✓	
Charitable contributions	All expensed	Limited to 10% of adjusted taxable income	✓	✓	✓
Loss on abandonment/casualty	Expense	Deduct			✓
Loss on worthless subsidiary	Expense	Deduct			✓
Depreciation: MACRS vs. straight-line	Slow depreciation	Fast depreciation	✓		
Section 179 depreciation	Not allowed (must depreciate)	$1,080,000 (2022)	✓		
Different basis of asset	Use GAAP basis	Use tax basis		✓	
Amortization: start-up/ organizational expenses	Expense	$5,000 maximum/amortize excess over 15 years	✓		
Franchise	Amortize	Amortize over 15 years	✓		
Goodwill	Impairment test	Amortize over 15 years	✓		
Depletion: percentage vs. straight-line (cost)	Cost over years	Percentage of sales	✓		
Percentage in excess of cost	Not allowed	Percentage of sales		✓	
Profit sharing and pension expense	Expense accrued	No deduction until paid	✓		
Accrued expense (50% owner/family)	Expense accrued	No deduction until paid	✓		
State taxes (paid)	Expense	Deduct			✓
Meals	Expense	Generally 50% deductible (100% for 2021 and 2022)		✓	

(continued on next page)

A   Differences Between Book and Tax Income

(continued)

GAAP Expense Items That Are Not Tax Deductions					
Life insurance expense (corporation)	Expense	Not deductible		✓	
Penalties	Expense	Not deductible		✓	
Lobbying/political expense	Expense	Not deductible		✓	
Federal income taxes	Expense	Not deductible		✓	
Entertainment expense	Expense	Not deductible		✓	
Special Items					
Net capital gain (NCG)	Income	Income			✓
Net capital loss (NCL)	Report as loss	Not deductible	✓		
Carryback/carryover (3 years back/5 years forward)	Not applicable	Offset NCGs in other years	✓		
Related shareholder	Report as a loss	Not deductible		✓	
Net operating loss	Report as a loss	Carryover indefinitely	✓		
Research and development	Expense	Expense/amortize/capitalize	✓	✓	✓

Question 1   MCQ-09469

In Year 6, Garland Corp. contributed $40,000 to a qualified charitable organization. Garland's Year 6 taxable income before the deduction for charitable contributions was $410,000. Included in that amount is a $20,000 dividends-received deduction. Garland also had carryover contributions of $5,000 from the prior year. In Year 6, what amount can Garland deduct as charitable contributions?

1. $40,000
2. $41,000
3. $43,000
4. $45,000

SCHEDULE M-1
Reconciliation of Income (Loss) per Books to Taxable Income

1	Net Income (or loss) per Books		$875,000
2	+	Federal Income Tax (per books)	$384,500
3	+	Excess Capital Losses over Gains	$5,000
4	+	Income subject to tax not recorded on books this year	
	+	Installment Sale Income	$8,500
	+	Rents Received in Advance	$15,000
5	+	Expenses recorded on books this year not on the tax return	
	+	Book Depreciation	$14,000
	+	Contribution Carryover	$0
	+	Meals	$4,200
	+	Allowance for Doubtful Accts. (Incr.)	$15,000
	+	Warranty Accrual	$8,500
	+	Different Basis of Assets	$0
	+	Expense of Organizational Costs	$0
	+	Goodwill Impairment per Books	$5,000
	+	Pension Expense Accrued	$12,000
	+	Penalties	$1,000
6	Add lines 1 through 5		$1,347,700

7	–	Income recorded on books this year not included on this return	
	–	Tax-exempt interest	$3,500
	–	Life Insurance proceeds	$100,000
8	–	Deductions on this return not charged against book income this year:	
	–	Tax Depreciation	$28,000
	–	Contribution Carryover	$0
	–	Section 179 Deduction	$20,000
	–	Direct Bad Debt Write-offs	$8,650
	–	Actual Warranty Costs	$7,500
	–	Different Basis of Assets	$0
	–	Amortization of Organizational Cost	$500
	–	Goodwill Amortization per Return	$9,200
	–	Pensions Paid	$11,350
9	Add lines 7 and 8		$188,700
10	Income (Line 28 Page 1) Line 6 minus Line 9		$1,159,000

This is taxable income per page 1 of the Form 1120 corporation income tax return, before the dividends-received deduction and the NOL carryforward deduction.

1 Corporate Formation

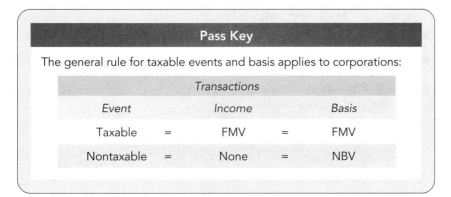

Pass Key				
The general rule for taxable events and basis applies to corporations:				
	Transactions			
Event		Income		Basis
Taxable	=	FMV	=	FMV
Nontaxable	=	None	=	NBV

1.1 Corporation Tax Consequences

1.1.1 No Gain or Loss Recognized

There is no gain or loss recognized when the corporation issues stock in exchange for property in the following transactions: (1) formation; (2) purchase of treasury stock; and (3) resale of treasury stock.

1.1.2 Basis of Property (Corporation Receives)

The basis of the property received from the transferor/shareholder is the greater of:

- the adjusted basis (net book value) of the shareholder plus any gain recognized by the shareholder; or
- debt assumed by the corporation.

1.2 Shareholder Tax Consequences

1.2.1 No Gain or Loss Recognized

Shareholders will not recognize gain or loss if the following conditions have been met:

- 80 percent control (must exist immediately after the transaction).
- No boot is received by the shareholder.

    The following items represent (taxable) boot and/or will trigger gain recognition:

    - Cash withdrawn.
    - Receipt of debt securities (e.g., bonds).

    The amount of liabilities that exceed the net book value of assets transferred into the corporation is not boot but generates gain.

Question 1   MCQ-09516

Gearty and Olinto organized The Worthington Corp., which issued voting common stock with a fair market value of $240,000. They each transferred property in exchange for stock as follows:

	Property	Adjusted Basis	Fair-Market Value	Percentage of the Worthington Corp. Stock Acquired
Gearty	Building	$80,000	$164,000	60%
Olinto	Land	$10,000	$ 96,000	40%

The building was subject to a $20,000 mortgage that was assumed by the Worthington Corp. What was The Worthington Corp.'s basis in the building?

1. $60,000
2. $80,000
3. $144,000
4. $164,000

2 Taxation of a C Corporation

2.1 Tax Calculation and Double Taxation

Corporations pay income tax at the corporate level at a flat tax rate of 21 percent. Dividends paid to the shareholders are also subject to tax at the shareholder level, thus creating the concept of double taxation.

2.2 Estimated Payments of Corporate Tax

■ Corporations other than large corporations pay the lower of:

- 100 percent of the tax shown on the return for the current year; or
- 100 percent of the tax shown on the return for the preceding year.

■ Large corporations must pay 100 percent of the tax as shown on the current year return

2.3 Charitable Contributions (10 Percent of Adjusted Taxable Income Limitation)

The charitable contributions deduction for corporations is limited to 10 percent of taxable income before "special deductions" (charitable contributions deduction and dividends-received deduction). Any disallowed charitable contributions may be carried forward for five years.

2.4 Dividends-Received Deduction

In an attempt to prevent triple taxation of earnings, domestic corporations (those that are not personal service corporations, personal holding companies, or personally taxed S corporations) are allowed a "dividends-received deduction." The amount of this deduction depends on the percentage that the corporation owns of the investee corporation that paid the dividends.

Percentage Ownership	Dividends-Received Deduction
0% to < 20%	50%
20% to < 80%	65%
80% to 100%	100%

2.5 Net Operating Losses (NOL)

NOLs that arise in 2018, 2019, and 2020 tax years can be carried back five years (oldest year first) and carried forward indefinitely. A taxpayer can elect to forgo the carryback and just carry forward. NOLs arising in 2021 and beyond cannot be carried back but can be carried forward indefinitely. Deduction of NOLs arising after 2017 that are carried forward to post-2020 tax years is limited to 80 percent of taxable income after deducting any pre-2018 NOL carryforwards.

2.6 Consolidated Returns

An affiliated group of corporations may elect to be taxed as a single unit, thereby eliminating intercompany gains and losses. An affiliated group means that a common parent directly owns:

1. 80 percent or more of the voting power of all outstanding stock; and

2. 80 percent or more of the value of all outstanding stock of each corporation.

Note

Not all corporations are allowed the privilege of filing a consolidated return. Examples of those that are denied the privilege include S corporations, foreign corporations, most real estate investment trusts (REITs), some insurance companies, and most tax-exempt organizations.

Question 2   MCQ-09484

In Year 6, Acorn Inc. had the following items of income and expense:

Sales	$500,000
Cost of sales	250,000
Dividends received	25,000

The dividends were received from a corporation of which Acorn owns 30%. In Acorn's Year 6 corporate income tax return, what amount should be reported as taxable income before special deductions?

1. $525,000
2. $505,000
3. $275,000
4. $250,000

3 Corporate Earnings and Profits (E&P)

3.1 General

■ Required for corporate income tax return preparation.

■ The starting point is corporate taxable income.

■ Affect corporate distributions and other activities—E&P is:

- a major factor in determining the ability of the corporation to pay a dividend to the shareholders.

- critical to the tax impact of corporate distributions, or nonliquidating dividends.

- a factor in the determination of corporate reorganizations, accumulated earnings tax, stock redemptions, partial liquidations, and the tax status of certain S corporations that have previously been C corporations.

3.2 Accumulated Earnings and Profits

Generally, the amount of "Accumulated E&P" is the amount of E&P that exists as of the end of the previous tax year. For any given year, the distinction between current E&P and accumulated E&P is necessary for the classification of corporate distributions.

3.2.1 General Calculation

The following formula is used to calculate the accumulated E&P to carry forward to the tax year after the current year:

Accumulated E&P as of the beginning of the year

Add/Subtract: Current E&P for the tax year less any distributions deemed from current E&P

Subtract: Distributions from accumulated E&P

Accumulated E&P as of the end of the year

3.2.2 Classification of Distribution

Corporate distributions are first applied to current E&P, then to accumulated E&P, and then to return of capital. If any excess remains, it is classified as "excess distributions" and reported as capital gain distributions (taxable income) by the shareholder. Distributions within the year are allocated based on the ratio of each distribution to the total distribution. Note that the allocation of the excess distribution to return of capital and capital gain distributions depends on the stock basis of the shareholder.

Question 3   MCQ-09632

On January 1, Year 5, Olinto Corp., an accrual-basis, calendar-year C corporation, had $35,000 in accumulated earnings and profits. For Year 5, Olinto had current earnings and profits of $15,000, and made two $40,000 cash distributions to its shareholders, one in April and one in September of Year 5. What amount of the Year 5 distributions is classified as dividend income to Olinto's shareholders?

1. $15,000
2. $35,000
3. $50,000
4. $80,000

---

4 Corporate Distributions

4.1 Shareholder Taxable Amount

The taxable amount of a dividend from a corporation's earnings and profits depends upon the type of entity the shareholder is:

4.1.1 Individual Shareholder

- **Cash Dividends:** Amount received.
- **Property Dividends:** FMV of property received.

4.1.2 Corporate Shareholders

Remember the dividends-received deduction.

- **Cash Dividends:** Amount received.
- **Property Dividends:** FMV of property received.

4.2 Corporation Paying Dividend— Taxable Amount

4.2.1 General Rule

The general rule is that the payment of a dividend does not create a taxable event. A dividend is a reduction of earnings and profits.

4.2.2 Property Dividends

If a corporation distributes appreciated property, the tax results are as follows:

- The corporation recognizes gain as if the property had been sold (i.e., FMV less adjusted basis). The gain increases current E&P.

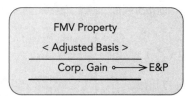

Question 4	MCQ-09619

Fox Corp. owned 2,000 shares of Duffy Corp., stock that it bought in Year 0 for $9 per share. In Year 8, when the fair market value of the Duffy stock was $20 per share, Fox distributed this stock to a noncorporate shareholder. Fox's recognized gain on this distribution was:

1. $40,000
2. $22,000
3. $18,000
4. $0

5 Corporate Liquidation

5.1 Corporation Sells Assets and Distributes Cash to Shareholders

- The corporation recognizes a gain or loss (as normal) on the sale of the assets; and

- Shareholders recognize gain or loss to the extent that cash differs from their adjusted basis of the stock.

5.2 Corporation Distributes Assets to Shareholders

- The corporation recognizes a gain or loss as if it sold the assets for FMV; and

- Shareholders recognize a gain or loss to the extent the FMV of the assets received differs from the adjusted basis of their stock.

Question 5   MCQ-09500

Krol Corp. distributed marketable securities in redemption of its stock in a complete liquidation. On the date of distribution, these securities had a basis of $100,000 and a fair market value of $150,000. What gain does Krol have as a result of the distribution?

   1. $0.

   2. $50,000 capital gain.

   3. $50,000 Section 1231 gain.

   4. $50,000 ordinary gain.

Notes

1 | S Corporation Eligibility

1.1 Eligible Shareholders

- Eligible shareholders include individuals, estates, and certain types of trusts.

- An individual shareholder may not be a nonresident alien.

- Qualified retirement plans and 501(c)(3) charitable organizations may be shareholders.

- Neither corporations nor partnerships are eligible shareholders.

1.1.1 Shareholder Limit

There may not be more than 100 shareholders. Family members (current/ former spouses, common ancestors, and/or their descendants) may elect to be treated as one shareholder.

1.1.2 One Class of Stock

There may not be more than one class of stock outstanding. However, differences in common stock voting rights are allowed. Preferred stock is not permitted.

1.2 S Election

S election requires unanimous consent of the shareholders.

- If election is filed by March 15 of the current tax year, it is effective January 1 of the current year.

- If election is filed after March 15 of the current tax year, it is effective January 1 of the following year.

Question 1	MCQ-09531

Village Corp., a calendar year corporation, began business in Year 1. Village made a valid S corporation election on December 5, Year 4, with the unanimous consent of its shareholders. The eligibility requirements for S status continued to be met throughout Year 5. On what date did Village's S status become effective?

    1. January 1, Year 4.

    2. January 1, Year 5.

    3. December 5, Year 4.

    4. December 5, Year 5.

2 Effect of S Corporation Election

2.1 No Tax on Corporation

Generally, there is no tax at the corporation level. All earnings are passed through to the shareholders (i.e., the entity is taxed similar to a partnership); however, if the S corporation was previously a C corporation, there are three exceptions: LIFO recapture tax, built-in gains tax, and passive investment income tax.

2.2 Effect of S Corporation Election on Shareholders

2.2.1 Pass-Through of Income and/or Losses

Net income (or loss) is passed through to shareholders on Schedule K-1.

- The following S corporation items flow through to the shareholder in a manner similar to a partnership (see Schedule K-1 for a complete list):
  - Ordinary business income/loss (not subject to S/E tax)
  - Rental income/loss
  - Portfolio income (including interest, dividends, and royalties)
  - Tax-exempt interest
  - Net capital gains and losses
  - Net Section 1231 gains and losses
  - Percentage depletion
  - Foreign income tax
  - Charitable contributions
  - Section 179 expense deduction

- Allocations to shareholders are made on a per-share, per-day basis.

- Losses are limited to the shareholder's adjusted basis in the S corporation stock plus direct shareholder loans to the corporation.

2.2.2 Effect on Basis in S Corporation Stock

Income, gains, and capital contributions increase basis; losses, deductions, and distributions decrease basis. Unlike partnership taxation, corporate debt does not increase a shareholder's basis in her or his stock of the S corporation.

Question 2 — MCQ-09515

Fox Corp., an S corporation, had an ordinary loss of $36,500 for the year ended December 31, Year 2. At January 1, Year 2, Duffy owned 50% of Fox's stock. Duffy held the stock for 40 days in Year 2 before selling the entire 50% interest to an unrelated third party. Duffy's basis for the stock was $10,000. Duffy was a full-time employee of Fox until the stock was sold. Duffy's share of Fox's loss was:

1. $0
2. $2,000
3. $10,000
4. $18,250

3 Termination of S Election

The S corporation status will terminate as a result of any of the following:

- A majority of the shareholders (any combination of voting and nonvoting) consent to a voluntary revocation. If no date is specified in the revocation, the effective date will be January 1 of the current year if the revocation is filed by March 15. If the revocation is filed after March 15, the effective date is January 1 of the following year.

- The corporation fails to meet the criteria that allow S corporation status (e.g., the number of shareholders exceeds 100). S corporation status terminates immediately.

- For each of three consecutive years, more than 25 percent of the corporation's gross receipts were from passive investment income and the corporation still had C corporation earnings and profits at the end of each year. In this case the S corporation status terminates at the beginning of the fourth year.

Question 3 — MCQ-09452

An S Corporation has 30,000 shares of voting common stock and 20,000 shares of nonvoting common stock issued and outstanding. The S election can be revoked voluntarily with the consent of the shareholders holding, on the day of the revocation:

	Shares of Voting Stock	Shares of Nonvoting Stock
1.	0	20,000
2.	7,500	5,000
3.	10,000	16,000
4.	20,000	0

Notes

1 Basis

The general rule for taxable events and basis applies to partnership taxation as well as individual taxation:

Transactions				
Event		*Income*		*Basis*
Taxable	=	FMV	=	FMV
Nontaxable	=	None	=	NBV

1.1 Basis of Contributing Partner's Interest

1.1.1 Initial Basis

The partner's initial basis shall be the following:

Cash contributed
+ Property contributed (adjusted basis)
+ Services provided (FMV, if capital interest)
< Liabilities transferred to partnership, assumed by other partners >
+ Partner's share of partnership liabilities

Partner's initial basis in partnership interest

1.1.2 Property Subject to an Excess Liability

When property contributed by a partner is subject to a liability and the decrease in the partner's individual liability exceeds his or her partnership basis, the excess amount is not boot, but is treated like boot in that it generates a gain to the partner.

D Partnerships

1.2 Partner Basis Formula

B	BEGINNING CAPITAL ACCOUNT	• cash • FMV services • NBV assets < liability transferred to partnership >
A	+ % ALL INCOME	• ordinary business income • separately stated income and gains • tax-exempt income
S	< % ALL LOSSES/DEDUCTIONS >*	• ordinary business loss • separately stated losses and deductions • nondeductible expenses
	< DISTRIBUTIONS >*	• cash • property—adjusted basis (NBV)
E	ENDING CAPITAL ACCOUNT % PARTNERSHIP LIABILITIES	• recourse unsecured (if personal liability) • nonrecourse secured (ownership percentage)
	ENDING TAX BASIS IN PARTNERSHIP INTEREST	

*Tax basis cannot be reduced below zero

Question 1 — MCQ-09470

Gray is a 50% partner in Fabco Partnership. Gray's tax basis in Fabco on January 1, Year 4, was $5,000. Fabco made no distributions to the partners during Year 4, and recorded the following:

Ordinary income	$20,000
Tax exempt income	$ 8,000
Portfolio income	$ 4,000

What is Gray's tax basis in Fabco on December 31, Year 4?

1. $21,000
2. $16,000
3. $12,000
4. $10,000

2 Determination of Ordinary Income/ Loss and Separately Stated Items

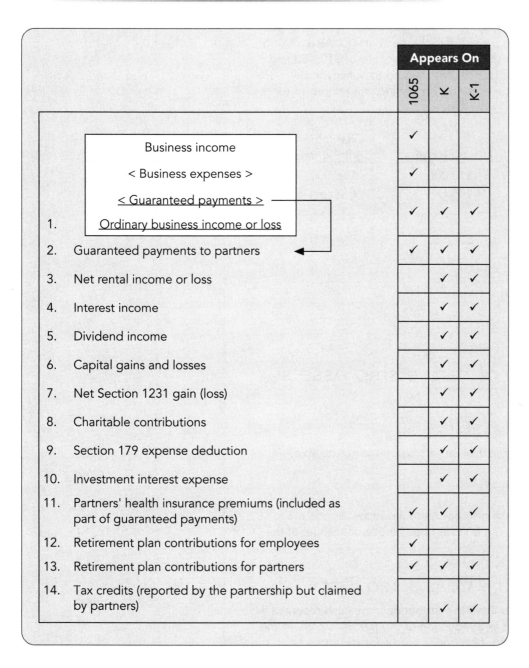

	Appears On		
	1065	K	K-1
Business income	✓		
< Business expenses >	✓		
< Guaranteed payments >	✓	✓	✓
1. Ordinary business income or loss			
2. Guaranteed payments to partners	✓	✓	✓
3. Net rental income or loss		✓	✓
4. Interest income		✓	✓
5. Dividend income		✓	✓
6. Capital gains and losses		✓	✓
7. Net Section 1231 gain (loss)		✓	✓
8. Charitable contributions		✓	✓
9. Section 179 expense deduction		✓	✓
10. Investment interest expense		✓	✓
11. Partners' health insurance premiums (included as part of guaranteed payments)	✓	✓	✓
12. Retirement plan contributions for employees	✓		
13. Retirement plan contributions for partners	✓	✓	✓
14. Tax credits (reported by the partnership but claimed by partners)		✓	✓

Question 2   MCQ-09652

Nick, Chris, Stacey, and Mike are each 25% partners in Liberty Partnership, a general partnership. During the current year, the partnership had revenues of $300,000 and non-separately stated business expenses of $100,000, including a guaranteed payment of $30,000 to Nick for services provided to the partnership. Also, during the current year, the partnership had interest income of $10,000 and charitable contributions of $16,000. With regard to activity in the partnership, what should Stacey report on her income tax return for the current year?

	Ordinary Income	Interest Income	Charitable Contributions
1.	$200,000	$10,000	$16,000
2.	$ 80,000	$ 2,500	$ 4,000
3.	$ 57,500	$ 2,500	$ 4,000
4.	$ 50,000	$ 2,500	$ 4,000

3 Distribution of Partnership Assets

3.1 General (Nontaxable)

In general, a nonliquidating distribution to a partner is nontaxable.

3.2 Basis Reduction

In general, distributions of cash or property to a partner reduce the partner's basis by the cash or the adjusted basis (net book value) of the property distributed.

3.3 Cash Received Is Considered First

In both nonliquidating and liquidating distributions, the cash received in the transaction is applied first as a reduction of the partner's basis in the partnership before any property distributions are considered.

3.4 Basis in Property Received

In a nonliquidating distribution, the basis of property received by the partner will be the same as the basis in the hands of the partnership immediately prior to the distribution.

3.5 Reduction (for Distribution) Limited to Partnership Basis

■ The assigned basis of the property received may not exceed the partner's basis in the partnership interest. Cash received is applied first.

■ If the amount of cash received exceeds the partner's basis in the partnership, gain is recognized to the extent of the excess. Any property received in the same transaction would have a basis to the partner of zero.

■ If the partnership's basis in property distributed exceeds the partner's basis in partnership interest (after reduction for cash distribution), the partner's basis in the property distributed is the remaining basis in the partnership interest.

Question 3	MCQ-09485

Day's adjusted basis in LMN Partnership interest is $50,000. During the year Day received a nonliquidating distribution of $25,000 cash plus land with an adjusted basis of $15,000 to LMN, and a fair market value of $20,000. How much is Day's basis in the land?

1. $10,000
2. $15,000
3. $20,000
4. $25,000

4 Ownership Changes and Liquidation

4.1 Complete Withdrawal (Liquidating Distribution)

In a complete liquidation, the partner's basis for the distributed property is the same as the adjusted basis of his partnership interest, reduced by any cash received in the same transaction.

4.1.1 Nontaxable Liquidation

> Beginning Capital Account
> Share of Income < Loss > Up to Withdrawal
> ───────────────────────
> Partner's Capital Account
> Share of Partnership Liabilities
> ───────────────────────
> Adjusted Basis in Partnership Interest @ Date of Withdrawal
> < Cash Distribution >
> ───────────────────────
> Remaining Basis to Be
> Allocated to Assets Distributed
> ═══════════════════════

The CPA Examination will require candidates to understand the difference in basis rules for nonliquidating and liquidating distributions.

Distribution	Basis in Property Received	Stopping Point
Nonliquidating	Adjusted Basis of Property	Stop at Zero
Liquidating	Partnership Interest	Must "Zero Out" Account

4.2 Sale of Partnership Interest

As a general rule, the partner has a capital gain or loss when transferring a partnership interest because a partnership interest is a capital asset. Any gain or loss that represents a partner's share of "hot assets" (unrealized cash basis receivables or appreciated inventory) is ordinary income or loss.

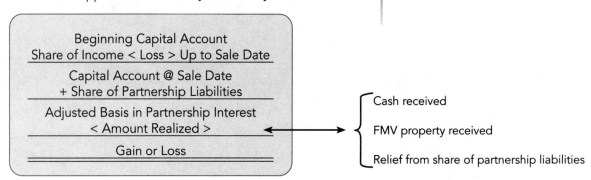

> Beginning Capital Account
> Share of Income < Loss > Up to Sale Date
> ───────────────────────
> Capital Account @ Sale Date
> + Share of Partnership Liabilities
> ───────────────────────
> Adjusted Basis in Partnership Interest
> < Amount Realized >
> ───────────────────────
> Gain or Loss
> ═══════════════════════

Cash received

FMV property received

Relief from share of partnership liabilities

Question 4
MCQ-09581

On December 31 of the current year, Fox sold his interest in a limited partnership for $50,000 cash and relief of all partnership liabilities. On that date, the adjusted basis of Fox's partnership interest, after the increase for his share of current year partnership income, was $60,000 consisting of his capital account of $35,000 and his share of the partnership liabilities of $25,000. The partnership has no unrealized receivables or substantially appreciated inventory. What is Fox's gain or loss on the sale of his partnership interest?

1. Ordinary loss of $10,000
2. Ordinary gain of $15,000
3. Capital loss of $10,000
4. Capital gain of $15,000

Notes

1 Separate Taxpaying Entities

Trusts are separate taxpaying entities. Distributions made by the trust are deductible by the trust and taxable to the recipient.

2 Simple Trusts vs. Complex Trusts

2.1 Simple Trusts

- A simple trust only makes distributions out of current income (i.e., it cannot make distributions from the trust corpus).
- A simple trust is required to distribute all of its income currently.
- A simple trust cannot take a deduction for a charitable contribution.
- A simple trust is entitled to a $300 exemption in arriving at its taxable income.

2.2 Complex Trusts

All trusts that are not simple trusts are complex trusts. A trust may be simple one year and complex the next.

- A complex trust may accumulate current income.
- A complex trust may distribute principal.
- A complex trust may deduct charitable contributions.
- A complex trust is permitted an exemption of $100 in arriving at its taxable income.

1 Types of Exempt Organizations

1.1 Section 501(c)(1) Organizations

- Section 501(c)(1) organizations are created by an act of Congress (e.g., federal credit union).

- Almost all other exempt organizations must make written application for exempt status, be approved by the IRS, become incorporated, and issue capital stock. Furthermore, the articles of organization must limit the purpose of the entity to the charitable/exempt purpose.

1.2 Section 501(c)(2) Organizations

Organized for an exclusive purpose to hold title to property, collect income from the property, and turn over the net income to an exempt organization.

1.3 Section 501(c)(3) Organizations

This is the most common type of exempt organization and includes:

- foundations organized and operated exclusively for religious, charitable, scientific, public safety testing, literary, or educational purposes;

- foundations organized to foster national and international amateur sports competitions; and

- foundations organized to prevent cruelty to children or animals.

1.4 Section 509 Private Foundations

These include all 501(c)(3) organizations except (1) maximum (60-percent-type) charitable deduction donees; (2) broadly publicly supported organizations receiving more than one third of their annual support from members and the public and less than one third from investment income and unrelated business income; (3) supporting organizations; and (4) public safety testing organizations.

2 Unrelated Business Income (UBI)

2.1 Definition

A tax-exempt organization may be subject to regular corporate income tax for unrelated business income (UBI). UBI is gross income, less related business deductions, that is:

- derived from an activity that constitutes a trade or business;
- regularly carried on; and
- not substantially related to the organization's tax-exempt purposes.

2.2 Excluded Trade or Business Activities

The following activities are excluded from the definition of unrelated trade or business:

- Bingo games (if legal, and limited to not-for-profit organizations and the jurisdiction where the game is played)
- Activity conducted for the convenience of an organization's members, students, patients, or employees
- Convention or trade show activity
- Exchange or rental of membership lists
- Sale of merchandise received as gifts or contributions (e.g., thrift shop)
- Sale of articles made by disabled persons as part of their rehabilitation
- Activity where substantially all the work is performed by unpaid volunteer workers

2.3 Excluded Types of Income

- Dividends, interest, annuities, and other investment income
- Royalties
- Rents from real property (generally)
- Income from research by a college, university, or hospital
- Gains and losses from disposition of property not held primarily for sale to customers in the ordinary course of business

2.4 Membership Organizations

If a membership organization, such as a social club or homeowners' association, makes a profit, that profit is generally taxable.

Note

The fact that an activity results in a loss does not exclude that activity from the definition of an unrelated business (if expenses exceed income, a net operating loss exists, which is subject to carryover provisions of net operating losses).

Question 1   MCQ-09657

Unrelated business income (UBI):

1. Includes unrelated income from an activity where all the work is performed by volunteers.

2. Does not apply if the activity results in a loss.

3. Includes proceeds from the sale of merchandise received as gifts or contributions.

4. Specifically excludes income from research by a college or hospital.

Class Question Explanations

Notes

Topic A

QUESTION 1 MCQ-09715

Choice "4" is correct.

Practitioners must apply due diligence standards to all written advice, including those by means of electronic communication, regarding one or more federal tax matters.

Choice "1" is incorrect. Prior to June 12, 2014, a different set of provisions applied to advice that was defined as a "covered" opinion.

Choice "2" is incorrect. The provisions in effect prior to June 12, 2014, excluded certain written opinions.

Choice "3" is incorrect. The requirements of Circular 230 apply to all applicable written advice, regardless of the principal purpose of the entity or plan.

QUESTION 2 MCQ-09712

Choice "4" is correct.

A compensated preparer is liable for a penalty if the preparer's understatement of taxpayer liability on a return or claim for refund is due to the preparer's negligent or intentional disregard of rules and regulations. In this situation, Mr. Powell knew that the income earned as an independent contractor by the taxpayer should be reported on the taxpayer's income tax return; however, he intentionally disregarded the rules associated with the reporting of this income.

Choice "1" is incorrect. Substantial authority refers to a standard that is used in determining whether or not a tax position taken in a tax return is supported by relevant tax authorities. A tax return preparer who takes an unreasonable position in a tax return that is not supported by substantial authority may be liable for the penalty associated with the understatement of the taxpayer's liability due to an *unreasonable position* by the *tax return preparer.*

Choice "2" is incorrect. Failure to file correct information returns refers to the penalty assessed on a person who employs a tax return preparer and fails to file an information return containing the name, taxpayer identification number, and place of work of each tax return preparer.

Choice "3" is incorrect. Wrongful disclosure and/or use of tax return information by the tax return preparer refers to the penalty imposed on a tax return preparer for wrongfully disclosing information provided by the taxpayer.

Regulation I

Topic B

QUESTION 1 MCQ-09719

Choice "3" is correct.

The U.S. Tax Court is the only forum in which taxpayers may litigate without first having to pay the disputed tax in full.

Choice "1" is incorrect. A case would not start in the U.S. Supreme Court. The U.S. Supreme Court only rarely hears tax cases. When a case makes it to the Supreme Court, it is typically when where there is a conflict among the Courts of Appeals or a tax issue of major importance.

Choice "2" is incorrect. A taxpayer who disagrees with the IRS may take his or her case to a U.S. District Court only after paying the disputed tax liability and then sue the IRS/government for a refund.

Choice "4" is incorrect. To start the litigation process in the U.S. Court of Federal Claims, the taxpayer must pay the disputed tax and sue the IRS/government for a refund.

QUESTION 2 MCQ-09705

Choice "2" is correct.

The failure-to-pay penalty will apply to Spayer, and the failure-to-pay penalty is generally 0.5 percent of the tax due for each month (or any fraction thereof) the tax is not paid, up to a maximum of 25 percent of the unpaid tax.

Choice "1" is incorrect. The failure-to-file penalty will apply to Spayer, but the failure-to-file penalty is generally 5 percent, not 10 percent, of the tax due for each month (or any fraction thereof), not year, the return is not filed, up to a maximum of 25 percent of the unpaid tax. If the return is more than 60 days late, as in this situation, the minimum penalty increases to the lesser of $450 or 100 percent of the tax due.

Choice "3" is incorrect. If both the failure-to-file penalty and the failure-to-pay penalty apply, the failure-to-file penalty is reduced by the amount of the failure-to-pay penalty. The penalty is thus not the total of the two penalties.

Choice "4" is incorrect. The penalty for failure to file a partnership or S corporation tax return is $220 for each month or part thereof (up to a maximum of 12 months) the return is late (or required information is missing) times the number of persons who are partners in the partnership, or shareholders in the S corporation, at any time during the year.

Topic C

QUESTION 1
MCQ-09540

Choice "2" is correct.

A client can recover from a CPA for negligence, gross negligence, or fraud. Negligence requires proof of the least culpable conduct, a failure to exercise due care.

Choice "1" is incorrect. Gross negligence (constructive fraud) occurs when an accountant, because of a reckless disregard for the truth, either makes a misrepresentation of a material fact or omits a material fact. Proving that Johnson acted recklessly would be more difficult than proving that Johnson failed to use reasonable care. Or, to put it simply, gross negligence requires a greater degree of culpability than ordinary negligence.

Choice "3" is incorrect. Fraud is an intentional tort. Rhodes would have to prove that Johnson acted with scienter. This would require proof that Johnson knowingly or intentionally failed to disclose the liability. Johnson could be liable for ordinary negligence even if it was unaware of the liability.

Choice "4" is incorrect. Johnson could be liable for ordinary negligence even if it was unaware of the liability. Failure to exercise due care requires proof of conduct less culpable than knowledge.

QUESTION 2
MCQ-09572

Choice "2" is correct.

Fraud has five elements: either a misrepresentation of a material fact or an omission of a material fact; scienter (intent to deceive or reckless disregard for the truth); reliance; intent to induce reliance; and damages. There can be no fraud if the false statements were immaterial.

Choice "1" is incorrect because lack of privity is only a defense to negligence. It is not a defense to fraud.

Choice "3" is incorrect. Whether or not the CPA financially benefited from the fraud is irrelevant.

Choice "4" is incorrect. Contributory negligence is only a defense to negligence. It is not a defense to fraud.

QUESTION 3
MCQ-09492

Choice "2" is correct.

Confidential client information may be revealed to a state CPA society voluntary quality control review board without the client's permission.

Choice "1" is incorrect because confidential client information may be revealed to others with the consent of the client. Thus, it can be waived by the client.

Choice "3" is incorrect. All states recognize the attorney-client privilege. Not all states recognize the accountant-client privilege.

Choice "4" is incorrect. The accountant-client privilege applies to oral and written communications.

Topic A

QUESTION 1

Choice "4" is correct.

If an agent has paid for the right to be appointed as an agent, the agency is coupled with an interest and may be revoked only by the agent. The principal may not terminate the agency, and the agency does not terminate by operation of law by the death of the principal.

Choices "1", "2", and "3" are incorrect, per the above explanation.

QUESTION 2

Choice "4" is correct.

If the principal fires an agent, the principal must give actual notice to persons with whom the agent has dealt and constructive notice to all others. Failure to give the required notice leaves the agent with apparent authority to act on behalf of the principal.

Choices "1", "2", and "3" are incorrect. An agency terminates by law and ends automatically if the agent loses a license required to fulfill his or her duties, the principal dies and the agent has notice of the death, or the principal becomes bankrupt.

QUESTION 3

Choice "4" is correct.

To ratify a contract, the principal must have knowledge of all material facts.

Choice "1" is incorrect. Ratification does not require notification to be effective (the third party already thinks he or she has a contract with the principal).

Choice "2" is incorrect. If the principal ratifies an unauthorized contract, the principal is bound even if the agent acted unreasonably.

Choice "3" is incorrect. There is no requirement that an agent be a general agent in order to give a principal the right to ratify; principals may ratify contracts of special agents as well. It may even be possible to ratify a contract entered into by someone who was not an agent of the principal but purported to be one.

QUESTION 4

Choice "4" is correct.

Generally, a principal is not liable for an agent's torts. However, an employer is liable for an employee's torts committed within the scope of the employment (i.e., while the employee was attending to the employer's business). Here, Ed completed the requested delivery and then continued 10 miles out of his way to get to his mother's house where the collision occurred. Thus, the collision occurred outside of the scope of the employment and Phil will not be held liable.

Choice "1" is incorrect because it is not enough merely that Ed was Phil's employee; the tort must also occur within the scope of the employment. As explained above, the collision here did not occur within the scope of Ed's employment. He was on a frolic of his own.

Choice "2" is incorrect. It is not enough merely that Ed was driving Phil's truck. Ed must be an employee and the tort must have been committed within the scope of the employment. See above.

Choice "3" is incorrect. It is not enough merely that Ed was negligent. Ed must be an employee and the tort must have been committed within the scope of the employment. See above.

Regulation II

Topic B

QUESTION 1
MCQ-09456

Choice "2" is correct.

Most offers can be revoked anytime prior to acceptance. This is true even if the offer states it will be held open.

Choice "1" is incorrect because an option contract requires consideration to support the promise to keep the offer open and none was given here.

Choices "3" and "4" are incorrect because the firm offer rule applies only to the sale of goods by a merchant, not to the sale of real estate.

QUESTION 2
MCQ-09612

Choice "4" is correct.

Specific performance is a court order requiring the breaching party to perform as promised under a contract. A court will not order a person to perform a non-assignable duty, as such an order would constitute involuntary servitude. The duties of a CPA are not assignable because they rely on the skills of the particular CPA.

Choices "1" and "3" are incorrect. By breaching the contract prior to the date of performance, Lark committed an anticipatory repudiation. An anticipatory repudiation permits Bale, the injured party, to sue Lark immediately or wait until the time of performance has passed and then sue.

Choice "2" is incorrect. Anytime there is a breach of contract, the injured party has the right to sue for compensatory damages and receive an award of money to compensate for all harm done.

QUESTION 3
MCQ-09505

Choice "4" is correct.

The statute of frauds requires a writing for most contracts for the sale of goods of $500 or more. A writing is not required, however, if the party admits in court that he made the contract.

Choices "1" and "2" are incorrect because part performance of a contract within the statute of frauds makes the contract enforceable only to the extent of the performance tendered and accepted. This question required the contract to be enforced in its entirety.

Choice "3" is incorrect because the contract involved the sale of goods of $500 or more.

QUESTION 4
MCQ-09489

Choice "2" is correct.

A buyer may reject any nonconforming delivery made by a seller. The seller has the right to correct or cure the nonconforming delivery by notifying the buyer it will be corrected on time. Thus, Kirk may deliver the freezer on June 23 by notifying Nix of its intent to do so.

Choice "1" is incorrect because notice is required to cure.

Choice "3" is incorrect because a buyer has an absolute right to reject a nonconforming delivery.

Choice "4" is incorrect because a seller has the right to cure or correct nonconforming deliveries if time is left before performance is due under the contract.

Topic C

QUESTION 1

Choice "2" is correct.

Contribution (a right to a pro rata payment of monies owed to a creditor) is a right a surety has against a cosurety.

Choices "1", "3", and "4" are incorrect. All three are available to a surety against the principal. Exoneration is the right to compel the principal to pay. Subrogation is the surety's right to succeed to the creditor's rights against the principal debtor after the surety pays the creditor. Reimbursement is the surety's right to recover from the principal whatever the surety pays the creditor.

QUESTION 2

Choice "3" is correct.

A debtor must wait at least eight years before receiving another discharge.

Choices "1", "2", and "4" are incorrect. They all are examples of specific debts that will not be discharged, but the mere fact that such debts are owed is not a ground for denying a discharge for a petitioner's other debts.

Topic D

QUESTION 1

Choice "2" is correct.

Self-employed persons do not pay into FUTA.

Choice "1" is incorrect. The liability is the responsibility of the employer, not the employees.

Choice "3" is incorrect. Employer payments into FUTA are deductible as an ordinary business expense.

Choice "4" is incorrect. Employers who meet a minimum quarterly payroll or who employ at least one person for 20 weeks in a year must participate. It is one or the other, not both.

QUESTION 2

Choice "1" is correct.

Under workers' compensation laws, employers pay for workers' compensation by purchasing insurance from the state or from a private carrier.

Choice "2" is incorrect. Workers' compensation programs are state-run, not federally run programs designed to enable employees to recover for injuries incurred while on the job.

Choice "3" is incorrect. Workers' compensation insurance premiums are ordinary business expenses deductible by the employer, not the employee.

Choice "4" is incorrect. An employee can collect workers' compensation even if the employee was negligent or grossly negligent. An employee cannot recover for injuries if the employee was intoxicated.

Regulation II

Topic E

QUESTION 1 MCQ-09103

Choice "3" is correct.

A partner can impose contract liability on the partnership and fellow partners when acting with apparent authority. It would be reasonable for a third party to believe that a partner could renew an existing lease.

Choice "1" is incorrect. Apparent authority depends on how things appear to third parties. It does not depend on a written partnership agreement.

Choice "2" is incorrect. A person is liable for his own torts and can be sued for them, regardless of whether the torts were committed on behalf of some business entity.

Choice "4" is incorrect because a partner has no apparent authority to admit liability in a lawsuit.

QUESTION 2 MCQ-09143

Choice "3" is correct.

A withdrawing partner is personally liable to creditors of the old partnership even if there is a hold harmless agreement. Fein was a partner in ABC. Thus, Fein is liable to the creditors of ABC. A hold harmless agreement allows Fein to recover from other partners any amounts he is required to pay to creditors.

Choices "1" and "2" are incorrect. A hold harmless agreement does not prevent creditors from holding an outgoing partner liable.

Choice "4" is incorrect. A hold harmless agreement allows Fein to recover from other partners any amounts he is required to pay to creditors. It is not limited to the amounts he has paid in excess of his proportionate share.

QUESTION 3 MCQ-09153

Choice "3" is correct.

A general partner may be a limited partner in the same partnership at the same time.

Choice "1" is incorrect. To form a limited partnership, there must be at least one general partner and one limited partner. General partners have unlimited liability.

Choice "2" is incorrect. Changes in limited partners do not cause dissolution.

Choice "4" is incorrect. The assignee does not become a substituted partner without the unanimous consent of all general and limited partners.

QUESTION 4 MCQ-09104

Choice "4" is correct.

Unless agreed otherwise, all LLC members have no liability beyond their investment. Thus, an LLC can be formed with limited liability for all members, unlike a limited partnership.

Choice "1" is incorrect. The articles of organization are filed with the state, not the operating agreement.

Choice "2" is incorrect. Unless otherwise agreed, an LLC is taxed like a partnership, not a corporation.

Choice "3" is incorrect. Virtually every state permits a one person LLC.

QUESTION 5 MCQ-09124

Choice "2" is correct.

The corporate entity may be disregarded and stockholders held personally liable for fraud, undercapitalization at the time of formation, or commingling of funds.

Choice "1" is incorrect because it is undercapitalization, not overcapitalization, that will permit piercing of the corporate veil.

Choice "3" is incorrect because a corporation may have more than one class of stock unless it is an S corporation.

Choice "4" is incorrect because it states one of the main reasons for incorporating—to shield the owner(s) from personal liability. That alone is not a ground for piercing the corporate veil.

Topic A

QUESTION 1   MCQ-09566

Choice "4" is correct.

There is no income tax on the value of inherited property. The gain on the sale is the difference between the sales price of $14,500 and Duffy's basis in the inherited property. Duffy's basis is the fair market value (FMV) of the property on the alternate valuation date elected by the executor. This is the FMV six months after date of death or date distributed if before six months. The property was distributed four months after death and the FMV on that day ($14,500) is used for the basis. $14,500 − $14,500 = 0.

Choice "1" is incorrect. There is no income tax on the value of inherited property.

Choice "2" is incorrect. This is the basis of the stock if the alternate date had not been used. Heirs are not taxed on inheritances. The income or loss results when inherited property is sold.

Choice "3" is incorrect. There is no income tax on the value of inherited property. The gain on the sale is the difference between the sales price of $14,500 and Duffy's basis. Duffy's basis is the FMV of the property on the alternate valuation elected by the executor.

QUESTION 2   MCQ-09529

Choice "1" is correct.

Alice has a realized gain of $5,000 on the transaction: $25,000 sales price less $20,000 purchase price. However, she can reduce the gain, but not below zero, by the amount of loss her father could not deduct on the sale to her. Thus, Alice can reduce her gain by up to $10,000, but not below zero. Here, the gain is $5,000, so it is reduced to zero. Conner should have sold the stock in the open market so that he could deduct the entire loss. Alice could then have purchased the stock in the open market.

Choice "2" is incorrect. $5,000 is Alice's realized gain on the sale. However, she can reduce the gain, but not below zero, by the amount of loss her father could not deduct on the sale to her. The holding period in related party transactions starts with the new owner's period of ownership; therefore, this would be a short-term transaction.

Choice "3" is incorrect. Alice has a realized gain of $5,000 on the sale. In addition, she can reduce the gain, but not below zero, by the amount of loss her father could not deduct on the sale to her. The holding period in related party transactions starts with the new owner's period of ownership; therefore, this would be a short-term transaction. The following as indicated in this option.

Choice "4" is incorrect. Alice has a realized gain of $5,000 on the sale. In addition, she can reduce the gain, but not below zero, by the amount of loss her father could not deduct on the sale to her. The holding period in related party transactions starts with the new owner's period of ownership; therefore, this would be a short-term transaction.

QUESTION 3   MCQ-09499

Choice "3" is correct.

Because the machine was a depreciable business use asset held more than 12 months, it was a Section 1231 asset. However, because it was sold at a gain, and the gain was less than the prior depreciation taken of $34,800 ($49,000 cost − $14,200 adjusted basis), all of the $30,800 gain ($45,000 selling price − $14,200 adjusted basis) is Section 1245 depreciation recapture gain and there is no Section 1231 gain.

      Regulation Final Review

Regulation III

Topic B

QUESTION 1 MCQ-09639

Choice "3" is correct.

Equipment is personal property. When over 40 percent of depreciable personal property is placed in service in the last quarter of the year (as is the case here), the MACRS mid-quarter convention applies to all personal property.

Choice "1" is incorrect. After the maximum amount of Section 179 depreciation (expense election) is taken, the remaining amount of property placed in service in the current year is depreciable using the regular tax depreciation rules. Because the maximum Section 179 expense elected does not create or increase a net loss on Sima's Schedule C, the entire Section 179 expense elected can be deducted in the current year. There is no carryforward of the excess amount of purchases over the Section 179 expense limit for the current year, as these may be depreciated under the regular tax rules.

Choice "2" is incorrect. The MACRS half-year convention generally applies to personal property (including equipment); however, in this case, it does not apply, as all current year personal property (clearly over 40 percent of the total) was purchased in the last quarter of the year.

Choice "4" is incorrect. Equipment is personal property. Real property is depreciated using the straight-line, mid-month convention.

Topic C

QUESTION 1 MCQ-09502

Choice "3" is correct.

Payments for college books, supplies, and dormitory fees on behalf of an individual unrelated to the donor requires filing a gift tax return. Only payment of tuition to a qualified educational institution receives an unlimited gift tax exclusion.

Choices "1" and "2" are incorrect. There is an unlimited exclusion for direct payments of tuition and medical expenses.

Choice "4" is incorrect. Campaign contributions are not considered a gift. They are nondeductible.

Topic A

QUESTION 1

MCQ-09545

Choice "2" is correct.

Jeff and Rhonda may claim a total of three (3) dependents on their joint income tax return.

■ Max is a qualifying child. He is a full-time student under the age of 24, lives at home when he is not away for temporary absence at school, and is supported more than 50 percent by Jeff and Rhonda. The gross income test does not apply. Max is a dependent.

■ Jen is also a qualifying child. While she is not a full-time student, she is still under the age of 19, lives at home, and is supported over 50 percent by her parents. The gross income test does not apply. Jen is a dependent.

■ Joanne is a qualifying relative. She receives all of her support from Jeff and Rhonda, makes less than the taxable gross income threshold amount, does not file a joint return, and is a relative. Joanne is a dependent.

Choices "1", "3", and "4" are incorrect, per the above explanation.

QUESTION 2

MCQ-09739

Choice "1" is correct.

Bob can only file as single. Bob does not meet the criteria to file as head of household. The head of household filing status is available to unmarried taxpayers who maintain a household for more than half the year for an unmarried son or daughter (not required to be a dependent, but must live with the taxpayer), father or mother (must be a dependent but not required to live with the taxpayer), or other dependent relative (must live with the taxpayer). In this case, Bob's mother does not meet the criteria to be considered his dependent. Specifically, she fails the qualifying relative taxable gross income test.

Choice "2" is incorrect. Bob's mother is not Bob's dependent. Therefore, he cannot file as head of household.

Choice "3" is incorrect. "Qualifying single" is not an actual filing status. The filing statuses are: single, head of household, married filing separately, qualifying widow(er), and married filing jointly.

Choice "4" is incorrect. "Supporting single" is not an actual filing status. The filing statuses are: single, head of household, married filing separately, qualifying widow(er), and married filing jointly.

Regulation IV

Topic B

QUESTION 1 MCQ-09481

Choice "1" is correct.

Rules: Alimony payments must be in cash, required by a divorce decree and be "periodic payments." Child support is nontaxable. Lump sum property settlements are not taxable. Alimony received per a divorce or separation agreement executed on or before December 31, 2018, is taxable to the recipient.

Total payments made by Kyle were $45,000. Of that, $20,000 represents the lump sum property settlement. The remainder, $25,000, must first be applied against child support. Child support for the year was $20,000; 10 months × $2,000 per month. The remaining $5,000 is classified as alimony and is taxable to Kaylie for 2018 because the divorce agreement was executed on or before December 31, 2018.

Choice "2" is incorrect. $20,000 is the amount of the property settlement or the child support, neither of which are taxable to Kaylie.

Choice "3" is incorrect. The child support payments must first be subtracted to arrive at the taxable portion that is characterized as alimony.

Choice "4" is incorrect. The lump sum property settlement and any amounts characterized as child support are not taxable to Kaylie.

QUESTION 2 MCQ-09450

Choice "3" is correct.

Amounts received as compensation for services ($6,000) are taxable. In addition, the amount of the scholarship not used for qualified expenditures is taxable ($1,500 room and board) for a total taxable amount of $7,500.

Rule: Scholarships and fellowships not used to pay for qualified expenditures (tuition, fees, books) are taxable income to the recipient.

Choice "1" is incorrect, as it ignores both items that are taxable.

Choice "2" is incorrect, as it does not consider the $1,500 of the scholarship not used for qualified expenditures.

Choice "4" is incorrect. Scholarships used to pay for qualified expenditures to a degree-seeking student are excludable from gross income. This answer identifies the total scholarship received and compensation for teaching as taxable.

Topic C

QUESTION 1
MCQ-09738

Choice "3" is correct.

The "mom and pop" rental real estate rule is an exception to the passive activity loss rules. Taxpayers may deduct up to $25,000 of net rental passive losses if they actively participate or manage the rental property and own more than 10 percent of the activity. The $25,000 is reduced by 50 percent of the excess of AGI over $100,000 and eliminated when AGI exceeds $150,000. The problem states that no AGI phase-out limitations apply, so Sam can deduct the entire $25,000 allowed.

Choice "1" is incorrect. The "mom and pop" rental real estate exception allows taxpayers to deduct up to $25,000 of net rental passive losses against ordinary income if the taxpayer actively participates in the rental activity.

Choice "2" is incorrect. The "mom and pop" rental real estate exception allows taxpayers to deduct up to $25,000 of net rental passive losses against ordinary income if the taxpayer actively participates in the rental activity.

Choice "4" is incorrect. The "mom and pop" rental real estate exception allows taxpayers to deduct up to $25,000 of net rental passive losses against ordinary income if the taxpayer actively participates in the rental activity.

Topic D

QUESTION 1
MCQ-09451

Choice "1" is correct.

Alimony payments received on a pre-2019 divorce or separation agreement are taxable as income to the recipient. However, payments that are required to be paid, even if the payee dies, are *not* considered to be payments for the support (alimony) and are considered to be amounts owed to the payee as part of the divorce settlement.

QUESTION 2
MCQ-09482

Choice "3" is correct.

Medical expenses include physical therapy (professional medical services) and insurance premiums providing reimbursement for medical care. Prescription drugs are considered medical care. Insurance against loss of income is not payment for medical care and therefore is not deductible. Qualified medical expenses must be reduced by insurance reimbursement ($2,000 + $500 − $1,500 = $1,000).

Choice "1" is incorrect. Insurance against loss of income is not payment for medical care and therefore is not deductible.

Choice "2" is incorrect. Medical expenses include physical therapy (professional medical services) and insurance premiums providing reimbursement for medical care.

Choice "4" is incorrect. Medical expenses include physical therapy (professional medical services) and insurance premiums providing reimbursement for medical care.

Regulation IV

Topic E

QUESTION 1 MCQ-09578

Choice "3" is correct.

The child tax credit is the only one of the above credits that is considered "refundable," which means that the credit can reduce tax below zero and result in a refund.

Choices "1", "2", and "4" are incorrect. All of these credits may only reduce total tax to zero.

Regulation V

Topic A

QUESTION 1

Choice "3" is correct.

The charitable contribution (CC) deduction is limited to 10 percent of taxable income before "special deductions" (charitable contributions deduction and dividends-received deduction). Taxable income $410,000 + $20,000 DRD = $430,000 × 10% = $43,000 Year 6 CC deduction limit. Total Year 6 CC deduction = $40,000 Year 6 CC + $3,000 Year 5 CC carryover = $43,000. The $2,000 remaining Year 5 CC carryover ($5,000 - $3,000 deducted in Year 6) is carried forward to Year 7.

Topic B

QUESTION 1

Choice "2" is correct.

As a general rule, the basis of property received by a corporation by a transferor/shareholder is the greater of the basis of the transferred asset in the hands of the transferor/shareholder, or the debt assumed by the corporation. Therefore, The Worthington Corp.'s basis in the building is the same as Gearty's basis immediately prior to its contribution to the corporation.

Choice "1" is incorrect. The Worthington Corp.'s basis in the building is computed separately from any debt that it assumes related to the building.

Choice "3" is incorrect. The Worthington Corp. uses Gearty's basis, not the building's fair market value, as its basis. Furthermore, the debt assumed by The Worthington Corp. does not affect the basis of the building to The Worthington Corp.

Choice "4" is incorrect. The Worthington Corp. uses Gearty's basis, not the building's fair market value, as its basis.

QUESTION 2

Choice "3" is correct.

Taxable income before special deductions includes sales, dividends received and cost of sales. It excludes the dividends received deduction, which is a "special" deduction.

Sales	$500,000
Cost of sales	(250,000)
Gross profit	250,000
Dividends received	25,000
Income before special deductions	$275,000

Choice "1" is incorrect. Cost of sales must be deducted.

Choice "2" is incorrect. Cost of sales must be deducted and 100%, not 80%, of the dividends received must be included in income before special deductions.

Choice "4" is incorrect. The $25,000 dividend must be included in income before special deduction.

Regulation V

QUESTION 3   MCQ-09632

Choice "3" is correct.

Dividends are distributions of a corporation's earnings and profits, including accumulated (prior year) and current year E&P. Because the corporation had both accumulated E&P of $35,000 and current E&P of $15,000, the total amount of distributions classified as dividends is $50,000.

Choice "1" is incorrect. If a corporation has accumulated E&P and/or current year E&P, the distribution (depending upon amount) should be taxable as a dividend.

Choice "2" is incorrect. The amount taxable as a dividend is total E&P, not just the accumulated E&P.

Choice "4" is incorrect. The total distributions exceeds E&P. The excess will be treated as a return of basis and any remaining excess will be capital gain.

QUESTION 4   MCQ-09619

Choice "2" is correct.

$22,000 gain.

Rule: A corporation generally must recognize gain when it distributes appreciated property to its shareholders in any ordinary, nonliquidating distribution to the extent that the fair market value of the property exceeds its adjusted basis.

Fair market value per share	$ 20
Basis per share	(9)
Appreciation in value per share	$ 11
Number of shares distributed	× 2,000
Recognized gain	$22,000

Choices "1", "3", and "4" are incorrect, per the above rule.

QUESTION 5   MCQ-09500

Choice "2" is correct.

$50,000 capital gain. Property distributed in a complete liquidation of a corporation will be deemed to have been sold by the corporation at its fair market value and any gain or loss will be recognized by the liquidating corporation as a capital gain or loss.

Fair market value	$ 150,000
Basis	(100,000)
Gain	$ 50,000

The assets distributed are capital assets as opposed to business assets; therefore, the gain is a capital gain.

Topic C

QUESTION 1

Choice "2" is correct.

Rule: In order to be effective for the current taxable year, the S corporation election must be made by the 15th day of the third month of the taxable year. If the election is made after that date, it becomes effective on the first day of the next taxable year, January 1, Year 5, in this case.

QUESTION 2

Choice "2" is correct.

Rule: If ownership interests of an S corporation change within the taxable year, the income and/or loss to be allocated among the various shareholders will be made on a "per share, per day" basis.

S corporation loss for the year:

$36,500 / 365 days =	$ 100	(per day)
Number of days Duffy was a shareholder	40	
Loss allocated to 40 days	$4,000	
Duffy's ownership interest	50%	
Loss allocated to Duffy for the year	$2,000	

QUESTION 3

Choice "3" is correct.

S corporation status can be revoked if shareholders owning more than 50% of the total number of issued and outstanding shares consent. The specific percentage of voting and nonvoting shareholders is not considered, just the total. Holders of more than 25,000 total shares must approve the revocation ([30,000 + 20,000 total shares] x 50% = 25,000).

Choices "1", "2", and "4" are incorrect. S corporation status can be revoked if shareholders owning more than 50% of the total number of issued and outstanding shares consent. The specific percentage of voting and nonvoting shareholders is not considered, just the total.

Regulation V

Topic D

QUESTION 1   MCQ-09470

Choice "1" is correct.

A partner's basis in a partnership interest is increased by the partner's share of partnership ordinary income, separately stated income, and tax-exempt income. $5,000 beginning tax basis + [($20,000 + $8,000 + $4,000) × 50%] = $21,000.

Choice "2" is incorrect. Gray's basis is increased by $16,000, but the question asks what his total basis is on December 31, Year 4.

Choice "3" is incorrect. Gray's basis is increased by 50% of $20,000 + $4,000, or $12,000, but it is also increased by 50% of tax exempt income. This increase is added to the beginning basis.

Choice "4" is incorrect. Gray's basis is increased by 50% of ordinary income, or $10,000, but it is also increased by tax exempt and portfolio income. This increase is added to the beginning basis.

QUESTION 2   MCQ-09652

Choice "4" is correct.

Stacey will report 25% of the ordinary business income of $200,000 ($300,000 − $100,000), or $50,000, as income from partnerships on her individual income tax return for the current year. The guaranteed payment is an allowable deduction for the partnership against ordinary income. Stacey will also report 25% of the interest income $2,500 on her Schedule B and 25% of the charitable contributions $4,000 on her Schedule A for the current year.

Choice "1" is incorrect. These are the amounts that will be reported for the partnership as a whole on Schedule K. The partnership will also report the detailed business revenues and expenses (including 100% of the guaranteed payment) on its Form 1065.

Choice "2" is incorrect. This answer shows the amounts that Nick would report on his tax return for the current year. The ordinary income would include $50,000 of income from partnerships and $30,000 ordinary income from the guaranteed payment (likely also subject to self-employment tax).

Choice "3" is incorrect. This answer assumes that the guaranteed payment is not an allowable expense of the partnership (or Stacey) and adds it back to the net ordinary business income of the partnership. ($300,000 − $100,000 + $30,000 = $230,000; $230,000 / 4 = $57,500.) The other columns are correct. Stacey will also report 25% of the interest income $2,500 on her Schedule B and 25% of the charitable contributions $4,000 on her Schedule A for the current year.

QUESTION 3   MCQ-09485

Choice "2" is correct.

In a nonliquidating distribution, the partner takes the partnership basis for assets distributed. This basis cannot exceed the partner's basis in the partnership.

Choice "1" is incorrect. This is Day's remaining basis in the partnership, not the basis for the land.

Choices "3" and "4" are incorrect. In a nonliquidating distribution, the partner takes the partnership basis for assets distributed.

QUESTION 4

MCQ-09581

Choice "4" is correct.

When Fox sells his partnership interest, capital gain or loss on the sale is recognized. To the extent that there are Sec. 751(a) hot assets (unrealized receivables or substantially appreciated inventory), the partner must recognize ordinary income or loss. In this case, the partnership has no Sec. 751(a) assets. The amount realized less the partner's basis in the partnership is a capital gain or loss. The amount realized is $75,000 ($50,000 cash received + $25,000 relief of debt). The partner's basis in the partnership is $60,000. Thus, the capital gain is $75,000 − $60,000, or $15,000.

Choice "1" is incorrect. Since there are no Sec. 751 assets, the gain or loss must be capital, not ordinary.

Choice "2" is incorrect. Since there are no Sec. 751 assets, the gain or loss must be capital, not ordinary.

Choice "3" is incorrect. The amount realized must include the $25,000 debt relief.

Topic F

QUESTION 1

MCQ-09657

Choice "4" is correct.

Although an organization may have tax-exempt status, it may become subject to regular corporate income tax on income from a business enterprise that is not related to its tax-exempt purpose (UBI). Income from certain types of activities are excluded from UBI. Income from the research of a college or hospital is one of the types of income that is specifically excluded.

Choice "1" is incorrect. Unrelated business income does not include any activity where all of the work is performed by unpaid workers (volunteers); thus, the fact that the organization uses unpaid workers makes the business or activity "related" and not taxable.

Choice "2" is incorrect. The fact that the activity results in a loss does not exclude that activity from the definition of an unrelated business. If expenses exceed income, a net operating loss exists, which is subject to carryback and carryover provisions of net operating losses.

Choice "3" is incorrect. Unrelated business income does not include income from the sale of merchandise received as gifts or contributions.

Regulation Final Review

You've got this.

This is the final stretch of your CPA Exam preparation – the Final Review. You've diligently studied these topics, and now it's crunch time. This Final Review has completely new content from the Becker CPA Exam Review and focuses on the key concepts on the CPA Exam. Remember, fortune favors the brave, but the CPA Exam favors the prepared.

Access Becker's Final Review

You can access Final Review under Additional Resources on each section home page when you log in to **cpa.becker.com** or when you use the mobile apps.

What's inside

Your Final Review is designed to mimic the actual CPA Exam, and has all-new task-based simulations and multiple-choice questions. If you need help at any point, remember that you still have access to the features of the CPA Exam Review, including:

- Access to 1-on-1 academic support from our experienced CPA instructors
- Unlimited practice tests to work on your weaknesses

You're not in it alone!

For tips, stories and advice, visit our blog at **becker.com/blog.** You can also collaborate with other Becker students studying AUD on our Facebook study group at **facebook.com/groups/ BeckerAUDStudyGroup/.**

Exam day tips

We want you to be prepared and confident when exam day rolls around. Here are some tips to keep in mind:

+ Arrive at least 30 minutes early on exam day.

+ Bring your NTS and two forms of identification.

+ Your cell phone is NOT allowed in the testing center, even during scheduled breaks.

+ No outside calculators are allowed. The testing software will have a built-in calculator for you to use.

+ Breathe. Relax. Ground yourself. You've got this.

S0-CPB-126

Becker™

This textbook contains information that was current at the time of printing.
Your course software will be updated on a regular basis as the content
that is tested on the CPA Exam evolves and as we improve our materials.
Note the version reference below and select your replacement textbook at
becker.com/cpa-replacements-upgrades to learn if a newer version of this
book is available to be ordered.

CPA Exam Review

Auditing
Final Review

For Exams Scheduled
After December 31, 2022

V 4.3

COURSE DEVELOPMENT TEAM

Timothy F. Gearty, CPA, MBA, JD, CGMA . . . . Editor in Chief, Financial/Regulation (Tax) National Editor

Angeline S. Brown, CPA, CGMA. . . . . Sr. Director, Product Management

Michael Potenza, CPA, JD. . . . . Director, Curriculum

Lauren Chin, CPA . . . . Sr. Manager, Curriculum

Stephen Bergens, CPA. . . . . Manager, Accounting Curriculum

Nancy Gauldie, CPA . . . . Sr. Specialist, Curriculum

Bill Karalius, CPA. . . . . Sr. Specialist, Curriculum

Tom Cox, CPA, CMA . . . . Financial (GASB & NFP) National Editor

Steven J. Levin, JD . . . . Regulation (Law) National Editor

Danita De Jane . . . . Director, Course Development

Joe Antonio . . . . Manager, Course Development

Shelly McCubbins, MBA. . . . . Project Manager, Course Development

CONTRIBUTING EDITORS

Teresa C. Anderson, CPA, CMA, MPA	Patrice W. Johnson, CPA
Valerie Funk Anderson, CPA	Julie D. McGinty, CPA
Heather Baiye, CPA, MBA	Sandra McGuire, CPA, MBA
Katie Barnette, CPA	Stephanie Morris, CPA, MAcc
Michael Brown, CPA, CMA	Michelle Moshe, CPA, DipIFR
Elliott G. Chester, CPA, CMA, CFE	Peter Olinto, JD, CPA
Courtney Chianello, CPA	Sandra Owen, JD, MBA, CPA
Cheryl Costello, CPA, CGMA	Michelle M. Pace, CPA
Jim DeSimpelare, CPA, MBA	Jennifer J. Rivers, CPA
Tara Z. Fisher, CPA	Josh Rosenberg, MBA, CPA, CFA, CFP
Melisa F. Galasso, CPA	Jonathan R. Rubin, CPA, MBA
R. Thomas Godwin, CPA, CGMA	Michael Rybak, CPA, CFA
Holly Hawk, CPA, CGMA	Jacob Shortt, CPA
Liliana Hickman-Riggs, CPA, CMA, CIA, CFE, CITP, CFF, CGMA, FCPA, MS	Denise M. Stefano, CPA, CGMA, MBA
	Elizabeth Lester Walsh, CPA, CITP

Auditing

Final Review Sections

Auditing Section I | *Ethics, Professional Responsibilities, and General Principles*

A   Terms of Engagement: Client Acceptance and Continuance

B   Terms of Engagement: Communication With the Predecessor Auditor

C   Terms of Engagement: Establishing an Understanding

D   Audit Documentation

E   Communication With Management and Those Charged With Governance

F   Communications Related to Internal Control

G   Ethics, Independence, and Professional Conduct

H   Quality Control

Auditing Section II | *Assessing Risk and Developing a Planned Response*

A   Planning an Engagement

B   Understanding an Entity's Internal Control

C   Assessing Risks Due to Fraud

D   Risk Assessment Procedures

E   Assessing the Risk of Material Misstatement

F   Responding to Assessed Risk

G   Materiality

H   Planning for and Using the Work of Others

I   Specific Areas of Engagement Risk: Related Parties and Noncompliance

J   Specific Areas of Engagement Risk: Accounting Estimates and Fair Value

(continued on next page)

(continued)

Auditing Section III | *Performing Further Procedures and Obtaining Evidence*

A   Understanding Sufficient Appropriate Evidence

B   Sampling Techniques

C   Tests of Controls

D   Analytical Procedures

E   Substantive Procedures

F   Confirmations

G   Performing Specific Procedures to Obtain Evidence

H   Specific Matters That Require Special Consideration: Inventory and Investments

I   Specific Matters That Require Special Consideration: Attorney Letter

J   Specific Matters That Require Special Consideration: Going Concern

K   Internal Control Deficiencies

L   Written Representations

M   Subsequent Events

N   Subsequent Discovery of Facts

O   Audit Data Analytics

Auditing Section IV | *Forming Conclusions and Reporting*

A   Reports on Auditing Engagements

B   Integrated Audit Reports

C   Reports on Internal Controls

D   Reports on Attestation Engagements

E   Accounting and Review Service Engagements

F   Accounting and Review Service Engagement Reports

G   Other Information

H   Reports Required by Government Auditing Standards

I   Special Reports

Introduction

Final Review is a condensed review that reinforces your understanding of the most heavily tested concepts on the CPA Exam. It is designed to help focus your study time during those final days between your Becker CPA Exam Review course and your exam date.

This Book

Becker's Final Review is arranged based on the AICPA's blueprints. The blueprints outline the technical content to be tested on each of the four parts of the CPA Exam. The blueprints can be found in the back sections of Becker's main CPA textbooks.

The Software

The Final Review software uses an interactive eBook (IEB) format. Watch the introduction video in the Final Review software for a tour of the IEB features.

We recommend progressing through this course in the following order:

- Review the IEB content, including the video introduction to each topic and the lecture audio associated with each page of the IEB.
- Work the embedded multiple-choice questions for each topic as you progress through the content.
- Work the related multiple-choice questions in the question bank for each topic.
- Once you have completed all of the IEB sections, topics, and multiple-choice questions, do the practice Simulations in the software.

Becker Customer and Academic Support

You can access Becker's Customer and Academic Support from within the course software by clicking Contact Support at the top at:

cpa.becker.com

You can also access customer service and technical support by calling 1-877-CPA-EXAM (outside the U.S. +1-630-472-2213).

Ethics, Professional Responsibilities, and General Principles

I

1 Client Acceptance and Continuance Policies

The auditor should consider the firm's client acceptance and continuance policies, including:

- The firm's ability to meet reporting deadlines.
- The firm's ability to staff the engagement.
- Independence.
- Integrity of client management.

2 Preconditions for an Audit

Before accepting an audit engagement, the auditor should establish that the preconditions for an audit are present.

2.1 Financial Reporting Framework

The auditor should determine whether the financial reporting framework used by the client is acceptable.

2.2 Management Responsibilities

The auditor should obtain the agreement of management that it acknowledges and understands its responsibility:

- For the preparation and fair presentation of the financial statements
- For the design, implementation, and maintenance of internal control
- To provide the auditor with:
  - access to all information of which management is aware that is relevant to the preparation and fair presentation of the financial statements;
  - additional information that the auditor may request from management for the purpose of the audit; and
  - unrestricted access to persons within the entity from whom the auditor determines it is necessary to obtain audit evidence.

Question 1   MCQ-09795

Which of the following auditor concerns most likely would be so serious that the auditor would conclude that a financial statement audit *cannot* be performed?

1. The CPA lacks experience in the client's operations and industry.

2. A portion of supporting evidence stored at an offsite storage facility was destroyed by a hurricane.

3. Management has imposed a restriction that the auditor believes will result in a qualified opinion.

4. There is substantial risk of management intentionally manipulating accounting records.

1 Communication Before Engagement Acceptance

Contact with the predecessor auditor before engagement acceptance is mandatory, but client permission is required. Inquiries can be oral or written. Inquiries should be made regarding:

- management integrity.

- disagreements with the predecessor auditor (principles, procedures, etc).

- reason for the change in auditors.

- any fraud, noncompliance with laws and regulations, or internal control matters and their communication to management, the audit committee, and those charged with governance.

- fee payment problems.

- nature of any significant or unusual transactions including those with related parties.

2 Communication During the Audit

- The auditor should obtain sufficient appropriate audit evidence about whether:

  - opening balances contain misstatements that could materially affect the current period financial statements; and

  - accounting policies reflected in the opening balances have been consistently applied.

- In order to do this, the auditor should request that management authorize the predecessor auditor to allow a review of the predecessor's audit documentation related to the most recently completed audit. The predecessor ordinarily allows a review of:

  - Planning documentation

  - Risk assessment procedures

  - Further audit procedures

  - Audit results

  - Matters of continuing accounting and audit significance

Question 1   MCQ-09796

A successor auditor's inquiries of the predecessor auditor should include questions regarding:

1. The number of engagement personnel the predecessor assigned to the engagement.

2. The assessment of the objectivity of the client's internal audit function.

3. Communications to management and those charged with governance regarding significant deficiencies in internal control.

4. The response rate for confirmations of accounts receivable.

1 Agree to the Terms of the Engagement

Establishing an agreement with the client is required to reduce the risk of misinterpretation. The agreement with the client should be documented through a written engagement letter. The agreement should include:

- The objective of the audit
- Management's responsibilities
- The auditor's responsibilities
- Limitations of the engagement
- Identification of the applicable financial reporting framework
- Reference to the expected form and content of any reports to be issued

On recurring audits, the auditor should assess whether circumstances require the terms of the engagement to be revised.

Question 1   MCQ-09799

An auditor's engagement letter most likely would include a statement regarding:

1. The advantages of statistical sampling.
2. The inherent limitations of an audit.
3. Billings to be paid in the form of stock of the entity.
4. The assessment of risk of material misstatement.

---

1 Audit Documentation (Working Papers)

Audit documentation is a written record of the work performed, evidence obtained, and conclusions reached. Audit documentation:

- is divided into permanent and current files.
- supports the auditor's report/opinion.
- aids in training and in the conduct/supervision of the audit.
- provides a record of accumulated evidence.
- must indicate that the accounting records reconcile with the financial statements, including disclosures.
- must contain enough information to allow an experienced auditor with no previous connection to the audit to understand the work that was performed.

2 Assembly and Retention

Audit documentation is required to be:

- assembled within 45 days (public company audits) or 60 days (other audits) following the report release date.
- kept for seven years (public company audits) or five years (other audits).

Question 1   MCQ-09811

According to PCAOB standards, audit documentation must be retained for:

1. One year.
2. Three years.
3. Five years.
4. Seven years.

---

3 Ownership and Confidentiality

Audit documentation is the independent auditor's property. It is confidential, but can be disclosed without client permission as part of:

- a quality review program.
- the subpoena process.
- an investigation conducted by the AICPA, state CPA society, or under state statute.

Question 2   MCQ-09844

According to professional standards, audit documentation should:

1. Be prepared in enough detail so that a new staff auditor who has no previous connection with the audit can understand the conclusions reached and any significant judgments made to reach those conclusions.

2. Monitor the effectiveness of the CPA firm's quality control activities.

3. Show who performed the work and the date the work was completed.

4. Include a flowchart to show the design and implementation of internal control.

---

4 Tickmarks

Auditors often use tickmarks, or symbols indicating the work that has been performed.

American Manufacturers Inc.
LONG-TERM DEBT
October 31, 20X7

Lender	Interest Rate	Payment Terms	Collateral	Balance 10/31/X6	Current Year Borrowings	Current Year Reductions	Balance 10/31/X7	Interest Paid To	Accrued Interest Payable 10/31/X7	Comments
▲ First National Bank	10%	Interest only on last day of each quarter; principal due in full on 9/30/X9.	Manufacturing equipment	500,000 ■	200,000 ◆ 3/31/X7	(100,000) O 6/30/X7	600,000 ✓	9/30/X7	5,000 ▛	First National confirms that interest payments are current and agrees with account balance.
▲ Second State Bank	9%	$10,000 principal plus interest due on the 1st of each month; due in full on 1/1/X0.	First mortgage on production facilities	380,000 ■	0	(110,000) +	270,000 ✓★	9/30/X7	2,025 ▛	Monthly payment for $12,025 was mailed on 11/3/X7; Second State agrees with account balance.
▲ Third Savings & Loan	12%	$5,000 principal plus interest due on the 15th of each month; due in full on 10/15/X9.	Second mortgage on production facilities	180,000 ■	0	(60,000)	120,000 ✱★	10/15/X7	600	Third Savings & Loan claims 10/15/X7 payment wasn't received as of 11/5/X7; adjusting entry proposed to increase balance $5,000 and increase accrued interest payable.
▲ A. Clark, majority stockholder	0%	Due in full 10/31/X9.	Unsecured	700,000 ■	0	(200,000) 10/28/X7	500,000 ✓		0	Borrowed additional $200,000 from Clark on 11/5/X7; need to investigate reborrowing just after year-end and consider imputed interest on 0% stockholder loan.
				1,760,000	200,000	(470,000)	1,490,000 ●		7,625 ●	

Tickmark Legend		
▲	Agreed interest rate, terms, and collateral to note & loan agreement.	✓ Confirmed, without exception.
■	Traced amount to prior year's audit documentation	★ Reclassification entry proposed for current portion of long-term debt.
◆	Agreed to loan agreement, validated bank deposit ticket, and board of director's authorization.	✱ Confirmed, with exception.
O	Agreed to canceled check and board of director's authorization.	● Traced amount to current year's trial balance and general ledger.
+	Agreed to canceled checks and lender's monthly statements.	▛ Tested reasonableness of calculations.

Auditing Final Review

1 Those Charged With Governance

Those charged with governance are those who bear responsibility to oversee the obligations and strategic direction of an entity, including the board of directors and the audit committee.

1.1 Audit Committee

An audit committee is a subgroup of those charged with governance. An audit committee consists of members of the board of directors, usually three to five "outside" directors, who are neither employees nor part of management and who do not have a material financial interest in the company. Audit committees are meant to strengthen the public's sense of the independence of the public accountant. Audit committee functions include:

- establishing the control environment.
- selecting and appointing the independent auditor.
- reviewing of the quality of the auditor's work.
- reviewing of the scope of the audit.
- responding to any auditor recommendations.
- helping to resolve disagreements related to the accounting treatment of material items.
- providing a bridge between the board of directors and the auditor.

2 Planned Scope and Timing of the Audit

- The auditor may communicate how significant risks of material misstatement will be addressed, the planned approach toward internal control, factors affecting materiality, the planned approach for addressing changes in the financial reporting framework or business environment, and any potential use of internal audit staff.
- The auditor may also solicit information from those charged with governance, such as the entity's objectives, strategies, and risks, or matters to which the auditor should pay particular attention.
- The communication may also include discussion of the attitudes, awareness, and actions of those charged with governance.
- When engaged to communicate key audit matters, the auditor may share preliminary views on areas requiring significant auditor attention.

Question 1   MCQ-09062

Which of the following statements is correct about an auditor's required communication with those charged with governance?

1. Any matters communicated to those charged with governance also are required to be communicated to the entity's management.

2. The auditor is required to inform those charged with governance about significant misstatements discovered by the auditor and subsequently corrected by management.

3. Disagreements with management about the application of accounting principles must be communicated in writing to those charged with governance.

4. The auditor should not communicate frequently recurring misstatements unless they are material.

1 Responsibility of the Auditor in a Financial Statement Audit Only

The auditor is not required to search for deficiencies that are less severe than a material weakness, or to express an opinion on internal control The auditor may, however, become aware of control deficiencies while performing the audit.

- Both significant deficiencies and material weaknesses must be communicated, in writing, to management and those charged with governance within 60 days of the report release date.

- Previously communicated significant deficiencies and material weaknesses that have not been corrected should be communicated again, in writing, during the current audit.

- The auditor should communicate to management only, in writing or orally, other deficiencies identified during the audit that are of sufficient importance to merit management's attention but that are not significant deficiencies or material weaknesses.

- The auditor may not report the absence of significant deficiencies, but may report on the absence of material weaknesses.

Question 1 MCQ-09061

Jefferson, CPA, has identified five significant deficiencies in internal control during the audit of Portico Industries, a nonissuer. Two of these conditions are considered to be material weaknesses. Which best describes Jefferson's communication requirements?

1. Communicate the two material weaknesses to Portico's management and those charged with governance, but not the three significant deficiencies that are not material weaknesses.

2. Communicate all five significant deficiencies to Portico's management and those charged with governance, distinguishing between significant deficiencies and material weaknesses.

3. Communicate all five significant deficiencies to Portico's management and those charged with governance, but only require a management response with respect to the two material weaknesses.

4. Communicate all five significant deficiencies to Portico's management and those charged with governance, without distinction among the deficiencies.

---

2 Internal Control Communication (Nonissuers)

Independent Auditor's Report

To Management and [*identify the body or individuals charged with governance*] of ABC Company:

In planning and performing our audit of the financial statements of ABC Company (the "Company") as of and for the year ended December 31, 20XX, in accordance with auditing standards generally accepted in the United States of America, we considered the Company's internal control over financial reporting (internal control) as a basis for designing audit procedures that are appropriate in the circumstances for the purpose of expressing our opinion on the financial statements, but not for the purpose of expressing an opinion on the effectiveness of the Company's internal control. Accordingly, we do not express an opinion on the effectiveness of the Company's internal control.

Our consideration of internal control was for the limited purpose described in the preceding paragraph and was not designed to identify all deficiencies in internal control that might be material weaknesses or significant deficiencies and therefore, material weaknesses or significant deficiencies may exist that were not identified. However, as discussed below, we identified certain deficiencies in internal control that we consider to be material weaknesses and significant deficiencies.

A deficiency in internal control exists when the design or operation of a control does not allow management or employees, in the normal course of performing their assigned functions, to prevent, or detect and correct, misstatements on a timely basis. A material weakness is a deficiency, or a combination of deficiencies, in internal control, such that there is a reasonable possibility that a material misstatement of the entity's financial statements will not be prevented, or detected and corrected on a timely basis. We consider the following deficiencies in the Company's internal control to be material weaknesses:

[*Describe the material weaknesses that were identified and an explanation of their potential effects.*]

A significant deficiency is a deficiency, or combination of deficiencies, in internal control that is less severe than a material weakness, yet important enough to merit attention by those charged with governance. We consider the following deficiencies in the Company's internal control to be significant deficiencies:

[*Describe the significant deficiencies that were identified and an explanation of their potential effects.*]

[*If the auditor is communicating significant deficiencies and did not identify any material weaknesses, the auditor may state that none of the identified deficiencies are considered to be material weaknesses.*]

This communication is intended solely for the information and use of management, [*identify the body or individuals charged with governance*], others within the organization, and [*identify any specified governmental authorities to which the auditor is required to report*] and is not intended to be, and should not be, used by anyone other than these specified parties.

[*Auditor's Signature*]
[*Date*]

---

1 AICPA Code of Professional Conduct

1.1 Independence Rule

1.1.1 Independence Requirement

- Independence is required for audits and attest services.

- It is not required for compilations, consulting services or tax work.

1.1.2 Independence Is Impaired in the Following Cases

- Independence is impaired if the CPA has a direct financial interest, regardless of materiality or a material indirect interest.

- Independence is impaired if audit fees remain unpaid for more than one year prior to the issuance of the current audit report. It is considered a loan.

- Independence is impaired if a CPA has a management position with a client or is an employee. The spouse of a CPA can be an employee, but cannot hold a management position.

- Independence is impaired if a CPA makes hiring decisions for a client. The CPA may recommend a job description, screen candidates for the position, and advise the client on hiring.

- Litigation can impair independence, but not for immaterial dollar amounts unrelated to the audit.

1.1.3 Independence Is Not Impaired in the Following Cases

- Independence is not impaired with a bank client by a checking account that is fully insured.

- Independence is not impaired by a fully collateralized auto loan.

1.2 Integrity and Objectivity Rule

- All engagements must be performed with objectivity and integrity.

- The CPA should be free of conflict of interests, although services may still be performed if a conflict is disclosed to the client and the client consents to the CPA performing the engagement.

1.3 General Standards Rule

The general standards apply to all engagements.

1.3.1 Professional Competence

Requires proper education and training. The CPA need not be an expert or attain specialty accreditation. The CPA can consult with or hire experts.

1.3.2 Due Professional Care

The CPA must exercise the same skill a reasonably prudent accountant would. The CPA must critically review the work done by others.

1.3.3 Adequate Planning and Supervision

All engagements must be adequately planned and supervised.

1.3.4 Sufficient Relevant Data

All decisions must be based on sufficient relevant data.

1.4 Compliance With Standards Rule and Accounting Principles Rule

- A CPA performing an engagement must comply with applicable standards.
- A CPA cannot state that financial statements or other data comply with GAAP if there are departures that would have a material effect on the financial statements.
- Unusual circumstances may justify a departure from GAAP if compliance would cause the financial statements to be misleading (e.g., new legislation or new form of business practice). The departure from GAAP must be described and explained.

1.5 Confidential Client Information Rule

Confidential client information cannot be revealed to others without the client's consent. Confidential information can be revealed in a lawsuit and it can be revealed to a state CPA society voluntary quality control review panel. It also can be revealed when subpoenaed and confidential audit documentation can be reviewed by a prospective purchaser of a CPA's practice if confidentiality is assured (but audit documentation may not be turned over to a purchaser without the client's consent).

1.6 Contingent Fees Rule

A contingent fee is a fee dependent upon attaining a specified result. It is not permitted for audits, reviews and most tax work. Contingent fees are permitted for compilations if the CPA discloses the lack of independence. It is also permitted if a CPA represents a client in an examination of a tax return by the IRS.

1.7 Acts Discreditable Rule

The following acts are considered discreditable to the profession:

- Retaining a client's records after the client has demanded that the records be returned or after the employment relationship has been terminated.
- Discrimination in employment.
- Failure to follow standards in audits or government audits.
- Negligently making false or misleading journal entries.

▧ Failure to timely file tax returns or remit payroll taxes.

▧ Soliciting or disclosing CPA exam questions or answers.

▧ Makes false, misleading, or deceptive claims about the member's abilities to provide professional services.

▧ Disclosure of confidential information, obtained from a prospective client or non-client without consent.

Question 1   MCQ-09616

Smith and Company, CPAs, has been hired to perform the audit of Warehouse Company's Year 10 financial statements. Warehouse Company is an issuer. Under the ethical standards of the profession, which of the following employment relationships would not impair Smith and Company's independence?

1. The lead partner on the audit serves on Warehouse Company's board of directors.

2. The Warehouse Company's former controller, who left the company during Year 10, is assigned to the engagement team that will perform the Warehouse Company audit.

3. The wife of an audit engagement team member works in Warehouse Company's customer service department.

4. The former manager of the Warehouse engagement was hired as Warehouse Company's CFO during Year 10.

Question 2   MCQ-09477

The concept of materiality would be *least* important to an auditor when considering the:

1. Adequacy of disclosure of a client's illegal act.

2. Discovery of weaknesses in a client's internal control structure.

3. Effects of a direct financial interest in the client on the CPA's independence.

4. Decision whether to use positive or negative confirmations of accounts receivable.

---

2 AICPA Conceptual Framework Approach

The rules and interpretations of the AICPA Code of Professional Conduct (discussed above) seek to address many situations; however, they cannot address all relationships or circumstances that may arise. In the absence of an interpretation that addresses a particular relationship or circumstance, a member should apply the appropriate conceptual framework approach.

The conceptual framework approach requires entities to identify threats to compliance with the fundamental principles, evaluate the significance of the threat, and apply safeguards to eliminate threats or reduce threats to an acceptable level, whenever possible.

2.1 Threats to Compliance

Threats to compliance may fall into one or more of the following categories:

2.1.1 Adverse Interest Threat

The threat that a member will not act with objectivity because the member's interests are opposed to the interests of the client or employing organization.

2.1.2 Advocacy Threat

The threat that a member will promote the interests of the client or employing organization to the point that his or her objectivity or independence, as applicable, is compromised.

2.1.3 Familiarity Threat

The threat that, due to a long or close relationship with the client or employing organization, a member will become too accepting of the product or service and/or too sympathetic to the client's or employing organization's interests.

2.1.4 Management Participation Threat

The threat that a member will take on the role of client management or otherwise assume management responsibilities. This threat exits for members engaged in attest engagements.

2.1.5 Self-Interest Threat

The threat that a member could benefit financially or otherwise from an interest in, or relationship with, a client or employing organization, or persons associated with the client or employing organization.

2.1.6 Self-Review Threat

The threat that a member will not appropriately evaluate the results of a previous judgment made, or service performed or supervised, by the member or an individual in the member's firm or employing organization, and that the member will rely on that service in forming a judgment as part of another service.

2.1.7   Undue Influence Threat

The threat that a member will subordinate his or her judgment to an individual associated with a client or employing organization or any relevant third party due to that individual's reputation or expertise, aggressive or dominant personality, or attempts to coerce or exercise excessive influence over the member.

2.2   Safeguards

Safeguards may include those created by the profession, legislation, or regulation, implemented by the client or employing organization, and/or implemented by the firm (if applicable).

3 Sarbanes-Oxley Act of 2002

The Sarbanes-Oxley Act of 2002 created the Public Company Accounting Oversight Board (PCAOB) and outlined the following key standards and independence rules that apply to audits of issuers:

3.1   Records Retention

Audit workpapers and supporting documentation must be maintained for seven years.

3.2   Concurring Partner Review

A concurring or second partner review is required for each audit report.

3.3   Prohibited Services

A registered public accounting firm may not provide the following services for issuers:

- Bookkeeping
- Financial information systems design and implementation
- Appraisal and valuation services
- Actuarial services
- Management functions or human resources services
- Internal audit outsourcing services
- Services as a broker, dealer, investment advisor, or investment banker
- Legal services
- Expert services unrelated to the audit

Tax services may be performed if preapproved by the audit committee.

3.4 Audit Committee Preapproval and Reporting

All audit services and permitted non-audit services must be preapproved by the audit committee. Additionally, the auditor must report the following to the audit committees of audited corporations:

- Critical accounting policies and practices used

- Alternative accounting treatments discussed with management and the treatment preferred by the auditors

- Material written communications between the auditor and management

3.5 Audit Partner Rotation

The lead and reviewing partner must rotate off the audit every five years.

3.6 Conflicts of Interest

The audit firm cannot have employed the issuer's CEO, CFO, controller, or chief accounting officer, or equivalent, for a one-year period preceding the audit (the "cooling off" period).

Question 3   MCQ-09589

Which of the following is not a provision of the Sarbanes-Oxley Act of 2002?

   1. The auditor of an issuer may not provide internal audit outsourcing services for the issuer.

   2. Audit documentation must be maintained for five years.

   3. The lead and reviewing partners must rotate off the audit after five years.

   4. Tax services must be preapproved by the audit committee.

---

4 Public Company Accounting Oversight Board (PCAOB)

4.1 Interim Standards

The PCAOB's interim independence standards, as adopted from the AICPA Code of Professional Conduct, have been amended to align with the standards as outlined in Rule 2-01 of Regulation S-X as outlined in the following section. Additionally, the PCAOB has adopted certain permanent independence rules that impose incremental obligations on registered public accounting firms.

4.2 Independence Standards

The PCAOB has adopted independence rules to conform with Rule 2-01 of the U.S. Securities and Exchange Commission (SEC) Regulation S-X, as described in the following section, and has issued the following additional independence standards that apply to audits of issuers by registered firms:

4.2.1 Contingent Fees

A registered firm may not provide services or products for a contingent fee or commission.

4.2.2 Tax Services

A registered firm may not provide to audit clients any tax services related to certain confidential or aggressive tax transactions and may not provide tax services to corporate officers of audit clients, or the immediate family members of corporate officers.

Proposed tax services and related fees must be communicated to the audit committee in writing and the potential effects of the tax services on audit independence must be discussed with the audit committee and documented.

4.2.3 Non-audit Services Related to Internal Control Over Financial Reporting

Non-audit services related to internal control over financial reporting must be communicated to the audit committee in writing and the potential effects of the tax services on audit independence must be discussed with the audit committee and documented.

4.2.4 Communication With the Audit Committee Concerning Independence

Before accepting an initial engagement with an issuer, and at least annually for each issuer audit client, a registered firm must describe in writing to the audit committee all relationships that might affect independence and the effects of those relationships. As part of the annual communication, the firm must affirm its independence in writing as of the date of the communication.

5 U.S. Securities and Exchange Commission (SEC)

Rule 2-01 of SEC Regulation S-X outlines the independence rules that apply to the auditors of SEC registrants. The SOX independence rules have been incorporated into these rules and the PCAOB has adopted independence rules that conform to these standards. According to Regulation S-X, the following circumstances impair auditor independence:

5.1 Financial Relationships

Similar to the AICPA Code of Professional Conduct, the SEC prohibits any direct or material indirect financial interest in an audit client during the period of professional engagement, as well as loans to or from an audit client (other than loans from financial institutions under normal lending circumstances). Additionally, the audit client may not invest in the accounting firm or engage the accounting firm to provide investments services.

5.2 Employment Relationships

Independence is impaired by employment relationships between the accounting firm, covered members of the accounting firm, and the audit client, including:

- Employment of a covered person by the audit client or service on the audit client board of directors.
- Employment of a close family member of a covered person in an accounting or financial reporting role at an audit client.
- Employment at the audit client of a former member of the audit engagement team in an accounting or financial oversight role, unless the individual no longer influences the accounting firms operations, and has no capital balances or financial arrangements with the accounting firm.
- Employment at the audit client of a former member of the audit engagement team in a financial oversight role during the one-year preceding the commencement of audit procedures.
- Employment at the accounting firm of former employees of the audit client, unless the individual does not participate in or influence any audit related to the period in which the individual was employed by the client.

5.3 Performance of Non-audit Services

The prohibited non-audit services outlined under SOX (see above) are also prohibited by the SEC.

5.4 Contingent Fees

Independence is impaired by contingent fee or commission arrangements between the auditor and the audit client.

5.5   Failure to Rotate Partners

The SEC has enhanced the SOX partner rotation rules. The SEC requires the lead and concurring partner to rotate off the audit engagement after five years and requires other audit partners to rotate off the audit engagement after seven years. Lead and concurring partners are subject to a five-year time out period before returning to an engagement and other audit partners are subject to a two-year time out period.

5.6   Failure of the Audit Committee to Administer the Engagement

The audit committee must preapprove all audit, review, and attestation engagements and all permissible non-audit services. Consistent with SOX, the auditor must report the following to the audit committees of audited corporations:

- Critical accounting policies and practices used.
- Alternative accounting treatments discussed with management and the treatment preferred by the auditors.
- Material written communications between the auditor and management.

5.7   Certain Compensation Arrangements

An audit partner cannot earn or receive compensation based on selling engagements to audit clients for services other than audit, review or attest services.

6 U.S. Department of Labor

The U.S. Department of Labor (DOL) has established guidelines for determining when a qualified public accountant is independent for the purpose of rendering an opinion on an employee benefit plan under the Employee Retirement Income Security Act of 1974 (ERISA).

6.1   Independence Required

Auditor independence is required when auditing and rendering an opinion on the financial information required to be submitted to the Employee Benefits Security Administration of the DOL.

6.2   Impairment of Independence

The following situations impair independence with respect to an employee benefit plan:

- Any direct financial interest or a material indirect financial interest in the plan or the plan sponsor.

- Connection to the plan or the plan sponsor as a promoter, underwriter, investment advisor, voting trustee, director, officer, or employee.

- An accountant or a member of the accounting firm maintains financial records for the employee benefit plan.

6.3   Independence Not Impaired

An accountant's independence is not impaired when:

- A former officer or employee of the plan or plan sponsor is employed by the firm, the individual has completely disassociated for the plan or plan sponsor, and the individual does not participate in auditing the financial statements of the plan covering any period of his or her employment by the plan or plan sponsor.

- The accountant or the accountant's firm was engaged by the plan sponsor during the period of the professional engagement with the employee benefit plan.

- An actuary associated with the accountant or the accountant's firm rendered services to the plan.

Question 4   MCQ-09603

Which of the following will not impair independence under the U.S. Department of Labor's independence rules for audits of employee benefit plans?

1. An actuary employed by the audit firm performs services for the employee benefit plan.

2. The audit firm has a material indirect financial interest in the sponsor of the employee benefit plan.

3. A member of the audit firm maintains the financial records of the employee benefit plan.

4. A partner on the engagement team serves on the board of directors of the plan sponsor.

---

7 GAGAS Conceptual Framework for Independence

7.1 Requirements

The GAGAS independence conceptual framework steps require that an auditor:

- Identify threats to independence;
- Evaluate the significance of the threats identified, both individually and in the aggregate; and
- Apply safeguards as necessary to eliminate the threats or reduce them to an acceptable level.

If no safeguards are available to eliminate an unacceptable threat or reduce it to an acceptable level, independence would be considered to be impaired.

7.2 Threats to Independence

- Self-interest threat is the threat that a financial or other interest will inappropriately influence an auditor's judgment or behavior.
- Self-review threat is the threat that an auditor providing non-audit services will not appropriately evaluate the results of previous judgments made or services when significant to an audit.
- Bias threat is the threat that the auditor's position is not objective.
- Familiarity threat is the threat that aspects of a relationship, such as a close or long relationship, will lead an auditor to take a position that is not objective.
- Undue influence threat is the threat that external influences or pressures will impact an auditor's ability to make independent and objective judgments.
- Management participation threat is the threat that results from an auditor's taking on the role of management or otherwise performing management functions on behalf of the entity undergoing an audit.
- Structural threat is the threat that occurs when an audit organization's placement within a government entity might impact the audit organization's ability to perform work and report results objectively.

7.3 Safeguards

- Safeguards are controls designed to eliminate or reduce to an acceptable level threats to independence.
- Under the conceptual framework, the auditor applies safeguards that address the specific facts and circumstances under which threats to independence exist.

7.4 Evaluation of Non-audit Services

- The auditor should determine whether providing a non-audit service would create a threat to independence.
- A critical component of this determination is consideration of management's ability to effectively oversee the non-audit service to be performed.

Auditing Final Review

1 Quality Control Standards

1.1 System of Quality Control

CPA firms are required to adopt a system of quality control for their auditing, attestation, and accounting and review services.

1.1.1 Human Resources

A firm should have criteria for recruitment and hiring, determining capabilities and competencies, assigning personnel to engagements, professional development, and performance evaluation, compensation and advancement.

1.1.2 Engagement/Client Acceptance and Continuance

Policies and procedures should ensure that the firm minimizes the likelihood of association with a client whose management lacks integrity, undertakes only those engagements that the firm expects to complete with reasonable competence, and complies with legal and ethical requirements.

1.1.3 Leadership Responsibilities

The firm's leadership bears the ultimate responsibility for the firm's quality control system and should create a culture that emphasizes quality.

1.1.4 Engagement Performance

Policies and procedures should be established to ensure that the firm consistently achieves a high level of performance, that engagements are properly supervised, that confidentiality, safe custody, integrity, accessibility, retrievability, and retention of engagement documentation is maintained, that differences of opinion can be resolved, and that guidelines exist to determine when an engagement quality control review should be performed.

1.1.5 Monitoring

The firm should have reasonable assurance that its quality control system is relevant, adequate, operating effectively, and complied with in practice.

1.1.6 Ethical Requirements

Personnel should maintain independence in fact and appearance in all required circumstances, perform all professional responsibilities with integrity, and maintain objectivity in discharging professional responsibilities.

1.2 Deficiencies or Noncompliance

Deficiencies in, or noncompliance with, a firm's quality control standards do not necessarily imply that a specific engagement was not performed in accordance with appropriate standards.

Question 1   MCQ-09056

A CPA firm should adopt a system of quality control:

1. For all audit and attest services, but not necessarily for accounting and review services.

2. That encompasses human resource policies and practices.

3. Because it maximizes audit efficiency.

4. Because it ensures that all audit engagements will be conducted in accordance with generally accepted auditing standards.

II

Assessing Risk and Developing a Planned Response

1 Obtain Knowledge of Industry and Business

The auditor is not required to have prior experience with the client's business or industry before accepting the engagement, but must obtain an understanding of the business and industry once the engagement has been accepted.

1.1 Industry Knowledge

Industry knowledge can be obtained from:

- AICPA accounting and auditing guides
- Trade publications and professional trade associations
- Government publications
- GAAP Financial Statements - Best Practices in Presentation and Disclosure

1.2 Business Knowledge

Knowledge of the client's business can be obtained by:

- Touring client facilities
- Reviewing the client's financial history
- Obtaining an understanding of the client's accounting system
- Asking questions of client personnel

Question 1 — MCQ-09804

Which of the following procedures would a CPA *least likely* perform during the planning stage of the audit?

1. Determine the timing of testing.
2. Take a tour of the client's facilities.
3. Perform inquiries of outside legal counsel regarding pending litigation.
4. Determine the effect of information technology on the audit.

Planning an Engagement

2 Audit Strategy and Audit Plan

2.1 Audit Strategy

The auditor should establish an overall audit strategy, including preliminary assessments of materiality. The audit strategy outlines the scope of the audit engagement, the reporting objectives, timing of the audit, required communications, and the factors that determine the focus of the audit.

2.2 Audit Plan

The auditor is required to develop a written audit plan that outlines the nature, extent, and timing of the procedures to be performed during the audit, including:

- Risk assessment procedures
- Further audit procedures (tests of controls and substantive procedures)
- Other audit procedures

The audit strategy and audit plan can be modified as the audit progresses in response to new information or to the results of other procedures.

Question 2   MCQ-09072

Which of the following is required documentation in an audit in accordance with generally accepted auditing standards?

1. A flowchart or narrative of the information system relevant to financial reporting describing the recording and classification of transactions for financial reporting.

2. An audit plan setting forth in detail the procedures necessary to accomplish the engagement's objectives.

3. A planning memorandum establishing the timing of the audit procedures and coordinating the assistance of entity personnel.

4. An internal control questionnaire identifying controls that assure specific objectives will be achieved.

-2   II   *Auditing Final Review*   © Becker Professional Education Corporation. All rights reserved.

1 Overview of Internal Control

1.1 Definition

Internal control is a process designed to provide assurance that an entity's objectives will be achieved. Objectives include:

- Reliability of financial reporting
- Effectiveness and efficiency of operations
- Compliance with applicable laws and regulations

1.2 Inherent Limitations

- Human error
- Collusion, deliberate circumvention, fraud
- Management override

Question 1   MCQ-09071

Which of the following situations is *not* an example of an inherent limitation of internal control?

1. A programming error in the design of an automated control allows an employee to give himself an unauthorized pay increase.

2. A lack of physical controls over the safeguarding of assets allows an employee to steal company assets.

3. Management's failure to enforce control policies surrounding access to inventory allows employees to steal assets.

4. A fraud scheme whereby an employee orders personal goods and his supervisor, who is in on the scheme, signs the checks to pay for those goods.

---

2 Five Components of Internal Control

> Mnemonic = **CRIME**

2.1 Control Environment

Sets the tone of an organization and its policies and procedures.
Key points include:

- Integrity
- Competence
- Participation of those charged with governance
- Management philosophy
- Organizational structure
- Role assignment
- Promotion and training

2.2 Risk Assessment

Management identifies, analyzes, and manages risks that affect the
entity's ability to accomplish its major objectives. Once risks are identified,
management considers their significance, likelihood of occurrence, and
how they should be managed. Key points include:

- New products
- Rapid growth
- Other changes

2.3 Information and Communication Systems

Methods and records used to identify, capture, and exchange information.
Key points include:

- All transactions are recorded and complete
- Detailed enough to provide for adequate financial reporting disclosure
- Communication among management, employees, those charged with
  governance, and external parties

2.4 Monitoring

Procedures established to assess the quality of the internal control
structure, and to make necessary corrections. Key points include:

- Internal audit
- Review and independent checks
- Other procedures such as mailing customer statements

2.5 (Existing) Control Activities

Policies and procedures established to ensure that management objectives are carried out. Key points include:

Mnemonic = **PAID TIPS**

- **P**renumbering of documents
- **A**uthorization of transactions
- **I**ndependent checks to maintain asset accountability
- **D**ocumentation
- **T**imely and appropriate performance reviews
- **I**nformation processing controls
- **P**hysical controls for safeguarding assets
- **S**egregation of duties

3 Audit Requirements

The auditor should:

- understand the five components of internal control.
- evaluate the design of relevant controls and determine whether they have been implemented.
- assess risk.
- design appropriate audit procedures, based on assessed risk.

Question 2	MCQ-09054

Which of the following is true regarding performance of the following audit tasks while obtaining an understanding of internal control?

Audit Tasks:

I. Obtain an understanding of the design of controls.

II. Determine whether internal controls have been implemented.

III. Evaluate the operating effectiveness of controls.

   1. The auditor must perform I and II, and is allowed, but not required, to perform III.

   2. The auditor must perform I, II, and III.

   3. The auditor must perform I and II, but may not perform III.

   4. The auditor may, but is not required to, perform I, II, and III.

4 Service Organizations

4.1 Effect on Internal Control

A service organization's services are considered to be part of a user entity's information system when such services affect the initiation, execution, processing, or reporting of the user's transactions.

4.2 Service Organization Reports

The System and Organization Controls (SOC) reports are issued to evaluate "system-level controls" or "entity-level controls" for service-based firms.

- A SOC 1® report addresses a company's internal control over financial reporting.

- A SOC 2® report deals with the examination of controls of a service organization over privacy, confidentiality, processing integrity, availability, and security.

Each report can be issued as a Type 1 or a Type 2 report.

- **Report on Controls Placed in Operation (Type 1 Report):** Helps the auditor understand controls.

- **Report on Controls Placed in Operation and Tests of Operating Effectiveness (Type 2 Report):** Helps the auditor understand controls and may provide evidence supporting a reduction in the assessed level of control risk.

Question 3   MCQ-08111

Payroll Data Co. (PDC) processes payroll transactions for a retailer. Cook, CPA, is engaged to express an opinion on a description of PDC's internal controls placed in operation as of a specific date. These controls are relevant to the retailer's internal control, so Cook's report may be useful in providing the retailer's independent auditor with information necessary to plan a financial statement audit. Cook's report should:

1. Contain a disclaimer of opinion on the operating effectiveness of PDC's controls.

2. State whether PDC's controls were suitably designed to achieve the retailer's objectives.

3. Identify PDC's controls relevant to specific financial statement assertions.

4. Disclose Cook's assessed level of control risk for PDC.

---

5 The Effect of Information Technology (IT) on the Audit

A client's use of information technology affects both the evaluation of internal control and the gathering of evidence, but the audit objectives remain the same.

5.1 The IT Environment

An entity's IT environment may consist of multiple layers of supporting IT infrastructure. Examples of different layers include hardware, software, network, operations systems, and data storage.

5.2 Evidence Gathering in an Automated Environment

An auditor can use manual audit procedures, e.g., "auditing around the computer," computer-assisted audit techniques (CAAT), e.g., "auditing through the computer," or a combination of the two.

5.2.1 Auditing Around the Computer

An auditor tests input data, processes data independently, and then compares the independent results to program results.

- This is appropriate for simple batch systems with good audit trails.

- The risks include insufficient paper-based evidence and insufficient audit procedures.

5.2.2 Auditing Through the Computer

- **Transaction Tagging:** Electronically marks a transaction and allows the auditor to follow it through the client's system.

- **Embedded Audit Modules:** An application program collects transaction data for the auditor. The auditor must be involved with the program design.

- **Test Deck (Test Data):** Uses application program to process test data, the results of which are already known (client system, offline).

- **Integrated Test Facility (ITF):** Test data is commingled with live data (client system, auditor's data, online).

- **Parallel Simulation (Reperformance Test):** The auditor reprocesses some or all of the client's live data and compares the results with client files (auditor's system, client data).

- **Generalized Audit Software Packages (GASP):** Allow the auditor to perform tests of controls and substantive tests directly on the client's system.

5.3 The Effect of Information Technology on Internal Control

Information technology use often affects an entity's internal control. IT brings increased risks but may also provide additional benefits.

5.3.1 IT Risks

- Potential reliance on inaccurate systems
- Loss of data and/or data inaccuracies from unauthorized data access
- Unauthorized changes to data, systems, or programs
- Failure to make required changes/updates to systems or programs

5.3.2 IT Benefits

- Accurate and consistent processing of large data/transaction volume
- Improved timeliness and availability of information
- Facilitation of data analysis and performance monitoring
- Reduction in the risk that controls will be circumvented
- Effective implementation of security controls enhances segregation of duties

Note

The accuracy of the IT system is crucial, because even manual controls may be dependent to some extent on the effective functioning of IT.

5.4 Assessing Control Risk

When assessing internal control, the auditor should consider the effects of both risks and benefits. Control risk assessment procedures in a computerized environment are the same as in manual systems (inquiry, inspection, observation, and reperformance).

5.5 The Effect of Information Technology on Audit Testing

- To select appropriate audit procedures, the auditor should consider the extent and complexity of the entity's computer operations, and the availability of an audit trail.
- Substantive tests alone may not suffice. Tests of controls should be performed to assess control risk in entities with significant computerized operations.
- The auditor needs to identify and test both specific application controls, and relevant general controls on which the application controls depend.
- The auditor should obtain an understanding of the internal control in effect throughout the period. Testing for operational integrity at a single point in time is generally not a reliable test of program controls. Although the auditor may make an initial assessment that a control is functioning as planned, subsequent testing is needed to ensure that the control continues to function effectively.

Question 4 — MCQ-04383

An auditor most likely would introduce test data into a computerized payroll system to test internal controls related to the:

1. Existence of unclaimed payroll checks held by supervisors.
2. Early cashing of payroll checks by employees.
3. Discovery of invalid employee I.D. numbers.
4. Proper approval of overtime by supervisors.

Question 5 — MCQ-08126

When an auditor tests a computerized accounting system, which of the following is true of the test data approach?

1. Several transactions of each type must be tested.
2. Test data are processed by the client's computer programs under the auditor's control.
3. Test data must consist of all possible valid and invalid conditions.
4. The program tested is different from the program used throughout the year by the client.

1 Auditor Responsibility

The auditor must obtain reasonable assurance about whether the financial statements are free of material misstatements, whether caused by error or fraud.

1.1 Error

Error is an unintentional misstatement or omission.

1.2 Fraud

Fraud is an intentional misstatement or omission in the financial statements. Fraud often involves management because management is in a position to manipulate, directly or indirectly, accounting records. Management also can override established controls.

Question 1   MCQ-09030

The auditor's responsibility regarding material misstatements caused by *fraud* is:

1. Less than the auditor's responsibility regarding material misstatements caused by *error*.

2. Greater than the auditor's responsibility regarding material misstatements caused by *error*.

3. The same as the auditor's responsibility regarding material misstatements caused by *error*.

4. Either less than or greater than the auditor's responsibility regarding material misstatements caused by *error*, depending on the specific circumstances.

---

2 Categories of Fraud

Fraud is divided into two categories:

2.1 Fraudulent Financial Reporting

Intentional misstatements or omissions of amounts/disclosures in the financial statements; committed by management with the intent to deceive.

2.2 Misappropriation of Assets (Defalcation)

Theft of an entity's assets; committed by management, employees, or third parties.

3 Presumed Fraud Risk

There is a presumption in every audit that the following two risks exist:

- Improper revenue recognition
- Management override of controls

4 Fraud Risk Factors

Three conditions generally are present when fraud occurs:

- **Incentives/Pressures:** A reason to commit fraud.
- **Opportunity:** Ineffective controls or override of controls.
- **Rationalization/Attitude:** Justification of fraudulent behavior.

Question 2

Which of the following is *not* true regarding fraud risk factors?

1. They include incentives/pressures, opportunity, and rationalization.
2. Lack of observation of the three fraud risk factors implies that there is no fraud risk.
3. The existence of all three fraud risk factors is not an absolute indication that fraud has occurred.
4. Fraud risk factors are often present in circumstances where fraud has occurred.

5 Audit Procedures to Address Fraud Risk

The auditor must exercise professional skepticism throughout the audit process.

- Discuss fraud risk with engagement personnel.
- Obtain information to identify specific fraud risks.
- Assess fraud risk and develop an appropriate response.
- Evaluate audit evidence regarding fraud.
- Make appropriate communications about fraud.
- Document the auditor's consideration of fraud.

Question 3

Which of the following items is *not* required to be documented about the required fraud brainstorming session?

1. The auditor's responsibility to provide absolute assurance to uncover fraud.
2. The audit team members who participated.
3. How and when the discussion occurred.
4. Significant decisions reached.

6 Communication of Fraud

6.1 To Management and Those Charged With Governance

Fraud that causes a material financial statement misstatement should always be reported directly to management and those charged with governance.

- Obtain sufficient evidence of fraud and its effects on the financial statements.
- Discuss with an appropriate level of management at least one level higher than where fraud occurred.
- Suggest that client consult with legal counsel.

6.2 To Third Parties

Ordinarily, the auditor does not disclose fraud to third parties. However, in certain circumstances a duty to disclose to outsiders may exist:

- to the SEC in order to comply with certain legal and regulatory requirements, such as on Form 8-K and other required reports.
- to a successor auditor when they make inquiries.
- in a response to subpoena.
- to a funding agency that receives governmental financial assistance.

1 Audit Risk (AR)

AR is the risk that the auditor may unknowingly fail to modify appropriately the opinion on materially misstated financial statements. The auditor should plan the audit so that overall audit risk is limited to a low level. AR includes:

1.1 Risk of Material Misstatement (RMM)

The risk that the financial statements are materially misstated. It can be subdivided into:

1.1.1 Inherent Risk (IR)

Susceptibility of an assertion to a material misstatement assuming that there are no related controls.

- IR exists independently of the audit.
- The auditor cannot change this risk.

1.1.2 Control Risk (CR)

The risk that a material misstatement could occur in an assertion and not be prevented or detected on a timely basis by an entity's internal control.

- CR exists independently of the audit.
- The auditor cannot change this risk, but can change his/her assessment of the risk based on evidence gathered during the audit.
- The stronger the system of controls, the greater the reliance that may be placed on it, and the fewer the substantive tests (or the lower the quality) required.

1.2 Detection Risk (DR)

The risk that the auditor will not detect a material misstatement that exists in an assertion. DR relates to the auditor's procedures.

- The auditor can change this risk by varying the nature, extent, or timing of audit procedures.
- As the acceptable level of DR decreases, the assurance provided from substantive tests should increase.

1.3   The Audit Risk Model

| Audit risk (AR) | = | Risk of material misstatement (RMM) (assessed by auditor) | x | Detection risk (DR) (controlled by auditor) |

Risk of Material Misstatement	Acceptable Level of Detection Risk	Determine "NET" of Substantive Tests
High ↑ (Bad)	Lower ↓	High ↑
Low ↓ (Good)	Higher ↑	Low ↓

Question 1   MCQ-08828

After making a preliminary assessment of the risk of material misstatement during planning and beginning to apply audit procedures, an auditor determines that this risk is actually higher than anticipated. Which would be the *most likely* effect of this finding on the auditor's desired level of detection risk and the overall level of audit risk, as compared to the levels originally planned?

	Auditor's Desired Level of Detection Risk	*Overall Level of Audit Risk*
1.	Decrease	Same
2.	Increase	Same
3.	Same	Higher
4.	Decrease	Lower

Question 2   MCQ-09815

As the acceptable level of detection risk increases, an auditor may:

1. Change the nature of substantive tests from a less effective to a more effective procedure.
2. Postpone the planned timing of substantive tests from interim dates to year-end.
3. Lower the assessed level of inherent risk.
4. Select a smaller sample size.

2 Procedures

2.1 Overview

The auditor must perform the following procedures in order to assess and respond to risk:

▦ Obtain an understanding of the entity and its environment, including its internal control.

▦ Assess the risk of material misstatement.

▦ Respond to the assessed level of risk by performing further audit procedures (tests of controls and substantive tests).

▦ Evaluate audit evidence.

2.2 Obtaining an Understanding

The auditor should understand:

▦ Industry, regulatory, and other external factors.

- The applicable financial reporting framework.

- Technological factors.

▦ The nature of the entity.

▦ The entity's objectives, strategies, and business risks.

▦ The entity's financial performance.

▦ The entity's internal control:

- includes evaluating the design of controls and determining whether they have been implemented.

- does not require an evaluation of the operating effectiveness of controls (but the auditor may purposefully or incidentally obtain evidence about operating effectiveness at this time).

▦ Under PCAOB standards, the auditor of an issuer must also obtain an understanding of the company's selection and application of accounting principles.

2.3 Risk Assessment Procedures

The understanding is obtained by performing the following risk assessment procedures:

▦ Inquiry

▦ Analytical procedures

▦ Audit data analytics

▦ Observation and inspection

▦ Audit team discussion

Question 3   MCQ-09029

Analytical procedures used in planning an audit should focus on:

1. Reducing the scope of tests of controls and substantive tests.
2. Providing assurance that potential material misstatements will be identified.
3. Enhancing the auditor's understanding of the client's business.
4. Assessing the adequacy of the available audit evidence.

Question 4   MCQ-09817

Which one of the following is a true statement about the required risk assessment discussion?

1. The discussion about the susceptibility of the entity's financial statements to material misstatement must be held separately from the discussion about the susceptibility of the entity's financial statements to fraud.
2. The discussion should involve all members who participate on the audit team, including the engagement partner.
3. The discussion should include consideration of the risk of management override of controls.
4. The risk assessment discussion should occur during the overall review stage of the audit.

Assessing the Risk of Material Misstatement

1 Management Assertions (**COVERUP**)

Management makes assertions about transactions and events, account balances, and related disclosures.

1.1 Main Assertions

There are six main financial statement assertions (Note that under PCAOB standards, the main financial statement assertions are completeness; valuation or allocation; existence and occurrence; rights and obligations; and presentation and disclosure):

1.1.1 Completeness

All account balances, transactions, and disclosures that should have been recorded have been recorded and included in the financial statements.

1.1.2 Cutoff

Transactions have been recorded in the correct (proper) accounting period.

1.1.3 Valuation, Allocation, and Accuracy

Account balances, transactions, and disclosures are recorded and described fairly and measured at appropriate amounts, and any resulting valuation or allocation adjustments are appropriately recorded.

1.1.4 Existence and Occurrence

Account balances exist and transactions that have been recorded and disclosed have occurred and pertain to the entity.

1.1.5 Rights and Obligations

The entity holds or controls the rights to assets, and liabilities are the obligations of the entity.

1.1.6 Understandability of Presentation and Classification

Transactions have been recorded in the proper accounts and appropriately aggregated or disaggregated. Financial information is appropriately presented and described and disclosures are clearly expressed and understandable in the context of the applicable financial reporting framework.

1.2 Relevant Assertions

Relevant assertions are assertions that have a meaningful bearing on whether an account, transaction, or disclosure is fairly stated.

1.2.1   Transactions, Events, and Related Disclosures

For transactions, events, and the related disclosures, relevant assertions include completeness, cutoff, accuracy, classification, presentation, and occurrence.

1.2.2   Account Balances and Related Disclosures

For account balances and the related disclosures, relevant assertions include completeness, accuracy, allocation and valuation, rights and obligations, classification, presentation, and existence.

1.2.3   Other Disclosures

The assertions may also be used by the auditor in considering the different types of misstatements that may occur in disclosures not directly related to transactions, events, or account balances.

For presentation and disclosure, relevant assertions include completeness, understandability and classification, rights and obligations, and valuation and accuracy.

Question 1   MCQ-08123

In assessing control risk for purchases, an auditor vouches a sample of entries in the voucher register to the supporting documents. Which assertion would this test of controls most likely support?

1. Completeness.

2. Occurrence.

3. Allocation and valuation.

4. Rights and obligations.

Question 2   MCQ-09066

An auditor wishes to test the completeness assertion for sales. Which of the following audit tests would most likely accomplish this objective?

1. Select a sample of shipments occurring during the year and trace each one to inclusion in the sales journal.

2. Compare accounts receivable turnover (net credit sales / average gross receivables) in the current year to that achieved in the prior year.

3. Use common size analysis to compare recorded sales to sales recorded by other companies in the same industry.

4. Select large individual sales recorded during the year and review supporting documentation.

---

2 Assessing Risk

The auditor should:

■ Identify and assess specific risks at the assertion level and at the financial statement level.

■ Give special consideration to significant risks.

■ Identify relevant controls.

■ Document the following:

• Key elements of the understanding of the entity and its environment, including the components of internal control

• Identified risks and related controls

• Risk assessment procedures performed

• The auditor's risk assessment and the basis for this assessment

---

Question 3   MCQ-09806

Which of the following documentation is *not* required for an audit in accordance with generally accepted auditing standards?

1. A written audit plan setting forth the procedures necessary to accomplish the audit objectives.

2. The basis for the auditor's decision to perform tests of controls concurrently with obtaining an understanding of internal control.

3. The auditor's understanding of the entity's control activities that help ensure achievement of management's objectives.

4. The assessment of the risks of material misstatement at both the financial statement and relevant assertion levels.

---

1 Levels of Response

1.1 Overall Response

Overall responses to an assessed high risk of material misstatement include:

■ Communicate to the audit team an increased need for professional skepticism.

■ Assign staff with more experience or specialized skills.

■ Increase the level of supervision.

■ Incorporate a greater level of unpredictability into the audit.

■ Make changes to the nature, extent, and timing of tests.

1.2 Assertion Level Response

There should be a clear linkage between the assessed level of risk at the relevant assertion level and the nature, extent, and timing of further audit procedures, including tests of controls and substantive procedures.

1.3 Response to Significant Risks

If relying on the operating effectiveness of internal controls intended to mitigate significant risk, tests of controls must be performed in the current period. Substantive procedures can consist of tests of details only, or tests of details and substantive analytical procedures.

Question 1   MCQ-09865

Which of the following represents an appropriate overall response to an increase in financial statement level risk?

1. Providing management with more specific details about audit sampling procedures.

2. Changing the general approach of the audit to ensure control testing of all significant accounts.

3. Shifting substantive procedures to interim.

4. Increasing the level of supervision.

---

2 Further Audit Procedures

Based on assessed risk at the relevant assertion level, the auditor designs the nature, extent, and timing of further audit procedures.

- **Nature:** the purpose and type of test.
- **Extent:** the quantity of testing.
- **Timing:** interim or period end.

3 Audit Approaches

3.1 Substantive Approach

Under a substantive approach, only substantive procedures are performed.

3.2 Combined Approach

Under a combined approach, tests of the operating effectiveness of controls and substantive procedures (perhaps at a reduced level) are both performed. In a combined approach, the nature, extent, and timing of substantive testing is affected by the operating effectiveness of controls:

- The more effective a control, the lower the assessed level of control risk (CR). As CR decreases, the acceptable level of detection risk (DR) increases and the assurance required from substantive tests decreases.

- Conversely, as the acceptable level of DR decreases, the assurance that must be obtained from substantive tests increases.

- The stronger a control, the more it can be relied upon, and the fewer the required substantive tests (or the lower the quality).

When Do We Test Controls?		
Status of Controls	*Risk Level*	*Audit Work*
No controls	Maximum Risk	Do not test controls*
Weak controls	High Risk	Do not test controls*
Some controls	Moderate Risk	Test the controls
Strong controls	Low Risk	Test the controls
* Exception: If significant electronic processing is used, controls should be tested.		

Question 2   MCQ-08320

Using a combined approach most likely would involve:

1. Performing more extensive substantive tests with larger sample sizes than originally planned.

2. Reducing inherent risk for most of the assertions relevant to significant account balances.

3. Changing the timing of substantive tests by omitting interim-date testing and performing the tests at year-end.

4. Identifying specific internal controls relevant to specific assertions.

1 Materiality

Materiality is the amount of error or omission that would affect the judgment of a reasonable person. The auditor should make preliminary assessments of materiality and should revise those assessments as appropriate throughout the audit.

1.1 Materiality for the Financial Statements as a Whole

Materiality for the financial statements as a whole needs to be expressed as a specific amount.

■ Materiality should be based on the smallest level of misstatement that could be material to any one of the financial statements.

■ Both qualitative and quantitative factors should be used to assess materiality, including:

- The application of a percentage to an appropriate financial statement benchmark

- Prior period and current period financial results

- Known or expected changes in the entity's circumstances, the industry, or the economy

1.2 Performance Materiality

Performance materiality consists of the amount(s) set at less than materiality for the financial statements as a whole in order to reduce to an appropriately low level the probability that the aggregate of uncorrected and undetected misstatements exceeds the materiality for the financial statements as a whole.

1.3 Tolerable Misstatement

Tolerable misstatement is the application of performance materiality to a particular sampling procedure.

1.4 Materiality for Classes of Transactions, Account Balances, or Disclosures

A separate materiality level should be set for a particular class of transactions, account balances, or disclosures when misstatements of an amount less than materiality for the financial statements as a whole would influence the judgment made by a reasonable user.

Question 1

In which of the following circumstances would an auditor of an issuer be *least likely* to reevaluate established materiality levels?

1. The materiality level was established based on preliminary financial statement amounts that differ significantly from actual amounts.

2. The client disposed a major portion of the client's business.

3. The client released third-quarter results before the SEC-prescribed deadline.

4. Significant new contractual arrangements draw attention to a particular aspect of a client's business that is separately disclosed in the financial statements.

1 Internal Audit Function

Independent auditors cannot share responsibility for audit decisions, assessments, or for issuing the report with a client's internal auditor. However, the internal auditor may assist with routine tasks.

1.1 Critical Factors

An auditor wishing to make use of an internal auditor's work must consider critical factors, including:

- The competence of the internal audit function, as evidenced by education, professional certification, and the quality of internal audit documentation.

- The objectivity of the internal auditors, based on the organizational level to which the internal audit function reports.

- The application of a systematic and disciplined approach, as evidenced by the use of documented internal audit procedures and quality control policies.

Question 1	MCQ-08139

In assessing the competence and objectivity of an entity's internal auditor, an independent auditor would *least likely* consider information obtained from:

1. Discussions with management personnel.

2. External quality reviews of the internal auditor's work.

3. Previous experience with the internal auditor.

4. The results of analytical procedures.

2 Use of Specialists

Actuaries, appraisers, attorneys, and engineers (specialists) may be used to assist the auditor in considering valuation or complex transactions. The auditor should understand the specialist's field of expertise, competence, capabilities, and objectivity to determine the possibility of using the specialist's work.

2.1 Impact on Audit Report

If, as a result of the work performed by the specialist, the auditor decides to add explanatory language or depart from an unqualified opinion, the auditor may refer to the specialist in the report and should indicate that the reference to the specialist does not reduce the auditor's responsibility for the audit opinion. In addition, an auditor of an issuer may reference the specialist if it helps the users understand a critical audit matter. The auditor may need the permission of the specialist before making reference to the specialist.

Question 2	MCQ-09802

Which of the following procedures is the auditor *least likely* to perform when an auditor decides to use the work of an auditor's specialist as audit evidence?

1. Obtain knowledge of the specialist's qualifications.

2. Refer to the auditor's specialist in the audit report to indicate a division of responsibility.

3. Inquire of the entity and the auditor's specialist about any known interests that the entity has with the auditor's external specialist that may affect that specialist's objectivity.

4. Review the working papers of the auditor's specialist.

3 Use of an IT Auditor

Someone possessing specialized knowledge in information technology participating in the audit is called an IT auditor, not a specialist.

- The IT auditor is considered a member of the engagement team.
- The IT auditor may be used throughout the audit to obtain an understanding of internal control, assess risks, and perform control test work and substantive procedures.
- The audit partner supervises and reviews the work performed on the audit, including the work performed by any IT auditors.

4 Use of a Component Auditor

A component auditor performs work on the financial information of a component that will be used as audit evidence for a group audit.

- A component auditor may be engaged to obtain sufficient appropriate evidence over a component or may be required by law or regulation.
- The group auditor is responsible for determining the need for a component auditor and for evaluating the adequacy of the component auditor's work.
- The group auditor should use his or her understanding of each component auditor to determine whether to make reference to the individual component auditor in the auditor's report.

If the group engagement partner decides to assume responsibility for the work of a component auditor, then no reference to the component auditor should be made in the auditor's report.

1 Related Party Transactions

1.1 Auditor Responsibility

Throughout the audit process, the auditor must be alert for the existence of transactions with related parties, such as entity affiliates, principal owners, management, and members of their immediate families. The auditor's primary concern with respect to related party transactions is their proper disclosure in accordance with GAAP.

1.2 Audit Procedures

Specific procedures regarding material transactions with related parties may include:

- Evaluation of the company's procedures to identify and account for related party transactions.

- Inquiry of management and others within the company regarding the names of all related parties and the nature and business purpose of any significant transactions with related parties.

- Review of the reporting entity's filings with the SEC and other regulatory agencies concerning the names of officers and directors who occupy management or directorship positions in other businesses.

- Review of material transactions for related party evidence.

Question 1　　　　　　　　　　　　　　　　　　　MCQ-09074

Which of the following auditing procedures most likely would assist an auditor in identifying related party transactions?

1. Inspecting correspondence with lawyers for evidence of unreported contingent liabilities.

2. Vouching accounting records for recurring transactions recorded just after the balance sheet date.

3. Reviewing confirmations of loans receivable and payable for indications of guarantees.

4. Performing analytical procedures for indications of possible financial difficulties.

---

2 Noncompliance With Laws and Regulations

2.1 Noncompliance

Noncompliance is an act of omission or commission by an entity, whether intentional or unintentional, which is contrary to prevailing laws and regulations.

2.2 Management's Responsibility

Management and those charged with governance are responsible for ensuring that the entity's operations are conducted in accordance with applicable laws and regulations.

2.3 Auditor's Responsibility

The auditor is responsible for obtaining reasonable assurance that the financial statements are free of material misstatement due to noncompliance with laws and regulations.

- The auditor is not responsible for preventing noncompliance and cannot be expected to detect noncompliance with all laws and regulations.

- The further removed noncompliance is from the financial statements, the less likely the auditor is to recognize the noncompliance.

2.4 Procedures When Noncompliance Is Identified or Suspected

If the auditor suspects that noncompliance may exist, the auditor should discuss the matter with management at least one level above those suspected of noncompliance and, when appropriate, those charged with governance.

2.5 Reporting Noncompliance in the Auditor's Report

2.5.1 Material Effect on the Financial Statements

If the noncompliance has a material effect on the financial statements and has not been adequately reflected in the financial statements, a qualified opinion or adverse opinion should be issued.

2.5.2 Insufficient Evidence

If the auditor is unable to obtain sufficient appropriate audit evidence about the noncompliance or suspected noncompliance, a qualified opinion or a disclaimer of opinion should be expressed.

2.5.3 Client Response

If the client refuses to accept the auditor's report as modified, the auditor should withdraw from the engagement and notify those charged with governance in writing.

Question 2   MCQ-09822

Which of the following information discovered during an audit most likely would raise a question concerning possible noncompliance with laws and regulations?

1. A piece of obsolete office equipment was not retired.

2. Material internal control weaknesses previously reported to management were not corrected.

3. The client receives financial assistance from a federal government agency.

4. There was an illegal payment to a foreign official.

Auditing Final Review

1 Fair Value Measurements

■ Management is responsible for making fair value measurements and disclosures in accordance with GAAP.

■ The auditor tests such measurements and disclosures to provide reasonable assurance that they are in conformity with GAAP.

2 Accounting Estimates

The auditor should verify that:

■ Appropriate practices are used to develop estimates.

■ All material estimates are reasonable.

■ Estimates are presented in conformity with GAAP.

■ Estimates are properly disclosed.

Question 1   MCQ-08121

Which of the following best describes the auditor's responsibility with respect to fair values?

1. The auditor should determine whether management has the intent and ability to carry out courses of action that may affect fair values.

2. The auditor should assess the risk of material misstatement of fair value measurements.

3. The auditor should obtain sufficient competent audit evidence to provide reasonable assurance that fair value measurements and disclosures are in conformity with GAAP.

4. The auditor should make fair value measurements and disclosures in accordance with GAAP and should identify and support any significant assumptions used.

Question 2   MCQ-09065

With respect to accounting estimates, an auditor:

1. Is not responsible for auditing estimated amounts, since they may be based on subjective determinations made by management.

2. Should verify that all material estimates required by generally accepted accounting principles have been developed.

3. Should focus on assumptions that are objective, insensitive to variation, and don't deviate from historical patterns.

4. Bears responsibility for making reasonable estimates and including them in the financial statements.

III

Performing Further Procedures and Obtaining Evidence

1 Audit Evidence

Evidence consists of underlying accounting data and corroborating or contradictory evidence. Evidence must be sufficient and appropriate to afford a reasonable basis for an opinion regarding the assertions in the financial statements. When an auditor is evaluating the results of audit procedures and the information obtained to be used as audit evidence, the auditor must be aware of the potential impact that conscious or unconscious bias may have on professional judgment.

1.1 Sufficient Audit Evidence

The auditor must use professional judgment to determine the amounts and kinds of evidence sufficient to support an opinion. Sufficiency is influenced by:

■ The risk of material misstatement (More risk = More evidence)

■ The quality of the audit evidence (Low quality = More evidence)

1.2 Appropriate Audit Evidence

Appropriate audit evidence must be both reliable and relevant. Appropriateness depends on the source of the information and on the following key attributes of accuracy, completeness, authenticity, and susceptibility to management bias.

1.2.1 Reliability

Reliability is dependent on the circumstances under which evidence is gathered. From most reliable to least reliable:

■ Auditor's direct personal knowledge and observation

■ External evidence

■ Internal evidence

■ Oral evidence

1.2.2 Relevance

Relevance means the evidence is related to (i.e., tells something about) the assertion under consideration and to the time period covered by the audit. PCAOB standards state that the relevance of evidence depends on the design of the audit procedure (whether it is designed to test the assertion directly or whether it is designed to test for overstatement or understatement) and the timing of the audit procedure.

Question 1   MCQ-09858

Which of the following circumstances most likely would cause an auditor to suspect that there are material misstatements in an entity's financial statements?

1. The entity's management strictly enforces its integrity and ethical values.

2. Monthly bank reconciliations ordinarily include several outstanding checks.

3. Management outsources the internal audit function to another CPA firm.

4. The auditor identifies an inappropriate valuation method that is widely applied by the entity.

1 Statistical and Nonstatistical Sampling

Sampling can be statistical (mathematical) or nonstatistical. Both can provide sufficient audit evidence and are acceptable under GAAS; both require professional judgment. Only statistical sampling enables the auditor to measure the sufficiency of the evidence, design an efficient sample, and quantify sampling risk.

2 Types of Statistical Sampling

2.1 Attribute Sampling

Attributes sampling is used to estimate a rate of occurrence (whether or not an attribute is present); primarily used to test internal controls. Methods include:

- Discovery sampling
- Stop and go sampling
- Acceptance sampling

2.2 Variables Sampling

Variables sampling is used to estimate numerical value; typically used in substantive testing. The auditor estimates a population's true value by computing a point estimate of the population and a precision interval around the estimate. Methods include:

- Mean-per-unit estimation (MPU)
- Ratio estimation
- Difference estimation

2.2.1 PPS Sampling

Probability-proportional-to-size (PPS) sampling is a hybrid method that uses attribute sampling theory to express a conclusion in dollar amounts.

B   Sampling Techniques

Question 1   MCQ-08135

An advantage of using statistical over nonstatistical sampling methods in tests of controls is that the statistical methods:

1. Can more easily convert the sample into a dual-purpose test useful for substantive testing.
2. Eliminate the need to use judgment in determining appropriate sample sizes.
3. Afford greater assurance than a nonstatistical sample of equal size.
4. Provide an objective basis for quantitatively evaluating sample risk.

Question 2   MCQ-09024

An auditor is likely using attribute sampling when he or she selects a sample of:

1. Receivables and sends confirmations to client customers.
2. Purchase orders and examines them for indication of proper approval.
3. Invoices to verify proper extensions and footings.
4. Cash receipts and traces them to the accounts receivable subsidiary ledger.

3 Sampling Risk

Sampling risk is the risk that the sample is not representative, and that the auditor's conclusion would be different from the conclusion if the auditor had examined 100 percent of the population.

3.1 Confidence Interval

Numerically, sampling risk is the complement of reliability, or confidence level (e.g., a 5 percent sampling risk reflects a 95 percent confidence level).

3.2 Sampling Risks in Tests of Controls (Attribute Sampling)

3.2.1 Risk of Assessing Control Risk Too Low

The risk of assessing control risk too low is the risk that a properly drawn sample will support the auditor's planned degree of reliance when the true compliance rate does not justify such reliance (risk of overreliance).

3.2.2 Risk of Assessing Control Risk Too High

The risk of assessing control risk too high is the risk that a properly drawn sample will not support the auditor's planned degree of reliance when the true compliance rate does justify such reliance (risk of under-reliance).

		Diagram 1: Attribute Sampling Risks	
		The true operation of the control is:	
		OK	Not OK
The sample indicates that the operation of the control is:	OK	Correct decision	Incorrect decision **Risk of assessing control risk too low** *Not effective*
	Not OK	Incorrect decision **Risk of assessing control risk too high** *Not efficient*	Correct decision

3.3 Sampling Risks in Substantive Testing (Variables Sampling)

3.3.1 Risk of Incorrect Acceptance

The risk of incorrect acceptance is the risk that a properly drawn sample supports a balance as not being materially misstated when in fact it is materially misstated.

3.3.2 Risk of Incorrect Rejection

The risk of incorrect rejection is the risk that a properly drawn sample supports a balance as materially misstated when in fact it is not materially misstated.

Diagram 2: Variables Sampling Risks

The recorded value of the population is:

		OK	Not OK
The sample indicates that the population is:	**OK**	Correct decision	Incorrect decision **Risk of incorrect acceptance** *Not effective*
	Not OK	Incorrect decision **Risk of incorrect rejection** *Not efficient*	Correct decision

3.4 Effect of Sampling Risk on the Audit

3.4.1 Effectiveness

The risk of assessing control risk too low and the risk of incorrect acceptance are concerned with the effectiveness of the audit. This type of risk is more critical because it can result in the auditor mistakenly relying on an ineffective control or unknowingly accepting a misstatement in the balance being tested and thereby issuing an inappropriate audit opinion.

3.4.2 Efficiency

The risk of assessing control risk too high and the risk of incorrect rejection are concerned with the efficiency of the audit. An audit conclusion in this direction causes the auditor to do more work than is really necessary.

Question 3   MCQ-04494

In assessing sampling risk, the risk of incorrect rejection and the risk of assessing control risk too high relate to the:

1. Efficiency of the audit.
2. Effectiveness of the audit.
3. Selection of the items in the sample.
4. Audit quality controls.

---

4 Steps in the Sampling Process

Attribute Sampling	Variables Sampling
1. Define the objective: This is the purpose of the test.	
Percentage of sales orders missing credit approval (i.e., what is the percentage of control failure).	True dollar value of sales for year 20X5.
2. Define the population: This is the aggregate group or set of items about which the auditor wishes to draw conclusions.	
All new customer sales orders during 20X5.	All sales dollars for year 20X5.
3. Define the sampling unit: This is the actual item or element from which the auditor will collect data.	
Individual sales orders.	Individual sales dollars.
4. Define the attribute of interest: This is the data to be collected.	
Credit approval (e.g., manager's signature). Missing approvals or missing sales orders are deviations.	Sales dollars.
5. Determine the sample size: This is the number of items to be selected for testing. The decision is based on statistical considerations, plus the auditor's judgment.	
Sample size is affected by the risk of assessing control risk too low (inverse relationship), the tolerable deviation rate (inverse), and the expected deviation rate (direct). Population size (>5000 items) generally does not matter.	Sample size is affected by expected misstatement, standard deviation, and the assessed level of risk (direct effects), as well as by tolerable misstatement and the acceptable level of risk (inverse effects).

6. Select the sample: The actual selection of a representative set of items for testing.

Random selection: Best method (used with prenumbered population).

Systematic selection: Every nth item (ineffective if population is systematically ordered).

Stratification: Divide the population into subpopulations based on strata.

Block or cluster: Not a desirable approach.

PPS: Every nth dollar, uses a random start, automatically stratifies population but does not test negative or zero balances.

7. Evaluate the sample results: This tells the auditor if the control can be relied on (attribute sampling) or if the account does not appear to be materially misstated (variables sampling).

Compare upper deviation rate to tolerable deviation rate.	Auditor projects misstatements to population utilizing a projected misstatement (point estimate). An allowance for sampling risk (or precision interval) is added to this estimate.
Sample deviation rate + Allowance for sampling risk = **Upper deviation rate**	
Tolerable deviation rate: maximum rate of deviation from prescribed controls that the auditor will tolerate without modifying planned reliance on the control. (Based on professional judgment.)	Sample error + recorded balance = point estimate
	Form conclusions about the account balances/ transactions tested:
Sample deviation rate: error rate in the sample; the auditor's best estimate of the deviation rate in the population from which the sample was selected.	Accept book value if it falls within an acceptable range (point estimate +/− allowance for sampling risk).
	Likely misstatement = Projected misstatement
	Tolerable misstatement: misstatement in the related account balance or class of transactions that may exist without causing the FS to be materially misstated.

8. Document sampling procedures.

A number of factors influence the sample size for a substantive test of details of an account balance. All other factors being equal, which of the following would lead to a larger sample size?

1. Greater reliance on internal control.

2. Greater reliance on analytical procedures.

3. Smaller expected frequency of errors.

4. Smaller measure of tolerable misstatement.

5 Example of Evaluating Sample Results for Attribute Sampling

- Sample deviation rate = (Number of errors)/(Sample size)

   10 errors/1000 sample size = 1%

- Sample deviation rate + Allowance for sampling risk = Upper deviation rate

   1.0% + 3.7% = 4.7%

- Compare upper deviation rate (UDR) to tolerable rate (TR).

   UDR ≤ TR   Assume TR = 6.0%

                   No change in preliminary assessment of control risk is needed

                   No change in NET of substantive tests is needed

                   4.7% < 6.0% would be a "good" result

   UDR > TR   Assume TR = 3.0%

                   Increase the assessment of control risk, resulting in a change in NET of substantive tests:

                   Nature: Select a more effective substantive test.

                   Extent: Increase the substantive test sample size.

                   Timing: Apply substantive tests at year-end instead of at interim.

                   4.7% > 3.0% would be a "bad" result

Question 5   MCQ-08127

An auditor who uses statistical sampling for attributes in testing internal controls should reduce the planned reliance on a prescribed control when the:

1. Sample rate of deviation plus the allowance for sampling risk equals the tolerable rate.

2. Sample rate of deviation is less than the expected rate of deviation used in planning the sample.

3. Tolerable rate less the allowance for sampling risk exceeds the sample rate of deviation.

4. Sample rate of deviation plus the allowance for sampling risk exceeds the tolerable rate.

6 Probability-Proportional-to-Size (PPS) Sampling

Under PPS sampling, the sampling unit is defined as an individual dollar in a population. Once the dollar is selected, the entire account is audited.

6.1 Advantage

Automatically emphasizes larger items, so if no errors are expected, PPS will require a smaller sample than other methods.

6.2 Disadvantage

Zero balances, negative balances, and understated balances generally require special design considerations.

6.3 Steps in PPS Sampling

- Sample size = recorded amount of the population/sampling interval.

- Sampling interval = tolerable misstatement/reliability factor.

- Reliability factors correspond to the risk of incorrect acceptance and are generally obtained from a table.

- **Sample Selection:** A random number between 1 and the sampling interval is selected; it determines the first item selected. The recorded amounts of the logical units throughout the population are then added and individual dollars (and their corresponding units) are selected based on the interval.

- **Evaluation of Sample Results:** If no errors are found, the error projection is zero and the allowance for sampling risk would not exceed the auditor's tolerable error. If errors are found, they need to be projected to the interval. If an account selected has a balance greater than the interval, the actual dollar amount of the error should be used.

	A Recorded Amount	B Audit Amount	A–B	A	(A–B)/A Tainting	Sample Interval	Projected Error
	$800	$600	$200	$800	25%	$5,000	$1,250
	4,350	4,350	0	4,350	0%	5,000	0
	4,900	0	4,900	4,900	100%	5,000	5,000
> 5,000	8,500	6,900	1,600	n/a	n/a	n/a	1,600
	1,500	1,200	300	1,500	20%	5,000	1,000
Totals	20,050	13,050	7,000				8,850

Probability-Proportional-to-Size

Known misstatement (sample errors)	7,000
Projected error	8,850
Allowance for sampling risk (calculation not shown)	2,500
Projected misstatement (likely misstatement)	11,350

If tolerable misstatement is 15,000, the book value is fairly stated (11,350 is less than 15,000)

7 Dual Purpose Samples

Auditors may use the same sample to perform both tests of controls and substantive tests; generally this would only be done when the auditor believes that there is an acceptably low risk that the deviation rate in the population exceeds the tolerable rate.

In evaluating dual-purpose samples, deviations from control procedures and monetary misstatements should be evaluated separately using appropriate risk levels.

1 Purpose

Tests of controls are used to evaluate the operating effectiveness of internal control in preventing or detecting material misstatements. Tests of controls are necessary when:

- The risk assessment is based on the operating effectiveness of internal control.
- Substantive procedures alone are insufficient because there is extensive use of information technology.

2 Tests of Operating Effectiveness

Testing the operating effectiveness of internal controls includes obtaining evidence regarding:

- Whether the controls were applied at relevant times
- How the controls were applied
- The consistency with which the controls were applied
- By whom or by what means the controls were applied

3 Nature, Extent, and Timing

3.1 Nature

The auditor should use a combination of procedures to obtain sufficient evidence of operating effectiveness. Acceptable procedures include:

- Reperformance
- Inspection
- Observation
- Inquiry

3.2 Extent

The auditor should consider the following factors to determine the extent of a control test:

- Frequency of performance of control
- Length of time over which the auditor intends to rely on the control
- Relevance and reliability of the evidence
- The extent to which other tests provide evidence about the assertion
- The extent to which the auditor intends to rely on the operating effectiveness of the control to reduce substantive procedures
- Expected deviation rate

3.3 Timing

Controls tested at a point in time provide evidence that the control operated effectively at that time, whereas controls tested throughout the period provide evidence of the operating effectiveness during the period.

4 Results

After performing tests of controls, the auditor may conclude that audit evidence indicates that:

- controls are operating effectively and can be relied upon.
- controls are not operating effectively, in which case the auditor can:
  - test alternative controls; or
  - respond to the assessed risk of material misstatement with more reliable and extensive substantive procedures.

Question 1   MCQ-08113

Which of the following is *least* likely to be evidence the auditor examines to determine whether controls are operating effectively?

1. Records documenting usage of computer programs.
2. Canceled supporting documents.
3. Confirmations of accounts receivable.
4. Signatures on authorization forms.

---

1 Use of Analytical Procedures in the Audit

Analytical procedures are evaluations of financial information made by a study of plausible relationships between financial and nonfinancial data.

1.1 Types of Analytical Procedures

Analytical procedures generally involve comparisons of recorded amounts to independent expectations developed by the auditor, including:

- Comparisons of financial data, such as comparison of current and prior year financial statements
- Ratio analysis

1.2 Use During the Audit

Analytical procedures are used during the planning, substantive procedure, and final review stages of the audit.

Phase	Requirement	Purpose
Planning	Required	To assist the auditor in understanding the entity and its environment. Used for risk measurement to alert the auditor to problem areas requiring attention. This serves a vital planning function.
Substantive procedures	Not required	As a substantive test to obtain audit evidence about specific management assertions related to account balances or transactions. The evidence is circumstantial and generally additional corroborating evidence (such as documentation) must be obtained.
Final review	Required	To assist the auditor in the final review of the overall reasonableness of account balances.

An auditor notices that interest expense stayed approximately the same as the prior year even though the debt outstanding significantly increased from the prior year. The client only invests in debt that has a fixed interest rate. Which of the following best explains the reason for the above explanation?

1. The company paid off a significant portion of the debt.

2. The company acquired a new loan for construction of a building that began during the year under audit.

3. The Federal Reserve decreased interest rates in the current year.

4. The company acquired a new loan at midyear related to the acquisition of a competitor.

2 Ratio Analysis

2.1   Liquidity Ratios

Measures of a firm's short-term ability to pay maturing obligations.

$$\text{Working capital} = \text{Current assets} - \text{Current liabilities}$$

$$\text{Current ratio (working capital ratio)} = \frac{\text{Current assets}}{\text{Current liabilities}}$$

$$\text{Quick ratio} = \frac{\text{Cash and cash equivalents} + \text{Short-term marketable securities} + \text{Accounts receivable (net)}}{\text{Current liabilities}}$$

■ Generally, as the current/quick ratios increase, an entity's ability to meet short-term obligation improves (and vice versa).

2.2 Activity Ratios

Measures of how effectively an enterprise is using its assets.

$$\text{Accounts receivable turnover} = \frac{\text{Sales (net)}}{\text{Average accounts receivables (net)}}$$

■ This ratio indicates the receivables' quality and indicates the success of a firm in collecting outstanding receivables. Faster turnover is better.

$$\text{Days sales in accounts receivable} = \frac{\text{Ending accounts receivable (net)}}{(\text{Sales (net) / 365})}$$

$$\text{Inventory turnover} = \frac{\text{Cost of goods sold}}{\text{Average inventory}}$$

■ This ratio measures how quickly inventory is sold. The higher the turnover, the better the performance.

$$\text{Days in inventory} = \frac{\text{Ending inventory}}{(\text{Cost of goods sold / 365})}$$

$$\text{Operating cycle} = \text{Days sales in accounts receivable} + \text{Days in inventory}$$

■ Indicates the number of days between the acquisition of inventory and the realization of cash from selling the inventory—the "cash to cash" cycle.

$$\text{Working capital turnover} = \frac{\text{Sales (net)}}{\text{Average working capital}}$$

■ This ratio indicates how effectively working capital is used.

$$\text{Asset turnover} = \frac{\text{Sales (net)}}{\text{Average total assets}}$$

■ This ratio is indicative of a firm's effective use of its assets. A high ratio indicates effective asset use to generate sales.

2.3 Profitability Ratios

Measures of the success or failure of an enterprise for a given period of time.

$$\text{Net profit margin} = \frac{\text{Net income}}{\text{Net sales}}$$

$$\text{Net operating margin percentage} = \frac{\text{Net operating income}}{\text{Net sales}}$$

$$\text{Gross (profit) margin} = \frac{\text{Sales (net)} - \text{Cost of goods sold}}{\text{Sales (net)}}$$

$$\text{Return on assets} = \frac{\text{Net income}}{\text{Average total assets}}$$

2.4 Long-Term Debt-Paying Ability Ratios

Measures of security for long-term creditors/investors.

$$\text{Debt to equity} = \frac{\text{Total liabilities}}{\text{Total equity}}$$

$$\text{Total debt ratio} = \frac{\text{Total liabilities}}{\text{Total assets}}$$

These ratios indicate the degree of protection to creditors in case of insolvency. The lower these ratios, the better the company's position.

Question 2	MCQ-09069

Which of the following is *least* likely to be a reasonable explanation for an increase in accounts receivable turnover?

1. Early payment incentives for customers.
2. Tightening of credit policy.
3. Implementation of more aggressive collection policies.
4. Allowance of a new grace period for customer payments.

1 Types of Substantive Procedures

Substantive procedures are performed to detect material misstatements at the relevant assertion level. They are required for each material transaction class, account balance, or disclosure.

Substantive procedures include:

- Tests of details of transactions and balances.
- Analytical procedures.

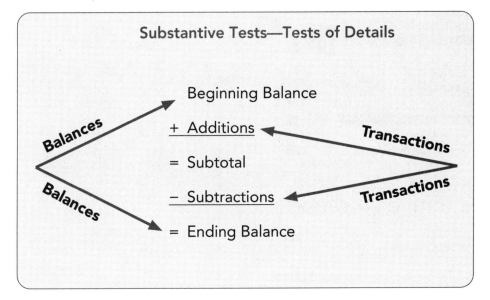

Substantive Tests—Tests of Details

2 Substantive Analytical Procedures

In certain situations, analytical procedures are a more effective and efficient means of gathering evidence than tests of details, and in those cases, analytical procedures may be used as substantive tests.

When using substantive analytical procedures, the auditor considers:

- Designing and performing substantive analytical procedures, including audit data analytics (ADAs) and any associated techniques, tools, graphics, and tables.
- Efficiency and effectiveness of analytical procedures.
- Limitations of analytical procedures.
- Documentation requirements.
- Analytical procedures used as an overall review.

3 Directional Testing

Directional testing refers to testing either forward or backward.

3.1 Tracing Forward

Tracing forward from source documents to journal entries or to the financial statements provides evidence of completeness.

3.2 Vouching Backward

Vouching backward from the financial statements or from journal entries to source documents provides evidence of existence or occurrence.

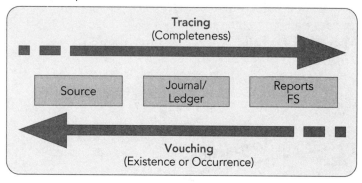

4 Common Substantive Auditing Procedures

- **F**ooting, cross-footing, and recalculation: Adding down and across; testing arithmetical accuracy of statements and schedules (valuation and allocation).
- **I**nquiry: Made of both internal and external sources.
- **V**ouching: Directional testing; looking for support for what has been recorded in the records and statements; going from the financial statement back to supporting documents (existence/occurrence).
- **E**xamination and inspection of documents/records; reading board of directors' (BOD) minutes; reviewing the financial statement (understandability and classification). May be aided by the use of automated tools such as text-recognition programs.
- **C**onfirmation: Direct written verification from independent third parties about account balances (existence) and transactions or events (occurrence). Also, perform **c**utoff review of year-end transactions (proper period).
- **A**nalytical procedures: Establish relationships and highlight risk areas. Also, **a**udit related accounts.
- **R**eperformance: Auditor independently performs control procedures.
- **R**econciliation: Substantiates the existence and valuation of accounts. Also, **r**ead necessary information such as meeting minutes from BOD/ shareholder meetings, and obtain management **r**epresentation letter.

- **O**bservation: Provides the auditor with direct knowledge; most persuasive form of evidence in providing assurance as to the existence or occurrence of an item. May be aided by the use of remote observation tools.

- **T**racing: Directional testing; starts with the source documents and traces forward to provide assurance that the event is being given proper recognition in the books and records (completeness; accuracy).

- **C**utoff review: The auditor should perform a cutoff review of year-end transactions, especially inventory, cash, purchases, sales, and accruals.

- **A**uditing related accounts simultaneously: Certain accounts can be audited simultaneously, including long-term liabilities and interest expense, capital additions to PP&E and repairs and maintenance expense, and investments and investment income.

- **R**epresentation letter: At the conclusion of fieldwork, the independent auditor must obtain a management representation letter from the client.

- **S**ubsequent events review: Procedures required for the period after the balance sheet date up to the date of the auditor's report.

Question 1 — MCQ-08112

Which financial statement assertion is violated when an expense occurring in one year is *not* recorded until the following year?

1. Accuracy
2. Classification
3. Completeness
4. Occurrence

---

5 Interim Substantive Procedures

- Performing substantive procedures at an interim date requires additional work to extend audit conclusions to period end.

- Interim substantive procedures should only be performed when the risk of material misstatement is low.

Question 2 — MCQ-09839

Which of the following is a substantive procedure?

1. Verifying that the vouchers payable package is appropriately approved.
2. Observing the payroll distribution on an unannounced basis.
3. Observing the preparation of the accounts receivable aging schedule.
4. Examining open vouchers as part of the search for unrecorded liabilities.

---

1 Auditing Accounts Receivable

1.1 Accounts Receivable Confirmations

Confirmation of accounts receivable is required unless:

- receivables are immaterial; or
- confirmation would be ineffective; or
- inherent and control risks are very low and evidence provided by other procedures sufficiently reduces audit risk.

The auditor must document the basis for omission of confirmation procedures.

1.2 Positive Confirmations

Positive confirmations should be used for large receivables. The customers are requested to return a statement to the auditor indicating that they agree with the amount. Positive confirmations should be sent for:

- Large individual accounts
- Expected errors
- Items in dispute
- Weak internal control
- Old balances

1.3 Negative Confirmations

Negative confirmations are less effective than positive confirmations. When negative confirmations are used, an answer is requested only if the amount stated is incorrect. Negative confirmations may be used when:

- inherent and control risks are low; and
- a large number of small balances are being confirmed; and
- there is no reason to expect that the recipients will ignore the confirmations.

1.4 Confirmation Nonresponses

When the auditor has not received replies to positive confirmation requests, the auditor should apply alternative procedures to the nonresponsive accounts to reduce audit risk to an acceptably low level. The nature of alternative procedures varies with the account and the assertion.

The omission of alternative procedures may be warranted when:

- the auditor has not identified unusual qualitative factors or systematic characteristics related to the nonresponses; and

- treating the aggregate nonresponses as 100 percent misstatements would not affect the auditor's conclusion about whether the financial statements are materially misstated.

1.5 Accounts Receivable Confirmation Exceptions

Confirmation exceptions occur when there is a disparity between the amount of the receivable recorded in the client's accounting records and the amount of the receivable confirmed by the client's customer. For confirmation exceptions, the auditor should determine whether the exception is due to a timing difference or a misstatement.

1.6 Evaluating Results

- The auditor should evaluate the evidence provided by confirmations and alternative procedures to determine whether sufficient evidence has been obtained about all the applicable financial statement assertions.

- If the evidence gathered is not sufficient, the auditor should request additional confirmations or extend other tests.

Question 1	MCQ-09833

After multiple attempts, an auditor is unable to obtain a response for several positive requests for year-end accounts receivable confirmations. An appropriate alternative procedure to verify the existence of accounts receivable is:

1. Visit the customer selected for confirmation and review documents in their possession.

2. Obtain the aging of accounts receivable and trace it to the general ledger control account.

3. Examine the applicable sales order, shipping document, and subsequent cash receipts.

4. Examine subsequent cash disbursements and related receiving reports.

2 Auditing Cash

2.1 Bank Confirmations

Bank confirmations should be sent to all banks with whom the entity has done business. Bank transfer schedules, bank reconciliations, and cutoff bank statements should also be used.

2.2 Fraudulent Cash Schemes

The auditor should look for fraudulent cash schemes during the audit.

2.2.1 Kiting

- Kiting occurs when a check drawn on one bank is deposited in another bank and no record is made of the first disbursement.

- To detect kiting, cash deposits at the end of a period and paid checks returned with the bank statements of the next period should be examined (bank transfer schedule). Check dates will indicate whether the receiving bank recorded the receipt before the recorded disbursement date.

2.2.2 Lapping

- Lapping occurs when current receipts of cash/checks are withheld (i.e., stolen) and not recorded. Subsequent receipts are applied to the prior accounts.

- Safeguard—Use a lockbox system.

- To detect lapping, use the deposit slip test—trace deposit items from the deposit slip to posting in the customer account.

Question 2   MCQ-09835

At KRM Corporation, an employee performed the following scheme:

Customer	*Employee*
Andrew Vent came in with $100 cash to pay off his outstanding receivable.	The employee stole the $100 cash.
Bob Butterfield paid off $100 of his outstanding receivable.	The employee credited Andrew Kent's account for $100.
Chris Copper paid off $200 of his outstanding receivable.	The employee credited Bob Butterfield's account for $100 and stole the remainder $100.

What best describes this scheme?

1. Kiting

2. Lapping

3. Identity theft

4. Fraudulent financial reporting

1 Auditing Revenue

1.1 Flowchart—Cash Receipts and Accounts Receivable

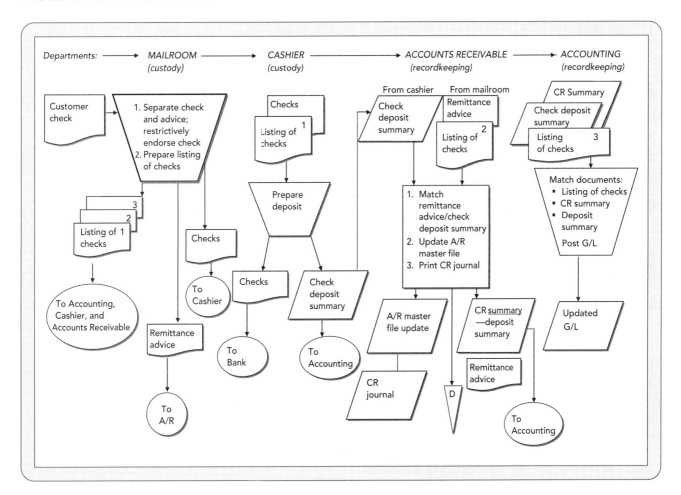

1.2 Segregation of Duties

- **Authorization:** Sales order and credit
- **Record Keeping:** Billing/accounts receivable/accounting
- **Custody:** Warehouse and shipping

1.3 Risk of Overstatement

Management may be pressured to overstate revenues to meet EPS targets and improve balance sheet ratios. For these reasons, management may:

- Record fictitious sales (existence assertion).

- Hold open the sales journal into next year (cutoff).

- Ship goods not ordered, which will be returned next year (improper revenue recognition).

1.4 Substantive Procedures

In addition to auditing the presentation and disclosure related to the revenue cycle, the auditor should perform the following procedures related to accounts receivable and sales transactions.

1.4.1 Auditing Accounts Receivable

- **Completeness**

  The auditor should obtain an aged trial balance of accounts receivable and trace the total to the general ledger control account. The auditor should also evaluate the related disclosures to ensure that all required information is included.

- **Valuation, Allocation, and Accuracy**

  The auditor should examine the results of confirmations and test the adequacy of the allowance for uncollectible accounts. The auditor should also review disclosures to determine whether the related information is presented at the appropriate amounts.

- **Existence and Occurrence**

  The auditor should confirm a sample of accounts receivable (see the discussion of accounts receivable confirmations below).

- **Rights and Obligations**

  The auditor should review bank confirmations and debt agreements for liens on receivables. The auditor should also inquire of management and review debt agreements and board minutes for evidence that accounts receivable have been factored or sold. The auditor should determine whether any receivables have been pledged, assigned, or discounted and, if so, determine whether disclosure is required.

- **Understandability of Presentation and Classification**

  The auditor should review all accounts receivable balances to ensure proper presentation at net realizable value and for proper classification between current and long-term assets (generally current is appropriate). Additionally, the auditor should read all related disclosures to ensure that they are understandable.

1.4.2 Auditing Sales Transactions

The following tests of details may also be performed as tests of controls or dual-purpose tests. The cutoff procedure is performed most often as a substantive procedure.

Completeness

The auditor should trace a sample of shipping documents to the corresponding sales invoices and to the sales journal and accounts receivable subsidiary ledger. The auditor should also evaluate the related disclosures to ensure that all required information is included.

Cutoff

The auditor should compare a sample of sales invoices from shortly before and after year-end with the shipment dates and with the dates the sales were recorded in the sales journal. The auditor should also analyze the record of sales returns after year-end.

Valuation, Allocation, and Accuracy

The auditor should compare prices and terms on a sample of sales invoices with authorized price lists and terms of trade to determine whether sales are recorded at the appropriate amount. The auditor should also review disclosures to determine whether the related information is presented at the appropriate amounts.

Existence and Occurrence

The auditor should vouch a sample of sales transactions from the sales journal to the sales invoice back to the customer order and shipping documents.

Understandability of Presentation and Classification

The auditor should examine a sample of sales invoices for proper classification into the appropriate revenue accounts. The auditor should also read all related disclosures to ensure that they are understandable.

Question 1   MCQ-01625

Which of the following controls most likely would assure that all billed sales are correctly posted to the accounts receivable ledger?

1. Daily sales summaries are compared to daily postings to the accounts receivable ledger.
2. Each sales invoice is supported by a prenumbered shipping document.
3. The accounts receivable ledger is reconciled daily to the control account in the general ledger.
4. Each shipment on credit is supported by a prenumbered sales invoice.

Question 2   MCQ-09847

Tracing shipping documents to sales invoices provides evidence that:

1. Sales billed to customers were actually shipped.
2. Shipments to customers were properly invoiced.
3. Shipments to customers were recorded as sales.
4. All goods ordered by customers were shipped.

2 Auditing Expenditures

2.1 Segregation of Duties

- **Purchasing Department:** Approve and prepare purchase order.
- **Receiving Department:** Receive goods, match with purchase order (blind copy), and prepare receiving reports.
- **Vouchers Payable Department:** Match documents, purchase order, receiving reports, invoice; prepare and approve voucher, verify accuracy.
- **Treasury Department:** Review documents, prepare check & remittance advice, sign checks, cancel voucher package.

2.2 Substantive Procedures

In addition to auditing the presentation and disclosure related to the expenditure cycle, the auditor should perform the following procedures related to accounts payable and purchase transactions.

2.2.1 Auditing Accounts Payable

- **Completeness**

  The auditor should perform a search for unrecorded liabilities. The auditor should also ensure that all required disclosures have been included in the financial statements.

- **Valuation, Allocation, and Accuracy**

  The auditor should obtain the accounts payable listing, foot the listing, and agree the listing to the general ledger, obtain a sample of vendor statements and agree the amounts to the vendor accounts, and review the results of any accounts payable confirmations. The auditor should also read the related disclosures to ensure that the information is presented at the accurate amounts.

- **Existence and Occurrence**

  The auditor should vouch selected amounts from the accounts payable listing to the voucher packages. The auditor may also confirm accounts payable. Accounts payable confirmations are not required because good external evidence to support accounts payable is generally available. However, confirmations of accounts payable may be sent when internal control is weak, when there are disputed amounts, or when monthly vendor statements are not available. Typically, vendors with small or zero balances would be selected for confirmation. The auditor should also compare disclosures with audit evidence and ensure that all disclosed information has occurred.

- **Rights and Obligations**

  The auditor should review a sample of voucher packages for the presence of the purchase requisition, purchase order, receiving report and vendor invoice to verify that the accounts payable are owed by the entity.

▣ **Understandability of Presentation and Classification**

The auditor should read all related disclosures to ensure that they are understandable and determine whether any specific items require separate disclosure.

2.2.2 Auditing Purchase Transactions

The following substantive tests may also be performed as tests of controls or dual-purpose tests.

▣ **Completeness**

The auditor should trace a sample of vouchers to the purchase journal. The auditor should also ensure that all required disclosures have been included in the financial statements.

▣ **Cutoff**

The auditor should compare dates on a sample of vouchers with the dates the transactions were recorded in the purchase journal. The auditor should also examine purchases before and after year-end to determine if they were recorded in the proper period.

▣ **Valuation, Allocation, and Accuracy**

The auditor should recompute the mathematical accuracy of a sample of vendor invoices. The auditor should also read the related disclosures to ensure that the information is presented at the accurate amounts.

▣ **Existence and Occurrence**

The auditor should test a sample of vouchers for authorization and the presence of the receiving report. The auditor should also compare disclosures with audit evidence and ensure that all disclosed information has occurred.

▣ **Understandability of Presentation and Classification**

The auditor should verify the account classification of a sample of purchases and read all related disclosures to ensure that they are understandable.

Question 3	MCQ-09849

An auditor searching for unrecorded payables most likely would:

   1. Obtain a sample of vendor invoices and recalculate the invoice amount.

   2. Obtain the accounts payable listing and agree to subsequent cash payments.

   3. Compare cash disbursements made prior to year-end with vendor invoices.

   4. Compare subsequent bank statements with the accounts payable listing.

---

3 Auditing PP&E

The property, plant, and equipment cycle includes all tangible long-term asset functions (e.g., purchasing, maintenance and repair, depreciation, retirement).

- **Purchases and Retirements:** Verify that proper authorization was obtained, and that proper procedures were followed. The auditor should vouch additions to fixed assets by examining documentation and inspecting the actual asset (existence). The auditor should also select older fixed assets from the subsidiary ledger and try to locate the assets as a means of testing for unrecorded retirements (existence). The auditor should review related repair and maintenance accounts for any improper classification of additions and repairs as expenses (completeness and classification).

- **Authorization:** Verify Board approval of substantial purchases.

- **Physical Security:** Serially numbered plates should be on assets; the control account should include all appropriate information.

- **Depreciation:** Verify that written policies and records are maintained; recalculate expense and ensure conformity with GAAP (valuation and accuracy).

- **Impairments:** Check for adjustments for impairments (valuation and accuracy).

Question 4 MCQ-08325

An auditor analyzes repair and maintenance accounts primarily to obtain evidence in support of the audit assertion that all:

1. Noncapitalizable expenditures for repairs and maintenance have been recorded in the proper period.

2. Expenditures for property and equipment have been recorded in the proper period.

3. Noncapitalizable expenditures for repairs and maintenance have been properly charged to expense.

4. Expenditures for property and equipment have not been charged to expense.

---

4 Auditing Payroll

4.1 Segregation of Duties

Controls including proper segregation of duties are essential to prevent common problems in the payroll and personnel cycle—fictitious employees and falsification of hours.

4.1.1 Authorization

- **Authorization to Employ and Pay:** The human resource department's function is to hire new employees and maintain personnel records (hire date, salary, and position).

- **Supervision:** All pay base data (hours, absences, and time off) should be approved by an employee's immediate supervisor.

4.1.2 Record Keeping

- **Timekeeping and Cost Accounting:** Data on which pay is based should be accumulated independent of any other function. Hourly employees should use time clocks. Supervisors should compare job time tickets to signed employee clock cards.

- **Payroll Check Preparation:** The payroll department computes salary based on information received. This department is responsible for issuing the unsigned payroll checks.

4.1.3 Custody of Assets

The treasurer is responsible for signing the payroll checks.

4.1.4 Auditing Payroll and Personnel

- The auditor reviews the payroll account to determine that only authorized people are being paid, and that they are receiving the right amounts. The auditor should verify time records, and perform recalculations of payroll amounts and any year-end accruals (valuation assertion).

- A person who has no other payroll function should distribute the payroll checks. This person is often referred to as the paymaster. Employees should be required to show ID before receiving paychecks.

4.2 Substantive Procedures

When internal control over payroll is effective, the auditor generally focuses substantive procedures on the valuation and accuracy assertion. The following audit procedures should be performed to verify the accuracy of payroll amounts:

- Vouch time on payroll summaries by selecting a payroll register entry and comparing to time cards and approved time reports.

- Compare total recorded payroll with total payroll checks issued.

- Test extensions and footings of payroll.
- Verify pay rates and payroll deductions with employee records from personnel.
- Recalculate gross and net pay on a test basis.
- Recalculate any year-end accruals.
- Compare payroll costs with standards or budgets.

Substantive tests should be extended if unusual fluctuations or significant errors are noted.

Question 5   MCQ-08124

In auditing the payroll function of a client, an auditor would least likely:

1. Request specific management representations related to payroll.
2. Verify proper segregation of duties.
3. Recalculate year-end payroll accruals.
4. Apply analytical procedures.

---

5 Auditing Liabilities

When auditing debt, the auditor reviews board minutes for evidence of new debt, obtains new debt agreements, and traces new debt to the financial statements (completeness), recomputes gains and losses, interest expense and interest payable (valuation and accuracy), and verifies proper presentation and disclosure.

6 Auditing Owners' Equity and Treasury Stock

The audit of owners' equity and treasury stock includes examining transactions related to the sale and repurchase of stock, related payments, dividends, and retained earnings.

6.1   Substantive Procedures

■ **Treasury Stock:** Examine and reconcile the number of shares in the treasury stock account, and trace all transactions to the accounting records and the board minutes (existence and completeness).

■ **Stock Transactions:** Vouch all transactions to supporting documentation (existence).

■ **Minutes of Board Meetings:** Verify that all stock issuances, dividends declared, and treasury stock transactions have been authorized by the board.

■ **Articles of Incorporation:** Read the articles and prepare excerpts for the permanent file.

■ **Stock Transfer Agents:** Use third-party confirmations to provide evidence of shares authorized, issued, and outstanding (completeness and existence).

■ **Stock Certificate Book:** If there is no transfer agent, review the stock certificate book to provide evidence of proper stock transaction accounting (completeness and existence).

■ **Retained Earnings:** Analyze retained earnings account since inception (or since the last audit) and review the propriety of any direct entries to retained earnings (valuation), and determine whether any appropriations are necessary (understandability and classification).

Question 6   MCQ-08868

An audit program for the examination of the retained earnings account should include a step that requires verification of the:

1. Market value used to charge retained earnings to account for a two-for-one stock split.

2. Approval of the adjustment to the beginning balance as a result of a write-down of an account receivable.

3. Authorization for both cash and stock dividends.

4. Gain or loss resulting from disposition of treasury shares.

---

1 Auditing Inventory

- **Controls:** Good controls should exist between purchasing, receiving, storage, and shipping.

- **Observation:** Observation of the physical inventory count is required, although failure to observe can be mitigated by alternative procedures. Observation and test counts provide evidence related to existence and completeness.

- **Calculation:** The auditor should test the physical inventory report by tracing test counts and verifying mathematical accuracy.

- **Consigned Goods:** The auditor should ascertain that consigned inventory on hand is excluded from the physical count, while goods out on consignment are included in inventory.

- **Related Accounts:** Simultaneous procedures should be undertaken for accounts related to inventory (purchases, sales, returns, and allowances).

- **Quantity:** Cutoff procedures should be performed for purchases and sales.

- **Presentation:** GAAP should be followed.

- **Analytical Review:** Overall reasonableness of amounts and disclosures should be evaluated; ratio analysis may be used.

- **Obsolete or Damaged Goods:** The inventory listing should be reviewed for slow-moving items; inquiries should be made regarding obsolete or damaged goods.

Question 1
MCQ-09830

In auditing a manufacturing entity, which of the following procedures would an auditor most likely perform to determine whether slow-moving, defective, and obsolete items included in inventory are properly identified?

1. Test the mathematical accuracy of the inventory report.
2. Inquire of management about whether inventory has been pledged or assigned.
3. Tour the manufacturing plant or production facility.
4. Test the computation of standard overhead rates.

---

2 Auditing Investments

The auditor must ensure that GAAP is consistently applied, gains and losses are accurately computed and disclosed, investment income is properly reported, valuation is fairly stated and disclosed, and the investments in fact exist and are owned by the entity under audit.

- **Segregation of Duties:** Authorization (usually the board of directors), the custodial function, and record keeping should be segregated.

- **Confirmation From Third Parties:** This should be obtained if investments are held by an independent, third-party custodian.

- **Physical Inspection:** For securities on hand, a physical inspection should be performed.

- **Cutoff Procedures:** These procedures should be applied to purchases, sales, and investment income.

- **Conformance With GAAP:** Derivative, fair value through net income method/equity method, trading, available-for-sale, and held-to-maturity classifications should be used.

- **Computations:** Gains, losses, discount or premium amortization, and interest or dividend income should be independently calculated.

- **Management Representations:** The auditor should inquire of management and obtain written representation concerning management's intent and ability to hold or to exercise significant influence over investments.

- **Reasonableness and Appropriateness:** These factors should be evaluated as they relate to assumptions, market variables, valuation models, and any decline in fair value.

- **Special Skill or Knowledge:** The auditor may need special skill or knowledge to plan and perform auditing procedures for certain assertions about derivatives and securities.

Question 2   MCQ-08905

Which of the following provides the best evidence supporting the existence of marketable securities included in the client's financial statements?

1. A custodial statement received and held by the client.
2. The client's securities ledger.
3. Broker's advice regarding purchases and sales of marketable securities.
4. A year-end listing of market prices for the securities obtained by reference to the Wall Street Journal.

---

1 Overview

When audit procedures indicate that there are actual or potential litigation, claims, or assessments, the auditor should seek direct communication with the entity's external legal counsel through a letter of inquiry regarding litigation, claims and assessments.

- The auditor should inquire about specific litigation (if identified), including the timing and the degree of probability of an unfavorable outcome.

- The lawyer's response is sent directly to the auditor.

- No response or a refusal to cooperate is considered a scope limitation.

Question 1 — MCQ-09851

Which limitation on response from an attorney in response to auditor's inquiry may result in a qualified opinion?

1. The client's refusal to permit inquiry of the attorney.

2. The attorney's refusal to respond when the attorney has given substantial attention to the matter.

3. An inherent uncertainty making it difficult for a lawyer to form conclusions regarding pending litigation.

4. The attorney limits replies to matters to which he or she has given substantial attention.

Question 2 — MCQ-09047

Which of the following best describes the purpose of an auditor's external inquiry sent to the client's attorney?

1. To develop an appropriate understanding of controls in place with respect to the recognition of litigation, claims, and assessments.

2. To evaluate the operating effectiveness of controls in place with respect to the recognition of litigation, claims, and assessments.

3. To corroborate information provided by management with respect to litigation, claims, and assessments.

4. To obtain reasonable assurance from the client's attorney regarding fair presentation of litigation, claims, and assessments in the financial statements.

2 Sample Attorney Letter

Letter of Audit Inquiry

[*Company Letterhead*]

[*Appropriate Addressee*]:

In connection with an audit of our financial statements at (balance sheet date) and for the (period) then ended, management of the Company has prepared, and furnished to our auditors (name and address of auditors), a description and evaluation of certain contingencies, including those set forth below involving matters with respect to which you have been engaged and to which you have devoted substantive attention on behalf of the Company in the form of legal consultation or representation. These contingencies are regarded by management of the Company as material for this purpose (management may indicate a materiality limit if an understanding has been reached with the auditor). Your response should include matters that existed at (balance sheet date) and during the period from that date to the date of your response.

Pending or Threatened Litigation

[*Ordinarily management's information would include (i) the nature of the litigation, (ii) the progress of the case to date, (iii) how management is responding or intends to respond to the litigation, and (iv) an evaluation of the likelihood of an unfavorable outcome and an estimate, if one can be made, of the amount or range of potential loss.*]

This letter will serve as our consent for you to furnish to our auditor all the information requested therein. Accordingly, please furnish to our auditors such explanation, if any, that you consider necessary to supplement the foregoing information, including an explanation of those matters as to which your views may differ from those stated and an identification of the omission of any pending or threatened litigation, claims, and assessments or a statement that the list of such matters is complete.

Unasserted Claims and Assessments

[*Ordinarily management's information would include (i) the nature of the matter, (ii) how management intends to respond if the claim is asserted, and (iii) an evaluation of the likelihood of an unfavorable outcome and an estimate, if one can be made, of the amount or range of potential loss.*]

Please furnish to our auditors such explanation, if any, that you consider necessary to supplement the foregoing information, including an explanation of those matters as to which your views may differ from those stated.

We understand that whenever, in the course of performing legal services for us with respect to a matter recognized to involve an unasserted possible claim or assessment that may call for financial statement disclosure, if you have formed a professional conclusion that we should disclose or consider disclosure concerning such possible claim or assessment, as a matter of professional responsibility to us, you will so advise us and will consult with us concerning the question of such disclosure and the applicable requirements of Financial Accounting Standards Board (FASB) Accounting Standards Codification (ASC) 450, Contingencies. Please specifically confirm to our auditors that our understanding is correct.

Please specifically identify the nature of and reasons for any limitations on your response.

Very truly yours,

[*Name*]

---

1 Auditor Responsibility

The auditor is responsible for evaluating audit evidence to determine whether there is *"substantial doubt"* that the client will be able to continue as a going concern for a reasonable period of time, as defined by the financial reporting framework used (FASB—one year after financial statements are issued or available to be issued; GASB—one year beyond the date of the financial statements).

2 Going Concern: Impact to Auditor's Report

If substantial doubt exists about the auditor's ability to continue as a going concern, a separate section (nonissuer) or explanatory paragraph (issuer) stating the auditor's concerns should be added to the auditor's opinion.

> **Substantial Doubt About the Company's Ability to Continue as a Going Concern**
>
> The accompanying financial statements have been prepared assuming that the Company will continue as a going concern. As discussed in Note X to the financial statements, the Company has suffered recurring losses from operations, has a net capital deficiency, and has stated that substantial doubt exists about the Company's ability to continue as a going concern. Management's evaluation of the events and conditions and management's plans regarding these matters are also described in Note X. The financial statements do not include any adjustments that might result from the outcome of this uncertainty. Our opinion is not modified with respect to this matter.

Question 1   MCQ-14949

Calibro, CPA, believes that there is substantial doubt about the ability of Canto Company, a nonissuer, to continue as a going concern and the concern has not been alleviated based on management's plans. This matter is appropriately disclosed in Canto's financial statements. Calibro should:

1. Issue an unmodified opinion with an other-matter paragraph describing the situation.

2. Issue a qualified opinion due to the fact that there is substantial doubt about the ability of Canto Company to continue as a going concern.

3. Issue an unmodified opinion and add a separate section with the heading "Substantial Doubt About the Entity's Ability to Continue as a Going Concern" describing the situation.

4. Withdraw from the engagement, to minimize the association with financial statements that may be misleading.

3 Audit Approach

The auditor identifies conditions and events that may be indicative of substantial doubt about the entity's ability to continue as a going concern for a reasonable period of time.

3.1 Conditions

Conditions (FINE) that may indicate a problem include:

■ **F**inancial difficulties

■ **I**nternal matters (e.g., work stoppages, labor difficulties)

■ **N**egative financial trends

■ **E**xternal matters (e.g., legal proceedings, new legislation)

3.2 Mitigating Factors

The auditor should consider *mitigating factors*. Both intent and ability are required.

3.3 Subsequent Periods

If doubt is removed in a subsequent period, the going concern paragraph need not be repeated.

Question 2
MCQ-08128

Davis, CPA, believes there is substantial doubt about the ability of Hill Co. to continue as a going concern for a reasonable period of time. In evaluating Hill's plans for dealing with the adverse effects of future conditions and events, Davis most likely would consider, as a mitigating factor, Hill's plans to:

1. Accelerate research and development projects related to future products.

2. Accumulate treasury stock at prices favorable to Hill's historic price range.

3. Purchase equipment and production facilities currently being leased.

4. Negotiate reductions in required dividends being paid on preferred stock.

1 Control Deficiency

A control deficiency exists when the design or operation of a control does not allow management or employees, in the normal course of their assigned functions, **to prevent, or detect and correct** [*prevent and detect*], misstatements on a timely basis.

2 Significant Deficiency

Note

Wording for nonissuers is shown in **bold**; wording for issuers is shown in [*brackets*].

A significant deficiency is a deficiency (or a combination of deficiencies) in internal control [*over financial reporting*] that is less severe than a material weakness, yet important enough to merit attention by **those charged with governance** [*responsible for oversight of the company's financial reporting*].

3 Material Weakness

A material weakness is a deficiency (or a combination of deficiencies) in internal control [*over financial reporting*] such that there is a reasonable possibility that a material misstatement of the **entity's** [*company's annual or interim*] financial statements will not be **prevented, or detected and corrected,** [*prevented or detected*] on a timely basis.

3.1 Reasonable Possibility

"Reasonable possibility" implies that the likelihood of an event is either reasonably possible or probable.

3.2 Indicators of Material Weakness

The following situations are indicators of material weakness in internal control:

- Identification of any level of fraud (even immaterial fraud) perpetrated by senior management.

- Restatement of previously issued financial statements to correct a material misstatement.

- Identification by the auditor of a material misstatement that would not have been detected by the entity's internal control.

- Ineffective oversight by those charged with governance.

Question 1   MCQ-09707

Significant deficiencies are control deficiencies that come to an auditor's attention that are:

1. Disclosures of information that significantly contradict the auditor's going concern assumption.

2. Material fraud or illegal acts perpetrated by high-level management.

3. Important enough to merit attention by those charged with governance.

4. Manipulation or falsification of accounting records or documents from which financial statements are prepared.

---

1 Overview

At the conclusion of fieldwork, the auditor must obtain a letter (signed by the CEO and CFO), dated as of the date of the auditor's report.

1.1 Purpose

The purposes of the representation letter are:

- to ensure that management accepts its responsibility for the assertions in the entity's financial statements; and
- to document the client's representations and responses to inquiries concerning various aspects of the audit.

1.2 Timing

The representation letter is the final piece of audit evidence. When reporting on comparative financial statements, it should address all periods covered by the report. This letter is mandatory; omission of this letter constitutes a scope limitation.

Question 1   MCQ-09834

According to U.S. GAAS, the date of the management representation letter should be:

1. As near as possible to, but not after, the date of the auditor's report.

2. The same as the date of the auditor's report.

3. As near as possible to, but not after, the date of the financial statements.

4. The same as the date of the financial statements.

---

2 Sample Representation Letter

[Entity Letterhead]

To *[Auditor]*   *[Date]*

This letter is provided in connection with your audit of the financial statements of ABC Company, which comprise the balance sheet as of December 31, 20XX, and the related statements of income, changes in stockholders' equity, and cash flows for the year then ended, and the related notes to the financial statements, for the purpose of expressing an opinion on whether the financial statements are presented fairly, in all material respects, in accordance with accounting principles generally accepted in the United States (U.S. GAAP).

Certain representations in this letter are described as being limited to matters that are material. Items are considered material, regardless of size, if they involve an omission or misstatement of accounting information that, in the light of surrounding circumstances, makes it probable that the judgment of a reasonable person relying on the information would be changed or influenced by the omission or misstatement.

Except where otherwise stated below, immaterial matters less than $*[insert amount]* collectively are not considered to be exceptions that require disclosure for the purpose of the following representations. This amount is not necessarily indicative of amounts that would require adjustment to or disclosure in the financial statements.

We confirm that, [*to the best of our knowledge and belief, having made such inquiries as we considered necessary for the purpose of appropriately informing ourselves*] [*as of (date of auditor's report)*]:

Financial Statements

1. We have fulfilled our responsibilities, as set out in the terms of the audit engagement dated *[insert date]*, for the preparation and fair presentation of the financial statements in accordance with U.S. GAAP.

2. We acknowledge our responsibility for the design, implementation, and maintenance of internal control relevant to the preparation and fair presentation of financial statements that are free from material misstatement, whether due to fraud or error.

3. We acknowledge our responsibility for the design, implementation, and maintenance of internal control to prevent and detect fraud.

4. Significant assumptions used by us in making accounting estimates, including those measured at fair value, are reasonable.

5. Related party relationships and transactions have been appropriately accounted for and disclosed in accordance with the requirements of U.S. GAAP.

6. All events subsequent to the date of the financial statements and for which U.S. GAAP requires adjustment or disclosure have been adjusted or disclosed.

7. The effects of uncorrected misstatements are immaterial, both individually and in the aggregate, to the financial statements as a whole. A list of the uncorrected misstatements is attached to the representation letter.

8. The effects of all known or possible litigation and claims have been accounted for and disclosed in accordance with U.S. GAAP.

[Any other matters that the auditor may consider appropriate.]

(continued)

(continued)

Information Provided

9. We have provided you with:

   a. Access to all information, of which we are aware that is relevant to the preparation and fair presentation of the financial statements such as records, documentation and other matters;

   b. Additional information that you have requested from us for the purpose of the audit; and

   c. Unrestricted access to persons within the entity from whom you determined it necessary to obtain audit evidence.

10. All transactions have been recorded in the accounting records and are reflected in the financial statements.

11. We have disclosed to you the results of our assessment of the risk that the financial statements may be materially misstated as a result of fraud.

12. We have [*no knowledge of any*] [*disclosed to you all information that we are aware of regarding*] fraud or suspected fraud affecting the entity and involves:

   a. Management,

   b. Employees who have significant roles in internal control, or

   c. Others where the fraud could have a material effect on the financial statements.

13. We have [*no knowledge of any*] [*disclosed to you all information that we are aware of regarding*] allegations of fraud, or suspected fraud, affecting the entity's financial statements communicated by employees, former employees, analysts, regulators, or others.

14. We disclosed to you all known instances of noncompliance or suspected noncompliance with laws and regulations whose effects should be considered when preparing financial statements.

15. We [*have disclosed to you all known actual or possible*][*are not aware of any pending or threatened*] litigation and claims whose effects should be considered when preparing financial statements [*and we have not consulted legal counsel concerning litigation or claims*].

16. We have disclosed to you the identity of the entity's related parties and all the related party relationships and transactions of which we are aware.

[*Any other matters that the auditor may consider necessary.*]

_____

[*Name of Chief Executive Officer and Title*]

_____

[*Name of Chief Financial Officer and Title*]

1 Types of Subsequent Events

A subsequent event occurs between the balance sheet date and the date the financial statements are issued. Subsequent events may require either adjustment to the financial statements or additional disclosure. Subsequent events are divided into two categories.

1.1 Recognized Events

Recognized events are conditions existing on or before the balance sheet date. Recognized events usually require adjustment to the financial statements.

1.2 Nonrecognized Events

Nonrecognized events are conditions existing after the balance sheet date. Nonrecognized events usually require disclosure, but no financial statement adjustment.

Question 1   MCQ-08118

A client acquired 25% of its outstanding capital stock after year-end but prior to the date of the auditor's report. The auditor should:

1. Advise management to adjust the balance sheet to reflect the acquisition.

2. Issue pro forma financial statements giving effect to the acquisition as if it had occurred at year-end.

3. Advise management to disclose the acquisition in the notes to the financial statements.

4. Disclose the acquisition in the opinion paragraph of the auditor's report.

Auditing Final Review

2 Auditor's Responsibility

The auditor has an active responsibility to investigate subsequent events during the period from the balance sheet date to the date of the auditor's report. Responsibilities include:

- Reviewing **p**ost balance sheet transactions.
- Obtaining a **r**epresentation letter from management.
- **I**nquiry
- Reading the **m**inutes of stockholder, director, and other committee meetings.
- **E**xamining the latest available interim statements.

3 Responsibility After the Auditor's Report Date

The auditor has no active responsibility after the date of the auditor's report, but cannot ignore information coming to his/her attention. If subsequent events result in adjustments or disclosures that are made after the original date of the auditor's report, the auditor may dual date the report to extend responsibility only for the particular subsequent event.

Question 2   MCQ-09050

An auditor issues a report dated 2/12/Year 2 on financial statements for the year ended 12/31/Year 1. Which best describes the auditor's responsibility for an event occurring on 2/1/Year 2 and an event occurring on 3/1/Year 2?

1. The auditor has an active responsibility to investigate both events.
2. The auditor has an active responsibility to investigate the 2/1/Year 2 event, but no responsibility concerning the 3/1/Year 2 event.
3. The auditor has an active responsibility to investigate the 2/1/Year 2 event, and must also consider the effect of the 3/1/Year 2 event if it comes to his/her attention.
4. The auditor has no responsibility for either event, since both occur after the date of the financial statements.

---

1 Auditor Action

If the auditor becomes aware of material information after the report's issuance and knows persons are currently relying or likely to rely on the financial statements, the auditor should advise the client to immediately disclose the information and its impact on the financial statements. If the financial impact cannot be timely ascertained, notification should be made that the financial statements cannot be relied upon.

2 Client Refuses to Follow Procedures

The auditor must be satisfied with the client's action; if not, the auditor should notify the board of directors and the client that the audit report cannot be associated with the financial statements. The auditor should also notify any regulatory agencies and any persons known to be relying on the statements and report.

Question 1	MCQ-09775

Which of the following events occurring after the issuance of the auditor's report most likely would cause the auditor to make further inquiries about the previously issued financial statements?

1. The company issues a bond for a material amount.
2. Loss of a plant as the result of a fire.
3. Purchase of a business that has revenues equivalent to the entity.
4. The discovery of information regarding a material unrecorded expense that occurred during the year under audit.

1 Defining Audit Data Analytics

Audit data analytics (ADAs) are data analytic techniques that enable auditors to analyze and review both financial and nonfinancial data to discover patterns, relationships, and anomalies during an audit.

The functions and benefits of ADAs include:

- Better understanding of clients and their operations.
- Advanced assessment of risk in areas that may have otherwise gone undiscovered.
- Expanded audit coverage through testing of entire populations.
- Insights gained from evaluating metadata and relationships among data both internal and external to the firm.
- Increased efficiency of applied procedures.
- Enhanced fraud detection.
- Improved communication through data visualizations and other reports.

2 Audit Data Analytics Tools and Techniques

2.1 Steps in Applying Data Analytics

When applying ADAs, the auditor should perform the following five steps:

1. Plan the ADA. Determine the objective and purpose of the ADA, including identifying which components of the entity are being tested.
2. Assess and obtain the data. This includes obtaining access to and sourcing the data from the appropriate data source and cleaning and validating the data.
3. Review and analyze the relevance and reliability of the sourced data.
4. Perform the ADA utilizing the selected tools and techniques.
5. Evaluate outcomes to ensure the proposed objective was achieved and the ADA was performed effectively.

2.2 ADA Tools and Technology

Most ADAs are performed using software, including spreadsheets, data transformation and cleaning software, data analytics software, data visualization software, data mining software, programming software, and robotic process animation (RBA) software.

2.3 ADA Techniques

Four broad categories of data analytics can be applied as ADAs:

■ **Descriptive analytics** explain what happened or what is happening with data. Examples of descriptive analytical techniques are summary statistics, data sorting, aging data, and data reduction.

■ **Diagnostic analytics** work to uncover correlations and patterns among data to explain outcomes. Common diagnostic analytical techniques include clustering, drill-down and drill-through analysis, data mining and discovery, variance analysis, period-over-period analysis, data profiling, and sequence checks.

■ **Predictive analytics** use historical data to make predictions, estimates, and assertions about future events. Common predictive analytical techniques include regression analysis, forecasting, time-series modeling, classification, and sentiment analysis.

■ **Prescriptive analytics** prescribe courses of action to help optimize decisions to reach desired outcomes. Common prescriptive analytical techniques include what-if analysis, decision support and automation, machine learning, and natural language processing.

3 Applying Audit Data Analytics

When planning an audit, the auditor should determine to which areas of the audit ADAs can and should be applied based on the nature and scope of the audit objectives and the data available. Then the specific techniques and tools to be used can be identified. A single ADA can be used to concurrently obtain evidence in multiple areas as long as the objectives of both types of procedures are met.

3.1 Risk Assessment

ADAs can be employed during the risk assessment process to identify risk, assess the risk of material misstatements, and identify and assess fraud risk.

3.2 Tests of Controls

ADAs can provide support and evidence in evaluating the design and operating effectiveness of internal controls.

3.3 Substantive Procedures

ADAs can be applied to both tests of details and analytical procedures.

- For tests of details, ADAs can perform sequence checks, test entire populations, compare transactions against external data, and evaluate source data to identify missing data.

- For analytical procedures used as substantive procedures, ADAs can be used to compare current year data with preceding year data, compare industry trends with those at the audited entity, develop expectations for transaction or balance amounts, and perform drill-down analyses of differences between expected and actual amounts.

3.4 Concluding the Audit

ADAs can assist when forming an overall conclusion and assuring that no material misstatements went unidentified during the audit.

4 Sourcing and Reviewing Data Used in Audit Data Analytics

ADAs are only as effective as the data they utilize. It is vital that the data be analyzed to ensure that it is complete, accurate, relevant, and reliable. The auditor must identify what data is needed for the ADA, where and how that data is sourced, and what procedures are needed to ensure reliability.

4.1 ADA Data Sources

Data may be sourced from the various information and management systems utilized by the entity.

Data can be stored in different data repositories based on the type of data, including databases, data lakes, data cubes, data warehouses, and data marts.

Internal data and data used in the compilation of financial statements provide sources for ADAs, including audited financial statements; transaction logs; general ledgers; source documents such as invoices, purchase orders, and receiving reports; and stand-alone data files such as spreadsheets.

Data may also be obtained from external sources such as governmental sources, private external sources, and service organizations that provide services to the organization, including cloud computing services.

4.2   ADA Data Types

Audit data analytics may be performed on either structured or unstructured data.

- Structured data is organized, has consistent data types and formats, and is easily searchable. Structured data includes data found in information systems, spreadsheets, databases, data warehouses, and data marts.

- Unstructured data is all data that is not structured. Unstructured data that may be utilized in an ADA includes social media posts, interview or phone transcripts, data sourced from sensors (Internet of Things), or nontraditional data types such as videos or images.

4.3   Attributes to Evaluate ADAs

Specific attributes of data obtained will determine the nature of the audit data analytic and its objective.

- Numeric (quantitative) data involves quantity, counts, or financial values (e.g., revenue for a given month, number of transactions at a specific store, or quantity ordered of inventory items).

- Text (qualitative) data provides descriptive values (e.g., customer satisfaction results, transcripts or customer support calls, or social media posts).

- Time data indicates when activities or transactions occur, including any level of detail about the time (e.g., years, quarters, months, specific dates, or even times during the day).

- Geographic data provides information about where operations or transactions take place.

4.4   Sourcing Data for ADAs

ADA data may be obtained from built-in reporting provided by information systems, custom queries, data mining, data pulls, walk-throughs, interviews with clients, as well as external sites.

4.5   ADA Data Reliability Verification

The majority of data is sourced from some type of information system. As a result, the audit will typically perform general IT controls (GITC) testing to ensure that there are sufficient internal controls for the information system and its functions.

Many procedures are available to determine the completeness, accuracy, and reliability of information utilized in an ADA, including flowcharts, data flow diagrams, tests of controls, confirmations, recalculations, SOC 1® reports, sequence tests, and use of a specialist, among others.

Reliability of data can be increased and/or improved based on the source of the data and how the extraction occurs. Audit evidence is more reliable if:

- The auditor sourced the data directly rather than requesting the data or through the use of narrative evidence.

- The data was sourced independently from the entity being audited.

- Controls surrounding the input, processing, and storage of the data are deemed effective.

- The original documents are provided rather than any type of reproduction.

- The evidence is documented rather than based on oral inquiries alone.

5 Procedures Performed on Visualizations and Reports

The efficacy of an ADA depends on how well it can be utilized by an auditor to gain insights and provide audit evidence. The output of an ADA must be in a format that the auditor can use to determine relationships among the variables, underlying trends, and outliers or anomalies. This allows the auditor to evaluate the risk of material misstatement, provide evidence to back up or dispute asserted findings, or trigger the need for additional procedures.

5.1 Determination of Appropriateness of ADA Application

The auditor must review the output of the ADA and evaluate whether the ADA was performed appropriately. This can be an iterative process in which the ADA technique, performance, or the underlying data may be further modified or refined with potential reperformance. Once the ADA is deemed appropriate, the auditor can review the output of the ADA to gain insights and review potential concerns.

5.2 Using Data Visualizations

Data visualizations take complex activities or content and transform them into easy-to-read graphs, charts, or other visuals that help the auditor gain insights to make decisions. When creating visualizations, the following items should be addressed to ensure ethical and effective decision making:

- **Choose the Right Type of Visualization:** A pie chart communicates different information from a scatter plot or a line chart.

- **Apply Correct Scaling:** Typically, scaling on the y-axis should start at zero to avoid misinterpretation of differences and variation.

- **Utilize Appropriate Colors:** Colors can change how a viewer interprets a visualization. Consider the audience and its culture when choosing a color scheme.

- **Emphasize Focus Areas:** Visualizations can be manipulated to draw the focus to specific outcomes. Design the visualization to focus on the objective the ADA was designed to achieve.

5.3 Interpreting Results

Relationships between variables allow the auditor to better understand the nature of the entity or specific accounts or activities. The analysis can be aided by numeric statistical output coupled with visualizations. Consider the following analysis techniques:

- **Regression Analysis:** Simple regression can be used to show the direction and strength of the relationship of an independent variable to a dependent variable. Regression analysis typically utilizes scatter plots where the data points are plotted with a regression line. If there is a strong correlation between the variables, the auditor may utilize the regression output to set expectations for given values and compare them with actual values.

- **Variance Analysis:** An auditor may run a variance analysis to compare forecasted or budgeted values against actual values. A bullet chart shows bar chart values against budgeted values. This type of analysis may lead the auditor to perform additional procedures on areas in which the variance is significant.

- **Period-Over-Period Analysis:** An auditor may compare financial or nonfinancial values across multiple periods. A bar or column chart comparing values allows easy identification of differences that may require further audit procedures for explanation.

- **Classification:** Classification is a predictive analytic that allows the auditor to utilize historic data to make predictions about what classes or categories would best fit a new data point. Scatter plots can be used to show where values fall in the analysis. In addition, pie charts or tree maps can be used to show the proportional makeup of a population by class or category.

- **Trend Analysis:** Trend analysis can be used to develop expectations of future results. Line charts can quickly show trends because they address the concept of time. If specific balances are inconsistent with trends in comparative data, further procedures may be required.

5.4 Evaluating and Grouping Potential Misstatements

The audit data analytic output may include a small or large number of items (potential misstatements) that require the auditor's attention. The auditor may divide the items into two broad categories: clearly inconsequential or not clearly inconsequential.

- **Clearly Inconsequential:** If the auditor concludes that the item or group of items do not pose a risk or material misstatement individually or in aggregate, the auditor will document the rationale as to why the items are inconsequential, including amounts or the nature of the item or group of items.

- **Not Clearly Inconsequential:** When there are possible misstatements found in the outcome of the audit data analytic that are not clearly inconsequential, the auditor must perform additional procedures. The auditor may group these possible misstatements by common characteristics and then determine the possible misstatements. Further analysis and procedures should be performed to determine whether the groups present no actual misstatements, misstatements that are clearly inconsequential, or misstatements that are not clearly inconsequential. This step should be thoroughly documented with detailed rationale on determinations. The items that remain not clearly inconsequential will trigger additional procedures.

5.5 Additional Procedures

The auditor should use judgment to determine the nature and scope of procedures that should be performed on the possible misstatements that have been categorized as not clearly inconsequential. These procedures should address the following:

- Consideration of quantitative and qualitative factors on the nature of the possible misstatement.

- Assessment to determine whether the possible misstatement is a result of fraudulent activity.

- Evaluation of the possible misstatement to determine whether it resulted from a control or process failure.

- Determination of the nature and extent of the substantive procedures to be applied.

Question 1   MCQ-14941

Andre has just begun an audit of Rousimoff Industries. As part of the audit, he will employ the use of audit data analytics. Which of the following is *not* a benefit of including audit data analytics in this engagement?

  1. The engagement will have enhanced fraud detection.

  2. Andre will gain absolute assurance of accuracy over every account balance.

  3. Andre will gain a better understanding of Rousimoff Industries and its operations.

  4. Andre will be able to improve communication of findings with data visualizations.

Question 2

Sophie wants to perform an analytic that will evaluate whether large sales should have been made to new customers. She will do this by creating a classification model using past transactions that were approved and rejected to determine whether the transactions being evaluated were in line with prior activities. What type of analytic is Sophie executing?

1. Descriptive analytic
2. Prescriptive analytic
3. Predictive analytic
4. Diagnostic analytic

IV | Forming Conclusions and Reporting

A   Reports on Auditing Engagements

B   Integrated Audit Reports

C   Reports on Internal Controls

D   Reports on Attestation Engagements

E   Accounting and Review Service Engagements

F   Accounting and Review Service Engagement Reports

G   Other Information

H   Reports Required by Government Auditing Standards

I   Special Reports

1 Opinion Types

1.1 Unmodified (Unqualified) Opinion

An unmodified opinion states that the financial statements present fairly, in all material respects, the financial position, results of operations, and cash flows of the entity, in conformity with the applicable financial reporting framework.

1.1.1 Emphasis-of-Matter, Other-Matter, Key Audit Matters Explanatory, and Critical Audit Matters Paragraphs

These are additional communications added to the auditor's report without modifying the auditor's opinion.

1.2 Modified Opinions

The auditor's report is modified when the auditor concludes that the financial statements as a whole are materially misstated (GAAP issue) or when the auditor is unable to obtain sufficient appropriate audit evidence to conclude that the financial statements as a whole are free from material misstatement (GAAS issue).

1.2.1 Qualified Opinion

A qualified opinion states that *except for* the effects of the matter(s) to which the qualification relates, "the financial statements present fairly…" It is used for GAAS or GAAP issues.

1.2.2 Adverse Opinion

An adverse opinion states that the financial statements do not present fairly. It is used for GAAP issues.

1.2.3 Disclaimer of Opinion

A disclaimer of opinion states that auditor does not express an opinion on the financial statements. It is used for GAAS issues.

2 Unmodified Opinion (Nonissuer)

Financial statements are presented fairly in all material respects. The following is an unmodified opinion for a nonissuer reporting on a single year.

Independent Auditor's Report

[*Appropriate Addressee*]

Report on the Audit of Financial Statements [1]

Opinion

We have audited the financial statements of ABC Company, which comprise the balance sheets as of December 31, 20X1 and 20X0, and the related statements of income, changes in stockholders' equity, and cash flows for the years then ended, and the related notes to the financial statements.

In our opinion, the accompanying financial statements present fairly, in all material respects, the financial position of ABC Company as of December 31, 20X1 and 20X0, and the results of its operations and its cash flows for the years then ended in accordance with accounting principles generally accepted in the United States of America.

Basis for Opinion

We conducted our audits in accordance with auditing standards generally accepted in the United States of America (GAAS). Our responsibilities under those standards are further described in the Auditor's Responsibilities for the Audit of the Financial Statements section of our report. We are required to be independent of ABC Company and to meet our other ethical responsibilities, in accordance with the relevant ethical requirements relating to our audits. We believe that the audit evidence we have obtained is sufficient and appropriate to provide a basis for our audit opinion.

Responsibilities of Management for the Financial Statements

Management is responsible for the preparation and fair presentation of the financial statements in accordance with accounting principles generally accepted in the United States of America, and for the design, implementation, and maintenance of internal control relevant to the preparation and fair presentation of financial statements that are free from material misstatement, whether due to fraud or error.

In preparing the financial statements, management is required to evaluate whether there are conditions or events, considered in the aggregate, that raise substantial doubt about ABC Company's ability to continue as a going concern for [*insert the time period set by the applicable financial reporting framework*].

Auditor's Responsibilities for the Audit of the Financial Statements

Our objectives are to obtain reasonable assurance about whether the financial statements as a whole are free from material misstatement, whether due to fraud or error, and to issue an auditor's report that includes our opinion. Reasonable assurance is a high level of assurance but is not absolute assurance and therefore is not a guarantee that an audit conducted in accordance with GAAS will always detect a material misstatement when it exists. The risk of not detecting a material misstatement resulting from fraud is higher than for one resulting from error, as fraud may involve collusion, forgery, intentional omissions, misrepresentations, or the override of internal control. Misstatements are considered material if there is a substantial likelihood that, individually or in the aggregate, they would influence the judgment made by a reasonable user based on the financial statements.

(continued on next page)

(continued)

In performing an audit in accordance with GAAS, we:

- Exercise professional judgment and maintain professional skepticism throughout the audit.

- Identify and assess the risks of material misstatement of the financial statements, whether due to fraud or error, and design and perform audit procedures responsive to those risks. Such procedures include examining, on a test basis, evidence regarding the amounts and disclosures in the financial statements.

- Obtain an understanding of internal control relevant to the audit in order to design audit procedures that are appropriate in the circumstances, but not for the purpose of expressing an opinion on the effectiveness of ABC Company's internal control. Accordingly, no such opinion is expressed. [2]

- Evaluate the appropriateness of accounting policies used and the reasonableness of significant accounting estimates made by management, as well as evaluate the overall presentation of the financial statements.

- Conclude whether, in our judgment, there are conditions or events, considered in the aggregate, that raise substantial doubt about ABC Company's ability to continue as a going concern for a reasonable period of time.

We are required to communicate with those charged with governance regarding, among other matters, the planned scope and timing of the audit, significant audit findings, and certain internal control–related matters that we identified during the audit.

Other Information [*Included in the Annual Report*]

Management is responsible for the other information [*included in the annual report*]. The other information comprises the [*information included in the annual report*] but does not include the financial statements and our auditor's report thereon. Our opinion on the financial statements does not cover the other information, and we do not express an opinion or any form of assurance thereon.

In connection with our audit of the financial statements, our responsibility is to read the other information and consider whether a material inconsistency exists between the other information and the financial statements, or the other information otherwise appears to be materially misstated. If, based on the work performed, we conclude that an uncorrected material misstatement of the other information exists, we are required to describe it in our report.

Report on Other Legal and Regulatory Requirements

[*The form and content of this section of the auditor's report would vary depending on the nature of the auditor's other reporting responsibilities.*]

[*Signature of the auditor's firm*]
[*City and state where the auditor's report is issued*]
[*Date of the auditor's report*]

---

[1] The subtitle "Report on the Audit of the Financial Statements" is unnecessary in circumstances in which the second subtitle, "Report on Other Legal and Regulatory Requirements," is not applicable.

[2] In circumstances in which the auditor also has a responsibility to express an opinion on the effectiveness of internal control in conjunction with the audit of the financial statements, omit the following: "but not for the purpose of expressing an opinion on the effectiveness of ABC Company's internal control. Accordingly, no such opinion is expressed."

3 Audits of Group Financial Statements

When an auditor acts as the auditor of group financial statements, the auditor must determine whether to make reference to any component auditors in the auditor's report on the group financial statements.

3.1 Making Reference to the Component Auditor

When making reference to the component auditor, the auditor's report on the group financial statements should clearly indicate that the component was audited by the component auditor and should include the magnitude of the portion of the financial statements audited by the component auditor.

3.1.1 U.S. GAAS

Under U.S. GAAS, the name of the component auditor may be included in the auditor's report only if permission is granted by the component auditor and the component auditor's report is presented with the auditor's report on the group financial statements.

3.1.2 Auditor's Report Referencing the Audit
of a Component Auditor (Nonissuer)

Independent Auditor's Report

[*Appropriate Addressee*]

Opinion

We have audited the consolidated financial statements of ABC Company and its subsidiaries, which comprise the consolidated balance sheets as of December 31, 20X1 and 20X0, and the related consolidated statements of income, changes in stockholders' equity, and cash flows for the years then ended, and the related notes to the financial statements.

In our opinion, based on our audits and the report of the other auditors, the accompanying consolidated financial statements present fairly, in all material respects, the financial position of ABC Company and its subsidiaries as of December 31, 20X1 and 20X0, and the results of their operations and their cash flows for the years then ended in accordance with accounting principles generally accepted in the United States of America.

We did not audit the financial statements of B Company, a wholly owned subsidiary, which statements reflect total assets constituting 20 percent and 22 percent, respectively, of consolidated total assets at December 31, 20X1 and 20X0, and total revenues constituting 18 percent and 20 percent, respectively, of consolidated total revenues for the years then ended. Those statements were audited by other auditors, whose report has been furnished to us, and our opinion, insofar as it relates to the amounts included for B Company, is based solely on the report of the other auditors.

Basis for Opinion

[*Same as standard nonissuer audit report.*]

Responsibilities of Management for the Financial Statements

[*Same as standard nonissuer audit report.*]

Auditor's Responsibilities for the Audit of the Financial Statements

[*Same as standard nonissuer audit report.*]

Report on Other Legal and Regulatory Requirements

[*Same as standard nonissuer audit report.*]

[*Signature of the auditor's firm*]
[*City and state where the auditor's report is issued*]
[*Date of the auditor's report*]

3.2 Assumption of Responsibility

When the group auditor decides to assume responsibility for the work of a component auditor, no reference to the component auditor is made in the auditor's report.

According to GAAS, which of the following procedures is *not* required when the group auditor decides to make reference to the component auditor in the auditor's report on the group financial statements?

1. The group auditor should be satisfied with the independence of the component auditor.

2. The component auditor's report is not restricted.

3. The group auditor should be satisfied with the competence of the component auditor.

4. The group auditor should determine the type of work to be performed on the financial information of the components.

4 Emphasis-of-Matter, Other-Matter, Key Audit Matters Explanatory, and Critical Audit Matters Paragraphs

4.1 Emphasis-of-Matter Paragraphs

An emphasis-of-matter paragraph is included in the auditor's report when required by GAAS or at the auditor's discretion. An emphasis-of-matter paragraph is used when referring to a matter that is appropriately presented or disclosed in the financial statements and is of such importance that it is fundamental to the users' understanding of the financial statements.

4.1.1 Report Requirements

When an emphasis-of-matter paragraph is included in the auditor's report, the auditor should:

- use the heading "Emphasis of Matter" or other appropriate heading (required to use the heading "Emphasis-of-Matter" when the auditor has been engaged to communicate key audit matters);

- describe the matter and the location of relevant disclosures; and

- state that the auditor's report is not modified with respect to the matter emphasized.

4.1.2 Lack of Consistency—Justified (Acceptable/Justified Change in Accounting Principle)

Consistency is implied in the auditor's report. *If a material change in GAAP has occurred* between periods and such change is justified, the auditor should *add an emphasis-of-matter paragraph* to the auditor's opinion describing the change and referring the reader to the note describing the change in detail.

4.2 Other-Matter Paragraphs

An other-matter paragraph is included in the auditor's report when required by GAAS or at the auditor's discretion. Other-matter paragraphs refer to matters other than those presented or disclosed in the financial statements that are relevant to the users' understanding of the audit, the auditor's responsibilities, or the auditor's report. When the auditor has been engaged to communicate key audit matters, the use of an other-matter paragraph is not appropriate for a matter identified as a key audit matter to be separately communicated.

4.2.1 Report Requirements

When an other-matter paragraph is included in the auditor's report, the auditor should:

■ use the heading "Other Matter" or other appropriate heading; and

■ describe the matter and the location of relevant disclosures.

4.2.2 Alert That Restricts the Use of the Auditor's Written Communication

The auditor may be required by GAAS or may decide that it is necessary to include language in the auditor's report (or other written communication) that restricts the use of the auditor's written communication. In the auditor's report, such language is included in an *other-matter paragraph*.

4.3 Key Audit Matters (Nonissuers Only)

Key audit matters (KAMs) are those matters that were of most significance in the audit of the financial statements of the current period. Such matters are selected from the matters communicated with those charged with governance. Entities have the option of whether or not to engage the auditor to communicate key audit matters but should consider the needs of the users of the financial statements when making this determination.

4.3.1 Reporting Requirements

When the auditor is engaged to communicate key audit matters, the audit report should include:

■ a separate section of the auditor's report with the heading "Key Audit Matters"; and

■ a description of why the matter was considered to be of most significance and how the matter was addressed.

If the auditor is engaged to communicate key audit matters, but determines, based on the facts and circumstances of the audit, that there are no items to communicate, a statement to this effect should be included in the auditor's report under the subheading "Key Audit Matters."

4.4   Explanatory Paragraphs

An explanatory paragraph is included in the auditor's report when required by PCAOB auditing standards or at the auditor's discretion. The inclusion of an explanatory paragraph in the auditor's report does not affect the auditor's opinion.

4.4.1   Report Requirements

When an explanatory paragraph is included in the auditor's report, the auditor generally should place the explanatory paragraph immediately after the opinion paragraph and describe the matter.

4.5   Critical Audit Matters (Issuers Only)

The auditor's report for audits of issuers must include any critical audit matters (CAMs) arising from the current period's audit of the financial statements, or state that the auditor determined that there were no CAMs.

A critical audit matter is a matter that was communicated or required to be communicated to the audit committee and that:

1. relates to accounts or disclosures that are material to the financial statements; and

2. involved especially challenging, subjective, or complex auditor judgment.

4.5.1   Reporting Requirements

For each CAM identified, the audit report should include:

- **identification** of the CAM;
- description of the **principal** considerations that led the auditor to determine that the matter was a CAM;
- description of how the CAM was **addressed** in the audit; and
- reference to the relevant financial statement accounts or **disclosures**.

Question 2   MCQ-14951

Which of the following circumstances requires the use of an emphasis-of-matter paragraph?

1. An alert in the audit report restricts the use of the audit report.

2. Prior to the audit report date, the auditor identifies a material inconsistency in other information that is included in the document containing audited financial statements that management refuses to revise.

3. The financial statements are prepared in accordance with a special purpose framework.

4. The auditor chooses to report on supplementary information presented with the financial statements in the auditor's report, rather than in a separate report.

---

5 GAAP Issues: Qualified or Adverse Opinion

The auditor uses professional judgment to determine whether to issue a qualified opinion or an adverse opinion when audit evidence indicates that there is material misstatement of the financial statements.

Materiality of Problem		Financial Statements Are Materially Misstated (GAAP Issues)	Inability to Obtain Sufficient Appropriate Audit Evidence (GAAS Issues)
None or immaterial	=	Unmodified	Unmodified
Material but not pervasive	=	Qualified opinion	Qualified opinion
Material and pervasive	=	Adverse opinion	Disclaimer of opinion

5.1 Qualified Opinion

A qualified opinion should be expressed when the auditor concludes that misstatements, individually or in the aggregate, are material but not pervasive to the financial statements.

5.2 Adverse Opinion

An adverse opinion should be expressed when the auditor concludes that misstatements, individually or in the aggregate, are both material and pervasive to the financial statements.

5.3 Form and Content of Auditor's Report

Nonissuers: When the auditor expresses a qualified or adverse opinion due to a material misstatement of the financial statements, the auditor's report includes a "Basis for Qualified Opinion" or "Basis for Adverse Opinion" section and a "Qualified Opinion" or "Adverse Opinion" section, as appropriate. The auditor should not include a section on key audit matters when the auditor expresses an adverse opinion.

Issuers: When the auditor expresses a qualified or adverse opinion due to material misstatement of the financial statements, the auditor's report will include an additional paragraph immediately following the opinion paragraph and the opinion paragraph will be modified. The auditor is not required to report critical audit matters in the auditor's report when the auditor expresses an adverse opinion.

5.3.1 Qualified Opinion—GAAP Problem (Nonissuer)

Independent Auditor's Report

[*Appropriate Addressee*]

Report on the Audit of Financial Statements

Qualified Opinion

We have audited the financial statements of ABC Company, which comprise the balance sheets as of December 31, 20X1 and 20X0, and the related statements of income, changes in stockholders' equity, and cash flows for the years then ended, and the related notes to the financial statements.

In our opinion, except for the effects of the matter described in the Basis for Qualified Opinion section of our report, the accompanying financial statements present fairly, in all material respects, the financial position of ABC Company as of December 31, 20X1 and 20X0, and the results of its operations and its cash flows for the years then ended in accordance with accounting principles generally accepted in the United States of America.

Basis for Qualified Opinion

ABC Company has stated inventories at cost in the accompanying balance sheets. Accounting principles generally accepted in the United States of America require inventories to be stated at the lower of cost or market. If the Company stated inventories at the lower of cost or market, a write-down of $XXX and $XXX would have been required as of December 31, 20X1 and 20X0, respectively. Accordingly, cost of sales would have been increased by $XXX and $XXX, and net income, income taxes, and stockholders' equity would have been reduced by $XXX, $XXX, and $XXX, and $XXX, $XXX, and $XXX, as of and for the years ended December 31, 20X1 and 20X0, respectively.

We conducted our audits in accordance with auditing standards generally accepted in the United States of America (GAAS). Our responsibilities under those standards are further described in the Auditor's Responsibilities for the Audit of the Financial Statements section of our report. We are required to be independent of ABC Company and to meet our other ethical responsibilities, in accordance with the relevant ethical requirements relating to our audits. We believe that the audit evidence we have obtained is sufficient and appropriate to provide a basis for our qualified audit opinion.

Responsibilities of Management for the Financial Statements

[*Same as standard nonissuer audit report.*]

Auditor's Responsibilities for the Audit of the Financial Statements

[*Same as standard nonissuer audit report.*]

Report on Other Legal and Regulatory Requirements

[*Same as standard nonissuer audit report.*]

[*Signature of the auditor's firm*]
[*City and state where the auditor's report is issued*]
[*Date of the auditor's report*]

5.3.2 Adverse Opinion (Nonissuer)

Independent Auditor's Report

[*Appropriate Addressee*]

Report on the Audit of Financial Statements

Adverse Opinion

We have audited the financial statements of ABC Company, which comprise the balance sheets as of December 31, 20X1 and 20X0, and the related statements of income, changes in stockholders' equity, and cash flows for the years then ended, and the related notes to the financial statements.

In our opinion, because of the significance of the matter discussed in the Basis for Adverse Opinion section of our report, the accompanying consolidated financial statements do not present fairly the financial position of ABC Company and its subsidiaries as of December 31, 20X1, or the results of their operations or their cash flows for the year then ended in accordance with accounting principles generally accepted in the United States of America.

Basis for Adverse Opinion

As described in Note X, ABC Company has not consolidated the financial statements of subsidiary XYZ Company that it acquired during 20X1 because it has not yet been able to ascertain the fair values of certain of the subsidiary's material assets and liabilities at the acquisition date. This investment is therefore accounted for on a cost basis by the Company. Under accounting principles generally accepted in the United States of America, the subsidiary should have been consolidated because it is controlled by the Company. Had XYZ Company been consolidated, many elements in the accompanying consolidated financial statements would have been materially affected. The effects on the consolidated financial statements of the failure to consolidate have not been determined.

We conducted our audit in accordance with auditing standards generally accepted in the United States of America (GAAS). Our responsibilities under those standards are further described in the Auditor's Responsibilities for the Audit of the Financial Statements section of our report. We are required to be independent of ABC Company and to meet our other ethical responsibilities, in accordance with the relevant ethical requirements relating to our audit. We believe that the audit evidence we have obtained is sufficient and appropriate to provide a basis for our adverse audit opinion.

Responsibilities of Management for the Financial Statements

[*Same as standard nonissuer audit report.*]

Auditor's Responsibilities for the Audit of the Financial Statements

[*Same as standard nonissuer audit report.*]

Report on Other Legal and Regulatory Requirements

[*Same as standard nonissuer audit report.*]

[*Signature of the auditor's firm*]
[*City and state where the auditor's report is issued*]
[*Date of the auditor's report*]

6 GAAS Issues—Qualified Opinion or Disclaimer

The auditor uses professional judgment to determine whether to issue a qualified opinion or a disclaimer of opinion due to a limitation on the scope of the audit. A scope limitation occurs when the auditor is unable to obtain sufficient appropriate audit evidence to conclude that the financial statements are free of material misstatement.

Materiality of Problem		Financial Statements Are Materially Misstated (GAAP Issues)	Inability to Obtain Sufficient Appropriate Audit Evidence (GAAS Issues)
None or immaterial	=	Unmodified	Unmodified
Material but not pervasive	=	Qualified opinion	Qualified opinion
Material and pervasive	=	Adverse opinion	Disclaimer of opinion

6.1 Qualified Opinion

A qualified opinion due to a GAAS issue should be expressed when the auditor is unable to obtain sufficient appropriate audit evidence on which to base an opinion and the auditor concludes that the possible effects of any undetected misstatements could be material but not pervasive.

6.2 Disclaimer of Opinion

A disclaimer of opinion should be expressed when the auditor is unable to obtain sufficient appropriate audit evidence on which to base an opinion and the auditor concludes that the possible effects of any undetected misstatements could be both material and pervasive.

6.3 Form and Content of the Auditor's Report

Nonissuer: When the auditor expresses a qualified opinion or disclaimer of opinion due to scope limitation, the auditor's report will include a "Disclaimer of Opinion" or "Qualified Opinion" section and a "Basis for Disclaimer of Opinion" or a "Basis for Qualified Opinion" section, as appropriate. When the auditor is expressing a disclaimer of opinion on the financial statements, the "Auditor's Responsibility for the Audit of the Financial Statements" section must be amended and the auditor should not include a "Key Audit Matters" section.

Issuer: When the auditor expresses a qualified opinion or disclaimer of opinion, a paragraph immediately following the opinion paragraph is added and the opinion paragraph is modified. A qualified opinion and disclaimer of opinion will include modified language in the basis for opinion section. The auditor is not required to report critical audit matters in the auditor's report when the auditor expresses a disclaimer of opinion.

6.3.1 Qualified Opinion—GAAS Problem (Nonissuer)

Independent Auditor's Report

[*Appropriate Addressee*]

Report on the Audit of Financial Statements

Qualified Opinion

We have audited the financial statements of ABC Company, which comprise the balance sheet as of December 31, 20X1, and the related statements of income, changes in stockholders' equity, and cash flows for the year then ended, and the related notes to the financial statements.

In our opinion, except for the possible effects of the matter described in the Basis for Qualified Opinion section of our report, the accompanying financial statements present fairly, in all material respects, the financial position of ABC Company as of December 31, 20X1, and the results of its operations and its cash flows for the year then ended in accordance with accounting principles generally accepted in the United States of America.

Basis for Qualified Opinion

ABC Company's investment in XYZ Company, a foreign affiliate acquired during the year and accounted for under the equity method, is carried at $XXX on the balance sheet at December 31, 20X1, and ABC Company's share of XYZ Company's net income of $XXX is included in ABC Company's net income for the year then ended. We were unable to obtain sufficient appropriate audit evidence about the carrying amount of ABC Company's investment in XYZ Company as of December 31, 20X1, and ABC Company's share of XYZ Company's net income for the year then ended because we were denied access to the financial information, management, and the auditors of XYZ Company. Consequently, we were unable to determine whether any adjustments to these amounts were necessary.

We conducted our audit in accordance with auditing standards generally accepted in the United States of America (GAAS). Our responsibilities under those standards are further described in the Auditor's Responsibilities for the Audit of the Financial Statements section of our report. We are required to be independent of ABC Company and to meet our other ethical responsibilities, in accordance with the relevant ethical requirements relating to our audit. We believe that the audit evidence we have obtained is sufficient and appropriate to provide a basis for our qualified audit opinion.

Responsibilities of Management for the Financial Statements

[*Same as standard nonissuer audit report.*]

Auditor's Responsibilities for the Audit of the Financial Statements

[*Same as standard nonissuer audit report.*]

Report on Other Legal and Regulatory Requirements

[*Same as standard nonissuer audit report.*]

[*Signature of the auditor's firm*]
[*City and state where the auditor's report is issued*]
[*Date of the auditor's report*]

6.3.2 Disclaimer of Opinion (Nonissuer)

Independent Auditor's Report

[*Appropriate Addressee*]

Report on the Audit of Financial Statements

Disclaimer of Opinion

We were engaged to audit the financial statements of ABC Company, which comprise the balance sheet as of December 31, 20X1, and the related statements of income, changes in stockholders' equity, and cash flows for the year then ended, and the related notes to the financial statements.

We do not express an opinion on the accompanying financial statements of ABC Company. Because of the significance of the matters described in the Basis for Disclaimer of Opinion section of our report, we have not been able to obtain sufficient appropriate audit evidence to provide a basis for an audit opinion on these financial statements.

Basis for Disclaimer of Opinion

We were not engaged as auditors of ABC Company until after December 31, 20X1, and, therefore, did not observe the counting of physical inventories at the beginning or end of the year. We were unable to satisfy ourselves by other auditing procedures concerning the inventory held at December 31, 20X1, which is stated in the balance sheet at $XXX. In addition, the introduction of a new computerized accounts receivable system in September 20X1 resulted in numerous misstatements in accounts receivable. As of the date of our audit report, management was still in the process of rectifying the system deficiencies and correcting the misstatements. We were unable to confirm or verify by alternative means accounts receivable included in the balance sheet at a total amount of $XXX at December 31, 20X1. As a result of these matters, we were unable to determine whether any adjustments might have been found necessary in respect of recorded or unrecorded inventories and accounts receivable, and the elements making up the statements of income, changes in stockholders' equity, and cash flows.

Responsibilities of Management for the Financial Statements

[*Same as standard nonissuer audit report.*]

Auditor's Responsibilities for the Audit of the Financial Statements

Our responsibility is to conduct an audit of ABC Company's financial statements in accordance with auditing standards generally accepted in the United States of America and to issue an auditor's report. However, because of the matters described in the Basis for Disclaimer of Opinion section of our report, we were not able to obtain sufficient appropriate audit evidence to provide a basis for an audit opinion on these financial statements.

We are required to be independent of ABC Company and to meet our other ethical responsibilities, in accordance with the relevant ethical requirements relating to our audit.

Report on Other Legal and Regulatory Requirements

[*Same as standard nonissuer audit report.*]

[*Signature of the auditor's firm*]
[*City and state where the auditor's report is issued*]
[*Date of the auditor's report*]

Question 3 MCQ-09764

Under which of the following situations would the expression of a disclaimer of opinion be inappropriate?

1. The entity's going concern disclosures are adequate.

2. Management refuses to allow the auditor to send a letter of inquiry to their attorneys.

3. The auditor is not independent.

4. Management fails to disclose a significant subsequent event.

---

7 Comparative Financial Statements

7.1 Change in Opinion

A prior opinion may be changed. The auditor should update (i.e., either reaffirm or change) the opinion on any previously issued financial statements shown in comparative statements.

If the updated opinion differs from the previous opinion, the auditor should disclose the reason(s) in an *emphasis-of-matter or other-matter paragraph* (nonissuer) or *explanatory paragraph* (issuer) that discloses the following:

- **D**ate of the previous auditor's report.
- **O**pinion type previously issued.
- **R**eason for the prior opinion.
- **C**hanges that have occurred.
- **S**tatement that "opinion … is different."

7.1.1 Sample Other-Matter Paragraph—Updating Prior Opinion

> *Other Matter*
>
> In our report dated March 1, 20X1, we expressed an opinion that the 20X0 financial statements did not fairly present the financial position, results of operations, and cash flows of ABC Company in accordance with accounting principles generally accepted in the United States of America because of two departures from such principles: (1) ABC Company carried its property, plant, and equipment at appraisal values, and provided for depreciation on the basis of such values; and (2) ABC Company did not provide for deferred income taxes with respect to differences between income for financial reporting purposes and taxable income. As described in Note X, the Company has changed its method of accounting for these items and restated its 20X0 financial statements to conform with accounting principles generally accepted in the United States of America. Accordingly, our present opinion on the restated 20X0 financial statements, as presented herein, is different from that expressed in our previous report.

7.2 Different Opinions

Some comparative reports will have different opinions for each year presented. Depending upon the situation, the appropriate paragraphs will be modified.

7.2.1 Report on Comparative Financial Statements— Different Opinions (Nonissuer)

Independent Auditor's Report

[Appropriate Addressee]

Report on the Audit of Financial Statements

Qualified Opinion

We have audited the financial statements of ABC Company, which comprise the balance sheets as of December 31, 20X1 and 20X0, and the related statements of income, changes in stockholders' equity, and cash flows for the years then ended, and the related notes to the financial statements.

In our opinion, except for the effects on the accompanying 20X1 financial statements of not capitalizing certain lease obligations as described in the Basis for Qualified Opinion section of our report, the financial statements present fairly, in all material respects, the financial position of ABC Company as of December 31, 20X1 and 20X0, and the results of its operations and its cash flows for the years then ended in accordance with accounting principles generally accepted in the United States of America.

Basis for Qualified Opinion

ABC Company has excluded, from property and debt in the accompanying 20X1 balance sheet, certain lease obligations that were entered into in 20X1 that, in our opinion, should be capitalized in accordance with accounting principles generally accepted in the United States of America. If these lease obligations were capitalized, property would be increased by $XXX, long-term debt by $XXX, and retained earnings by $XXX as of December 31, 20X1, and net income and earnings per share would be increased (decreased) by $XXX and $XXX, respectively, for the year then ended.

We conducted our audits in accordance with auditing standards generally accepted in the United States of America (GAAS). Our responsibilities under those standards are further described in the Auditor's Responsibilities for the Audit of the Financial Statements section of our report. We are required to be independent of ABC Company and to meet our other ethical responsibilities, in accordance with the relevant ethical requirements relating to our audit. We believe that the audit evidence we have obtained is sufficient and appropriate to provide a basis for our qualified audit opinion on the 20X1 financial statements and for our opinion on the 20X0 financial statements.

Responsibilities of Management for the Financial Statements

[Same as standard nonissuer audit report.]

Auditor's Responsibilities for the Audit of the Financial Statements

[Same as standard nonissuer audit report.]

Report on Other Legal and Regulatory Requirements

[Same as standard nonissuer audit report.]

[Signature of the auditor's firm]
[City and state where the auditor's report is issued]
[Date of the auditor's report]

Question 4 MCQ-09041

In Year 1, Randall, CPA, issued a qualified opinion on the financial statements of Celadon Industries, a nonissuer, due to the improper recording of lease obligations. During Year 2, Celadon restated the Year 1 financial statements to correct the error, and now plans to issue comparative financial statements for Year 1 and Year 2. Which of the following is true about Randall's report on the comparative financial statements?

1. Randall may not change the prior opinion, but may add an other-matter paragraph to the report indicating that the previous error has been corrected.

2. Randall may revise the prior opinion, but must include an emphasis-of-matter or other-matter paragraph describing the situation.

3. Randall may not change the prior opinion, and should not issue a report on the comparative financial statements.

4. Randall may revise the prior opinion and need not make mention of the change, as long as the comparative financial statements include the revised statements (and not the original statements) for Year 1.

8 Required Auditor Reporting of Certain Audit Participants

8.1 Filing of Form AP

An issuer must file Form AP with the PCAOB for each audit report issued. This form includes information about the audit, such as:

- Name of the firm.
- Name of the issuer whose financial statements are audited.
- Date of the audit report.
- The end date of the most recent period's financial statements identified in the audit report.
- The name of the engagement partner on the most recent period's audit and his/her current and prior ID number(s).
- The city and state (or city and country) of the office of the firm issuing the audit report.
- Whether the audit report is dual-dated.
- Whether other accounting firms participated in the audit.
- Whether the firm divided responsibility for the audit.
- Signature of partner or authorized officer.

Form AP must be filed by the 35th day after the audit report is first filed in a document with the SEC or within 10 days if the audit report is included in a registration statement.

8.2 Optional Inclusions

Although not required, the auditor of an issuer may elect to include in the auditor's report information regarding the engagement partner and/or other accounting firms participating in the audit.

1 Integrated Audits of Issuers

PCAOB standards, which apply to issuers, require that auditors perform an "integrated audit," auditing internal control in conjunction with the audit of the financial statements. The Dodd-Frank Act amended this rule, providing that integrated audits are required only for large accelerated filers and accelerated filers.

2 Integrated Audits of Nonissuers

SASs allow an auditor to audit and report on a nonissuer's internal control over financial reporting that is integrated with a financial statement audit. The rules governing integrated audits of nonissuers are very similar to the rules for issuers.

3 Impact on Tests of Controls

In both issuer and nonissuer integrated audits, tests of controls should be designed to provide sufficient appropriate evidence to support both the opinion on internal control and the control risk assessment in the financial statement audit.

3.1 Top-Down Approach

A top-down approach is used to select the controls to test. The auditor should:

- Evaluate overall risk at the financial statement level.
- Consider controls at the entity level.
- Focus tests of controls on accounts, disclosures, and assertions for which there is a reasonable possibility of material misstatement.

Question 1

In an integrated audit of an issuer, which of the following most likely would be considered an entity-level control?

1. The auditor's adherence to a system of quality control.

2. Management's procedures used to initiate, authorize, and record journal entries into the general ledger.

3. An aging schedule that is prepared by the accounts receivable department.

4. Upon receiving checks from customers by mail, an employee prepares a duplicate listing of checks received.

1 Communications With Management and Those Charged With Governance

The auditor is not required to search for control deficiencies or significant deficiencies in a financial statement audit only, but those that are identified should be communicated.

- Control deficiencies, significant deficiencies, and material weaknesses should be communicated to management in writing.

- Significant deficiencies and material weaknesses must also be communicated to the audit committee in writing.

- For issuers, material weaknesses should be communicated to management and the audit committee before the issuance of the auditor's report on internal control.

- For nonissuers, communication of significant deficiencies and material weaknesses should be made by the report release date and communication of control deficiencies should be made within 60 days of the report release date.

Question 1   MCQ-09064

With respect to the expression of an opinion regarding whether a client maintained effective internal control over financial reporting:

1. The auditor of a nonissuer may express an opinion as a result of an audit engagement.

2. The auditor of a nonissuer may express an opinion as a result of a financial statement audit.

3. The auditor of a nonissuer must express an opinion in every financial statement audit.

4. The auditor of a nonissuer must express an opinion whenever significant deficiencies or material weaknesses are noted.

---

2 Opinion on Internal Control

The auditor must express an opinion on the company's internal control over financial reporting in an integrated audit.

2.1 Separate or Combined Reports

This report may be combined with the report on the financial statements, or it may be presented separately. If separate reports are issued, each report should contain an explanatory paragraph making reference to the other report.

2.1.1 Sample Combined Report (Issuer)

Report of Independent Registered Public Accounting Firm

To the shareholders and the board of directors of W Company:

Opinions on the Financial Statements and Internal Control Over Financial Reporting

We have audited the accompanying balance sheets of W Company (the "Company") as of December 31, 20X8 and 20X7, and the related statements of income, comprehensive income, stockholders' equity, and cash flows for each of the years in the two-year period ended December 31, 20X8, and the related notes [*and schedules*] (collectively referred to as the "financial statements"). We also have audited the Company's internal control over financial reporting as of December 31, 20X8, based on [*identify control criteria, for example, "criteria established in Internal Control-Integrated Framework: (20XX) issued by the Committee of Sponsoring Organizations of the Treadway Commission (COSO)"*].

In our opinion, the financial statements referred to above present fairly, in all material respects, the financial position of the Company as of December 31, 20X8 and 20X7, and the results of its operations and its cash flows for each of the years in the two-year period ended December 31, 20X8, in conformity with accounting principles generally accepted in the United States of America. Also in our opinion, the Company maintained, in all material respects, effective internal control over financial reporting as of December 31, 20X8, based on [*identify control criteria, for example, "criteria established in Internal Control-Integrated Framework: (20XX) issued by COSO"*].

Basis for Opinion

The Company's management is responsible for these financial statements, for maintaining effective internal control over financial reporting, and for its assessment of the effectiveness of internal control over financial reporting, included in the accompanying [title of management's report]. Our responsibility is to express an opinion on the Company's financial statements and an opinion on the Company's internal control over financial reporting based on our audits. We are a public accounting firm registered with the Public Company Accounting Oversight Board (United States) (PCAOB) and are required to be independent with respect to the Company in accordance with the U.S. federal securities laws and the applicable rules and regulations of the Securities and Exchange Commission and the PCAOB.

We conducted our audits in accordance with the standards of the PCAOB. Those standards require that we plan and perform the audits to obtain reasonable assurance about whether the financial statements are free of material misstatement, whether due to error or fraud, and whether effective internal control over financial reporting was maintained in all material respects.

(continued on next page)

(continued)

Our audits of the financial statements included performing procedures to assess the risks of material misstatement of the financial statements, whether due to error or fraud, and performing procedures that respond to those risks. Such procedures included examining, on a test basis, evidence regarding the amounts and disclosures in the financial statements. Our audits also included evaluating the accounting principles used and significant estimates made by management, as well as evaluating the overall presentation of the financial statements. Our audit of internal control over financial reporting included obtaining an understanding of internal control over financial reporting, assessing the risk that a material weakness exists, and testing and evaluating the design and operating effectiveness of internal control based on the assessed risk. Our audits also included performing such other procedures as we considered necessary in the circumstances. We believe that our audits provide a reasonable basis for our opinions.

Definition and Limitations of Internal Control Over Financial Reporting

A company's internal control over financial reporting is a process designed to provide reasonable assurance regarding the reliability of financial reporting and the preparation of financial statements for external purposes in accordance with generally accepted accounting principles. A company's internal control over financial reporting includes those policies and procedures that (1) pertain to the maintenance of records that, in reasonable detail, accurately and fairly reflect the transactions and dispositions of the assets of the company; (2) provide reasonable assurance that transactions are recorded as necessary to permit preparation of financial statements in accordance with generally accepted accounting principles, and that receipts and expenditures of the company are being made only in accordance with authorizations of management and directors of the company; and (3) provide reasonable assurance regarding prevention or timely detection of unauthorized acquisition, use, or disposition of the company's assets that could have a material effect on the financial statements.

Because of its inherent limitations, internal control over financial reporting may not prevent or detect misstatements. Also, projections of any evaluation of effectiveness to future periods are subject to the risk that controls may become inadequate because of changes in conditions, or that the degree of compliance with the policies or procedures may deteriorate.

Critical Audit Matters

[*Include critical audit matters*]

[*Signature*]

We have served as the Company's auditor since [year].

[*City and State or Country*]

[*Date*]

2.1.2 Sample Combined Report (Nonissuer)

Independent Auditor's Report

[*Appropriate Addressee*]

Report on the Financial Statements and Internal Control

Opinions on the Financial Statements and Internal Control Over Financial Reporting

We have audited the financial statements of ABC Company, which comprise the balance sheet as of December 31, 20XX, and the related statements of income, changes in stockholders' equity, and cash flows for the year then ended, and the related notes to the financial statements. In our opinion, the accompanying financial statements present fairly, in all material respects, the financial position of ABC Company as of December 31, 20XX, and the results of its operations and its cash flows for the year then ended in accordance with accounting principles generally accepted in the United States of America.

We also have audited ABC Company's internal control over financial reporting as of December 31, 20XX, based on [*identify criteria*]. In our opinion, ABC Company maintained, in all material respects, effective internal control over financial reporting as of December 31, 20XX, based on [*identify criteria*].

Basis for Opinions

We conducted our audits in accordance with auditing standards generally accepted in the United States of America (GAAS). Our responsibilities under those standards are further described in the Auditor's Responsibilities for the Audits of the Financial Statements and Internal Control Over Financial Reporting section of our report. We are required to be independent of ABC Company and to meet our other ethical responsibilities, in accordance with the relevant ethical requirements relating to our audits. We believe that the audit evidence we have obtained is sufficient and appropriate to provide a basis for our audit opinions.

Responsibilities of Management for the Financial Statements and Internal Control Over Financial Reporting

Management is responsible for the preparation and fair presentation of the financial statements in accordance with accounting principles generally accepted in the United States of America, and for the design, implementation, and maintenance of effective internal control over financial reporting relevant to the preparation and fair presentation of financial statements that are free from material misstatement, whether due to fraud or error. Management is also responsible for its assessment about the effectiveness of internal control over financial reporting, included in the accompanying [*title of management's report*].

In preparing the financial statements, management is required to evaluate whether there are conditions or events, considered in the aggregate, that raise substantial doubt about ABC Company's ability to continue as a going concern [*insert the time period set by the applicable financial reporting framework*].

Auditor's Responsibilities for the Audits of the Financial Statements and Internal Control Over Financial Reporting

Our objectives are to obtain reasonable assurance about whether the financial statements as a whole are free from material misstatement, whether due to fraud or error, and about whether effective internal control over financial reporting was maintained in all material respects, and to issue an auditor's report that includes our opinions.

Reasonable assurance is a high level of assurance but is not absolute assurance and therefore is not a guarantee that an audit of financial statements or an audit of internal control over financial reporting conducted in accordance with GAAS will always detect a material misstatement or a material weakness when it exists. The risk of not detecting a material misstatement resulting from fraud is higher than for one resulting from error, as fraud may involve collusion, forgery, intentional omissions, misrepresentations, or the override of internal control. Misstatements are considered to be material if there is a substantial likelihood that, individually or in the aggregate, they would influence the judgment made by a reasonable user based on the financial statements.

(continued on next page)

(continued)

In performing an audit of financial statements and an audit of internal control over financial reporting in accordance with GAAS, we:

- Exercise professional judgment and maintain professional skepticism throughout the audits.

- Identify and assess the risks of material misstatement of the financial statements, whether due to fraud or error, and design and perform audit procedures responsive to those risks. Such procedures include examining, on a test basis, evidence regarding the amounts and disclosures in the financial statements.

- Obtain an understanding of internal control relevant to the statement audit in order to design audit procedures that are appropriate in the circumstances.

- Obtain an understanding of internal control over financial re-porting relevant to the audit of internal control over financial reporting, assess the risks that a material weakness exists, and test and evaluate the design and operating effectiveness of internal control over financial reporting based on the assessed risk.

- Evaluate the appropriateness of accounting policies used and the reasonableness of significant accounting estimates made by management, as well as evaluate the overall presentation of the financial statements.

- Conclude whether, in our judgment, there are conditions or events, considered in the aggregate, that raise substantial doubt about ABC Company's ability to continue as a going concern for a reasonable period of time.

We are required to communicate with those charged with governance regarding, among other matters, the planned scope and timing of the audit, significant audit findings, and certain internal control-related matters that we identified during the financial statement audit.

Definition and Inherent Limitations of Internal Control Over Financial Reporting

An entity's internal control over financial reporting is a process effected by those charged with governance, management, and other personnel, designed to provide reasonable assurance regarding the preparation of reliable financial statements in accordance with accounting principles generally accepted in the United States of America. An entity's internal control over financial reporting includes those policies and procedures that (1) pertain to the maintenance of records that, in reasonable detail, accurately and fairly reflect the transactions and dispositions of the assets of the entity; (2) provide reasonable assurance that transactions are recorded as necessary to permit preparation of financial statements in accordance with accounting principles generally accepted in the United States of America, and that receipts and expenditures of the entity are being made only in accordance with authorizations of management and those charged with governance; and (3) provide reasonable assurance regarding prevention, or timely detection and correction of unauthorized acquisition, use, or disposition of the entity's assets that could have a material effect on the financial statements.

Because of its inherent limitations, internal control over financial reporting may not prevent, or detect and correct, misstatements. Also, projections of any assessment of effectiveness to future periods are subject to the risk that controls may become inadequate because of changes in conditions, or that the degree of compliance with the policies or procedures may deteriorate.

Report on Other Legal and Regulatory Requirements

[*The form and content of this section of the auditor's report would vary depending on the nature of the auditor's other reporting responsibilities.*]

[*Signature of the auditor's firm*]
[*City and state where the auditor's report is issued*]
[*Date of the auditor's report*]

2.2 Modified Audit Opinions

2.2.1 Scope Limitation

A scope limitation requires the auditor to disclaim an opinion or to withdraw from the engagement.

2.2.2 Material Weakness

A material weakness requires the auditor to issue an adverse opinion. The adverse opinion should include:

- the definition of material weakness.

- a statement that a material weakness has been identified.

- an identification of the material weakness described in management's own assessment of internal control.

If the material weakness is not included in management's assessment, the report should state this and should include a description of the material weakness.

2.2.3 Absence of Control Deficiencies or Significant Deficiencies

The auditor should not report the absence of control deficiencies or significant deficiencies.

Question 2   MCQ-09861

During an integrated audit, an auditor uncovers one control deficiency in internal control such that there is a reasonable possibility that a material misstatement of the entity's financial statements will not be prevented, or detected and corrected on a timely basis. In this situation, the auditor should issue an opinion on internal control that is:

1. Unmodified
2. Qualified
3. Adverse
4. A disclaimer

---

1 Statements on Standards for Attestation Engagements

Statements on Standards for Attestation Engagements (SSAE) apply to engagements in which a practitioner is engaged to issue, or does issue, an examination, review, or agreed-upon procedures report on subject matter (or an assertion thereon) that is the responsibility of a party other than the practitioner. Independence is required.

1.1 Levels of Reports

There are three levels of reports that may be issued on the assertion or the associated subject matter:

1. Examination (reasonable assurance, with positive opinion, may be assertion-based or direct)

2. Review (limited assurance, with conclusion)

3. Agreed-upon procedures (no assurance, with list of findings)

Report Type			
Attestation Service	*Examination*	*Review*	*Agreed-Upon Procedures*
Agreed-upon procedures			✓
Prospective financial statements	✓		✓
Pro forma financial statements	✓	✓	
Compliance	✓		✓
MD&A	✓	✓	
Service organizations	✓		

Note that preparations and compilations are also allowed for prospective financial statements. However, with the issuance of SSAE 18, preparations and compilations of prospective financial statements are no longer addressed in the attestation standards and are instead governed by the SSARS standards.

2 "Agreed-Upon" Procedures Engagements

The practitioner is engaged to report findings using specific, agreed-upon procedures. Required conditions:

- **I**ndependence of the practitioner.

- **A**greement of parties—the practitioner and the engaging party agree, or will be able to agree, regarding procedures to be performed, the criteria to be used in the determination of findings, and any materiality limits used for reporting.

- **M**easurability and consistency—subject matter should be capable of reasonably consistent measurement, procedures should be expected to result in reasonably consistent findings, and evidential matter to support the report should be expected to exist.

- **S**ufficiency of procedures—the client takes responsibility for the sufficiency of the procedures to be performed to meet the intended purpose of the engagement.

- **U**se of the report can be general or restricted to specified parties.

- **R**esponsibility for subject matter. Either:
  - the client is responsible for (or has a reasonable basis for providing an assertion about) the subject matter; or
  - the client is able to provide evidence of a third party's responsibility for the subject matter.

- **E**ngagements to perform agreed-upon procedures on prospective financial statements.
  - Prospective financial statements must include a summary of significant assumptions.

Question 1   MCQ-14952

Which of the following should a practitioner perform as part of an engagement for agreed-upon procedures in accordance with *Statements on Standards for Attestation Engagements*?

1. Ensure the engagement procedures are comparable to those performed in a compilation.
2. Express a disclaimer of opinion on the subject matter.
3. Express positive assurance on findings of work performed.
4. Disclose responsibility for the sufficiency of procedures.

---

3 Financial Forecasts and Projections

Financial forecasts and projections are prospective financial statements. Allowable engagements for prospective financial statements are preparation, compilation, examination, and agreed-upon procedures. No review engagement is allowed.

Note: SSARS provides guidance for preparations and compilations of financial forecasts and projections. SSAE provides guidance for examinations and agreed-upon procedure engagements of financial forecasts and projections.

3.1 Financial Forecast

Financial forecasts are based on expected conditions and expected courses of action. Financial forecasts are available for general use or may be limited use.

3.1.1 Report on Compilation of a Financial Forecast*

[The responsible party] is responsible for the accompanying financial forecast of XYZ Company, which comprises the forecasted balance sheet as of December 31, 20X2, and the related forecasted statements of income, changes in stockholders' equity, and cash flows for the year then ending, and the related summaries of significant assumptions and accounting policies in accordance with guidelines for the presentation of a financial forecast established by the American Institute of Certified Public Accountants (AICPA). We have performed a compilation engagement in accordance with Statements on Standards for Accounting and Review Services promulgated by the Accounting and Review Services Committee of the AICPA. We did not examine or review the financial forecast nor were we required to perform any procedures to verify the accuracy or completeness of the information provided by management. Accordingly, we do not express an opinion, a conclusion, nor provide any form of assurance on the accompanying financial statements or assumptions.

The forecasted results may not be achieved as there will usually be differences between the forecasted and actual results, because events and circumstances frequently do no occur as expected, and these differences may be material. We have no responsibility to update this report for events and circumstances occurring after the date of this report.

[*Signature of practitioner's firm or accountant, as appropriate*]

[*Practitioner's city and state*]

[*Date of the practitioner's report*]

*With the issuance of SSAE 18, compilations of prospective financial statements are no longer addressed in the attestation standards and are instead governed by AR-C section 80 of the SSARS standards.

3.1.2 Report on Examination of a Financial Forecast

Independent Accountant's Report

[*Appropriate Addressee*]

We have examined the accompanying forecast of XYZ Company, which comprises, the forecasted balance sheet as of December 31, 20XX, and the related forecasted statements of income, stockholders' equity, and cash flows for the year then ending, based on the guidelines for the presentation of a forecast established by the American Institute of Certified Public Accountants. XYZ Company's management is responsible for preparing and presenting the forecast in accordance with the guidelines for the presentation of a forecast established by the American Institute of Certified Public Accountants. Our responsibility is to express an opinion on the forecast based on our examination.

Our examination was conducted in accordance with attestation standards established by the American Institute of Certified Public Accountants. Those standards require that we plan and perform the examination to obtain reasonable assurance about whether the forecast is presented in accordance with the guidelines for the presentation of a forecast established by the American Institute of Certified Public Accountants, in all material respects. An examination involves performing procedures to obtain evidence about the forecast. The nature, timing, and extent of the procedures selected depend on our judgment, including an assessment of the risks of material misstatement of the forecast, whether due to fraud or error. We believe that the evidence we obtained is sufficient and appropriate to provide a reasonable basis for our opinion.

In our opinion, the accompanying forecast is presented, in all material respects, in accordance with the guidelines for the presentation of a forecast established by the American Institute of Certified Public Accountants, and the underlying assumptions are suitably supported and provide a reasonable basis for management's forecast.

There will usually be differences between the forecasted and actual results because events and circumstances frequently do not occur as expected, and those differences may be material. We have no responsibility to update this report for events and circumstances occurring after the date of this report.

[*Practitioner's signature*]

[*Practitioner's city and state*]

[*Date of practitioner's report*]

3.2 Financial Projection

Financial projections are based on hypothetical ("what if") assumptions. Reports on financial projections are restricted use only and cannot be made available for general use.

3.2.1 Report on Compilation of a Financial Projection

The report on the compilation of a financial projection would be similar to the report on the compilation of a financial forecast, except that it would refer to a "financial projection" rather than "financial forecast."

3.2.2 Report on Examination of a Financial Projection

The report on an examination of a financial projection would be similar to the report on the examination of a financial forecast, except it would include a description of the purpose of the projection in the first paragraph, a reference to the hypothetical assumption in the third and fourth paragraphs, and a paragraph restricting the use of the report.

3.3 Prospective Financial Statement (PFS) Summary

General Procedures	Compilation Report*	Examination Report	Agreed-Upon Procedures
Prospective financial statements	Assemble	Evaluate	Apply specific procedures
Responsible party's assumptions	Assemble	Evaluate	Should be included in PFS
Are financial statements and significant assumptions in conformance with AICPA guidelines?	Look for obvious errors	Opinion	Disclaimer
Obtain agreed-upon scope from engaging party	—	—	Prior to report issuance

Reports Include a Statement Regarding:	Compilation Report*	Examination Report	Agreed-Upon Procedures
Identification of PFS	Yes	Yes	Yes
Compliance with AICPA standards	Yes	Yes	Yes
Limitation of scope	Yes	—	Yes
An enumeration of procedures performed	—	—	Yes
A caveat that prospective results may not be achieved	Yes	Yes	Yes
CPA has no responsibility for updating report	Yes	Yes	Yes
Opinion on PFS accordance with AICPA presentation guidelines	—	Yes	—
Limited use of report	Only required for projection	Only required for projection	Only required for projection

*With the issuance of SSAE 18, compilations of prospective financial statements are no longer addressed in the attestation standards and are instead governed by AR-C section 80 of the SSARS standards.

Question 2   MCQ-08129

Which of the following is a prospective financial statement for general use upon which an accountant may appropriately report?

1. Financial projection
2. Partial presentation
3. Pro forma financial statement
4. Financial forecast

---

1 Statements on Standards for Accounting and Review Services

SSARS (Statements on Standards for Accounting and Review Services) are issued by the AICPA Accounting and Review Services Committee. SSARS provide guidance with respect to preparations, compilations, and reviews of financial statements of nonissuers.

1.1 Engagement Letter

- All SSARS engagements require a written understanding with management and, when appropriate, those charged with governance, regarding the services to be performed.

- This engagement letter (or other suitable form of written agreement) should be signed by the accountant or the accountant's firm as well as management or those charged with governance.

1.2 Review Engagements

- Independence is required.

- Each page of the financial statements should be marked, "See accountant's review report."

- Review procedures, consisting principally of inquiry and analytical procedures, should be tailored to the specific engagement. The accountant should determine materiality for the financial statements as a whole in designing procedures and evaluating the results of those procedures.

1.2.1 Inquiry

In a review engagement, inquiries should be made about:

- Matters that have arisen during the course of the review.

- Identification of related parties and transactions and an understanding of the purpose for such transactions.

- Significant, unusual, or complex transactions, events, or matters that affected or may affect the financial statements.

- Material commitments, contractual obligations, or contingencies that affected or may affect the financial statements.

- Material nonmonetary transactions or transactions for no consideration in the financial statements.

- Accounting principles and practices used.

- Procedures for recording, classifying, and summarizing transactions.

- Changes in business or accounting.

- Subsequent events.

- Whether the financial statements have been prepared and fairly presented in accordance with the applicable financial reporting framework, including how management determined accounting estimates are reasonable.

- Actions authorized by stockholders or board of directors.

- Significant transactions near the end of the period.

- The status of uncorrected misstatements from previous engagements.

- Material fraud, suspected fraud, or noncompliance with provisions of the law and regulations.

- Significant journal entries and adjustments.

- Communications from regulatory agencies.

- Litigation, claims, and assessments.

- Entity's ability to continue as a going concern (and, if applicable, management's plans to mitigate the going concern issue).

1.2.2 Analytical Procedures

The accountant should compare current statements with prior statements, compare actual with budgets, and study specific predictable items. The accountant should also compare:

- Financial and relevant nonfinancial information.

- Ratios and indicators with those of other entities in the industry.

- Relationships among elements in the financial statements within the period and with corresponding prior period relationships.

1.2.3 Other Procedures

The accountant should also:

- Obtain an understanding of the client's business.

- Become familiar with the accounting principles used in the client's industry.

- Read the client's financial statements.

- Obtain reports of other accountants who have been engaged to audit or review significant components of the reporting entity.

- Evaluate the adequacy of work performed by other accountants or experts.

- Evaluate the impact of any going concern considerations.

- Remain alert for any related party relationships or transactions not previously disclosed by management.

- Evaluate the impact to review procedures of any matters that may cause the financial statements to be materially misstated. Perform additional procedures as necessary.

- Obtain evidence that the financial statements agree or reconcile with accounting records.

- Obtain a representation letter. Management representations should include:
  - Acknowledgment of responsibility to prevent/detect fraud.
  - Knowledge of any material fraud or suspected fraud.

- Issue a review report.

1.3 Compilation Engagements

- No independence is required and no assurance is expressed. Lack of independence must be disclosed in the compilation report. The accountant is permitted, but not required, to disclose the reason(s) for the lack of independence.

- The CPA presents in the form of financial statements, information that is management's representation.

1.3.1 Procedures

- Obtain knowledge of the client industry's accounting principles practices.

- Obtain an understanding of the client's business.

- Read the financial statements to ensure they are free of obvious clerical errors and obvious mistakes related to GAAP.

- Disclose lack of independence, if applicable.

- Issue a compilation report.

1.4 Preparation Engagements

- A preparation does not provide assurance.

- A preparation is considered a non-attest service, therefore, it does not require a determination of whether the accountant is independent of the entity.

- In a preparation, the CPA prepares financial statements in accordance with a specified financial reporting framework.

- The accountant may prepare financial statements that omit disclosures as long as the financial statements clearly indicate the omission.

1.4.1 Procedures

- Obtain knowledge of the client industry's accounting principles/practices.

- Obtain an understanding of the client's business.

- Prepare the financial statements.

- Ensure a statement on each page at a minimum stating "no assurance is provided." If no such statement can be included, the accountant should issue a disclaimer that makes clear no assurance is provided on the financial statements, perform a compilation engagement, or withdraw from the engagement and inform management of the reasons for the withdrawal. The accountant or accountant's firm name is not required to be included in prepared financial statements.

1.5 Change in Engagement

- If the client wishes to change an audit to a compilation or a review, the accountant should:

  - Inquire about the reasons for the change (e.g., a change in client requirements, a misunderstanding as to the service to be rendered, a scope restriction).

  - Consider the estimated additional cost/effort required to complete the engagement.

■ If the accountant decides that the change in engagement is justified, he/she must comply with standards for a compilation or review and issue an appropriate report.

Question 1   MCQ-04522

Which of the following accounting services may an accountant perform without being required to issue a compilation or review report under Statements on Standards for Accounting and Review Services?

I. Preparing a working trial balance.

II. Preparing standard monthly journal entries.

   1. I only.

   2. II only.

   3. Both I and II.

   4. Neither I nor II.

Question 2   MCQ-09051

Which of the following procedures would most likely be performed during an engagement to compile the financial statements of a nonissuer?

   1. Read the financial statements and consider whether they are appropriate in form and free from obvious material errors.

   2. Perform inquiry and analytical review procedures.

   3. Obtain a representation letter from management.

   4. Send accounts receivable confirmations.

Question 3   MCQ-09789

A client requests to change an engagement from an audit to a review of financial statements. Which of the following is most likely to be considered by the auditor as an acceptable reason for the change?

   1. Management is unwilling to sign the representation letter because management was not present for the entire period covered by the engagement.

   2. Management does not want the auditor to correspond with legal counsel.

   3. The bank the client is obtaining a loan from has changed the assurance required on the financial statements from positive to negative assurance.

   4. Audit procedures might discover that land is materially overstated.

Question 4   MCQ-09788

Before reissuing a compilation report on the financial statements of a nonissuer for the prior year, the predecessor accountant is required to perform all the following procedures, *except* for:

1. Read the financial statements and the report of the current period.

2. Obtain a letter of representation from management.

3. Compare the prior period financial statements with those issued previously and currently.

4. Obtain a letter from the successor accountants.

---

2 Review of Interim Financial Statements

A review of interim financial statements provides a basis for reporting whether the auditor is aware of any needed material modifications to interim financial information for GAAP conformity. Procedures include inquiries, analytical procedures, and other procedures.

2.1 Procedures

- The required procedures are:

  - **U**nderstanding with the client must be established.

  - **L**earn and/or obtain an understanding of the entity and its environment, including its internal control.

  - **I**nquiries should be addressed to appropriate individuals, including the predecessor auditor.

  - **A**nalytical procedures should be performed.

  - **R**eview—other procedures should be performed.

  - **C**lient representation letter should be obtained from management.

  - **P**rofessional judgment should be used to evaluate results.

  - **A**ccountant (CPA) should communicate results.

- In addition to the standard review analysis of aggregated amounts, analytical procedures should be applied to disaggregated revenue data (by month, by product line, etc.).

- The auditor is required to obtain evidence that interim data reconciles to accounting records.

- In addition to the usual representations, the auditor should also obtain management's written representations related to internal controls and fraud.

---

3 Comparison of SSARS and SAS Engagements

	Preparation Engagement	Compilation Engagement	Review Engagement			Audit Engagement
	SSARS	SSARS	SSARS	SAS	PCAOB	SAS/PCAOB
Level of Assurance	None	None	Limited			Reasonable.
Entities	Nonissuers only	Nonissuers only	Nonissuers	Nonissuers: Interim	Issuers: Interim	Nonissuers/Issuers
Knowledge Required	Knowledge of accounting principles and practices of industry; general understanding of client's business	Knowledge of accounting principles and practices of industry; general understanding of client's business	Same as compilation plus increased knowledge of client's business			Extensive knowledge of economy, industry, and client's business
Inquiry and Analytical Procedures Required	None unless information is questionable	None unless information is questionable	Inquiries of internal personnel Analytical procedures			Inquiries of external parties and internal personnel Analytical procedures Audit procedures
GAAP Disclosure Omitted	May omit, but need to disclose in the financial statement	May omit most without restricting use; warn with ending paragraph	All are required or modify review report			All required or "qualified/ adverse" opinion
GAAP Departures	May depart from GAAP, but need to disclose in the financial statement	Modify report to discuss GAAP departure	Modify report to discuss GAAP departure. Modify report "qualified/ adverse" conclusion			Modify report "qualified/ adverse" opinion
Independence	Not required (non-attest engagement)	Not required but disclosure is required	Required			Required
Engagement Letter	Presumptively mandatory	Presumptively mandatory	Presumptively mandatory			Presumptively mandatory
Representation Letter	Not required	Not required	Required			Required
Understanding of Internal Control	Not required (no test work)	Not required (no test work)	Not required (no test work)	Required		Required
Errors and Irregularities Detection	Only obvious errors found when preparing financial statements	Only obvious errors found when reading financial statements	Only errors discovered through inquiry and analytical procedures			Must be designed to provide reasonable assurance of detection of material misstatements
Noncompliance with Laws and Regulations Detection	None, but known acts must be evaluated	None, but known acts must be evaluated	Only direct and material effect, that could be disclosed by inquiry and analytical procedures			Must be designed to reasonably assure detection of direct and material noncompliance with laws and regulations
FS Reported on (BS/IS/RE/CF)	One or more financial statements allowed to be prepared	One or more financial statements allowed to be reported on	One or more financial statements allowed if scope of inquiry and analytical procedures has not been restricted			One or more financial statements allowed if scope of audit is not limited and all necessary procedures are applied
Communication with Predecessor	Not required	Not required	Not required	Required		Required
Subsequent Event Inquiries	Not required	Not required	Required			Required

1 SSARS Review Report

- The review report provides limited assurance (less assurance than is provided by an audit) that the financial statements are prepared in conformity with GAAP (or other appropriate financial reporting framework).

- The accountant should express a modified conclusion (qualified or adverse) when the accountant determines, based on the procedures performed and the review evidence obtained, that the financial statements are materially misstated, or the accountant may withdraw from the engagement.

SSARS Standard Review Report

Independent Accountant's Review Report

[*Appropriate Addressee*]

I (We) have reviewed the accompanying financial statements of XYZ Company, which comprise the balance sheet as of December 31, 20XX, and the related statements of income, changes in stockholders' equity, and cash flows for the year then ended, and the related notes to the financial statements. A review includes primarily applying analytical procedures to management's owners') financial data and making inquiries of company management (owners). A review is substantially less in scope than an audit, the objective of which is the expression of an opinion regarding the financial statements as a whole. Accordingly, I (we) do not express such an opinion.

Management's Responsibility for the Financial Statements

Management (Owners) is (are) responsible for the preparation and fair presentation of these financial statements in accordance with accounting principles generally accepted in the United States of America; this includes the design, implementation, and maintenance of internal control relevant to the preparation and fair presentation of financial statements that are free from material misstatement whether due to fraud or error.

Accountant's Responsibility

My (Our) responsibility is to conduct the review engagement in accordance with Statements on Standards for Accounting and Review Services promulgated by the Accounting and Review Services Committee of the AICPA. Those standards require me (us) to perform procedures to obtain limited assurance as a basis for reporting whether I am (we are) aware of any material modifications that should be made to the financial statements for them to be in accordance with accounting principles generally accepted in the United States of America. I (We) believe that the results of my (our) procedures provide a reasonable basis for my (our) conclusion.

We are required to be independent of XYZ Company and to meet our other ethical responsibilities, in accordance with the relevant ethical requirements related to our review.

Accountant's Conclusion

Based on my (our) review, I am (we are) not aware of any material modifications that should be made to the accompanying financial statements in order for them to be in accordance with accounting principles generally accepted in the United States of America.

[*Signature of accounting firm or accountant, as appropriate*]

[*Accountant's city and state*]

[*Date of the accountant's review report*]

Question 1   MCQ-14950

Financial statements of a nonissuer that have been reviewed by an accountant should be accompanied by a report stating that a review:

1. Provides a basis for expressing an opinion on the financial statements as a whole.

2. Includes examining, on a test basis, information that is the representation of management.

3. Includes primarily applying analytical procedures to management's financial data and making inquiries of company management.

4. Does not contemplate obtaining corroborating audit evidence or applying certain other procedures ordinarily performed during an audit.

2 SSARS Compilation Report

SSARS Compilation Report

Management is responsible for the accompanying financial statements of XYZ Company, which comprise the balance sheets as of December 31, 20X2 and 20X1 and the related statements of income, changes in stockholders' equity, and cash flows for the years then ended, and the related notes to the financial statements in accordance with accounting principles generally accepted in the United States of America. We have performed compilation engagements in accordance with Statements on Standards for Accounting and Review Services promulgated by the Accounting and Review Services Committee of the AICPA. We did not audit or review the financial statements nor were we required to perform any procedures to verify the accuracy or completeness of the information provided by management. Accordingly, we do not express an opinion, a conclusion, nor provide any form of assurance on these financial statements.

[*Signature of accounting firm or accountant*]

[*Accountant's city and state*]

[*Date*]

- GAAP departures should be disclosed in a separate paragraph of the report, or the accountant may withdraw from the engagement.

- If substantially all required disclosures are omitted, the accountants report should clearly indicate this omission.

3 Comparative Reporting

Different services may be provided in different years.

- Increase in level of service—If a service upgrade (from compiled to reviewed) occurs:
  - The prior year report should be updated and issued as the last paragraph of the current period report.

- Decrease in level of service—If a service downgrade (from reviewed to compiled) occurs, three options exist:
  - Issue a compilation report and add a paragraph to the report describing the responsibility for the prior period statements. Include the date of original report, and a statement that no review procedures were performed after that date.
  - Issue two separate reports.
  - Issue a combined report presenting both full reports with an added statement to the review report indicating that no review procedures have since been performed.

- Decrease in level of service—If a service downgrade to a preparation engagement (from reviewed or compiled to preparation) occurs, there is no requirement to reference the prior period service performed.

4 Interim Review Report

- The auditor expresses limited assurance on interim financial information covering the period from the last audit to the date of the interim statements.
- GAAP departures must be disclosed.
- If the auditor determines that the disclosure related to substantial doubt about the entities' ability to continue as a going concern is inadequate, resulting in a departure from the applicable financial reporting framework, the auditor should modify the report.
- For issuers: As long as going concern disclosure is adequate, the auditor is not required to include an explanatory paragraph.
- For nonissuers: Add a separate section in the auditor's report regarding going concern if management has included a statement that substantial doubt exists in its financial statements or (1) a going concern section was included in the prior year audit report, (2) the conditions of going concern still exist at interim, and (3) management's plans do not alleviate the substantial doubt.
- A lack of consistency paragraph is optional if there is adequate disclosure.

Independent Auditor's Review Report

[*Appropriate Addressee*]

Results of Review of Interim Financial Information

We have reviewed the accompanying [*describe the interim financial information or statements reviewed*] of ABC Company and subsidiaries as of September 30, 20X1, and for the three-month and nine-month periods then ended, and the related notes (collectively referred to as the interim financial information).

Based on our review, we are not aware of any material modifications that should be made to the accompanying interim financial information for it to be in accordance with [*identify the applicable financial reporting framework; for example, accounting principles generally accepted in the United States of America*].

Basis for Review Results

We conducted our review in accordance with auditing standards generally accepted in the United States of America (GAAS) applicable to reviews of interim financial information. A review of interim financial information consists principally of applying analytical procedures and making inquiries of persons re-sponsible for financial and accounting matters. A review of interim financial information is substantially less in scope than an audit conducted in accordance with GAAS, the objective of which is an expression of an opinion regarding the financial information as a whole, and accordingly, we do not express such an opinion. We are required to be independent of ABC Company and to meet our other ethical responsibilities in accordance with the relevant ethical requirements relating to our review. We believe that the review procedures provide a reasonable basis for our conclusion.

Responsibilities of Management for the Interim Financial Information

Management is responsible for the preparation and fair presentation of the interim financial information in accordance with [*identify the applicable financial reporting framework; for example, accounting principles generally accepted in the United States of America*] and for the design, implementation, and maintenance of internal control relevant to the preparation and fair presentation of interim financial information that is free from material misstatement, whether due to fraud or error.

[*Signature of the auditor's firm*]
[*City and state where the auditor's report is issued*]
[*Date of the auditor's report*]

1 Other Information in Documents Containing Audited Financial Statements

The auditor must read the information and should try to resolve any material inconsistencies or material misstatements of fact directly with the client. The auditor may issue a disclaimer of opinion, or may be engaged to express an opinion on such information.

Question 1 — MCQ-14953

In its annual report to shareholders, Walsh Co. (a nonissuer) included a letter to shareholders that contained financial summaries of the past two years. Walsh's auditor is expressing an unmodified opinion on Walsh's financial statements but has not been engaged to examine and report on this additional information. What is the auditor's responsibility concerning the financial summaries?

1. The auditor should express a qualified or adverse opinion because all financial statement information should be audited.

2. The auditor should include an emphasis-of-matter paragraph that includes a disclaimer of opinion on this information.

3. The auditor should inquire of management regarding the purpose of the supplementary information and the criteria used to prepare the information.

4. The auditor should read the letter to the shareholders and verify the information is materially consistent with the information presented in the audited financial statements.

2 Reporting on Supplementary Information in Relation to the Financial Statements as a Whole

An auditor may be engaged to report on supplementary information in relation to the financial statements as a whole.

2.1 Engagement Objectives

The auditor has two objectives in such engagements:

- to evaluate the presentation of the supplementary information in relation to the financial statements as a whole; and
- to report whether the supplementary information is fairly stated, in all material respects, in relation to the financial statements as a whole.

2.2 Auditor's Report

The auditor's report on the supplementary information may either be presented:

- in a separate report; or
- in the auditor's report on the financial statements as a separate section with the heading "Supplementary Information" (nonissuer) or as an additional paragraph (issuer).

3 Required Supplementary Information

Limited procedures should be performed. The auditor's report on the financial statements should include a separate section related to the required supplementary information. An opinion is permitted but not required.

Question 2   MCQ-09044

Jorge, CPA, has been asked to audit the financial statements of Capri Industries, which include supplementary information required by generally accepted accounting principles. Which best describes an appropriate response to this situation?

1. Jorge should not accept this engagement, since auditing information outside the basic financial statements goes beyond the scope of an audit.

2. Jorge may accept this engagement, but need not apply procedures specifically to the supplementary information, since it is outside the basic financial statements.

3. Jorge should not accept this engagement unless he is also hired to perform a separate attest engagement on the supplementary information.

4. Jorge may accept this engagement, but would need to perform certain procedures specifically with respect to the supplementary information.

---

4 Reports on Application of the Requirements of an Applicable Financial Reporting Framework

A reporting accountant may report on the application of the requirements of an applicable financial reporting framework to a specific transaction or the type of report that may be rendered on a specific entity's financial statements. The report should be restricted in use.

5 Reporting on Financial Statements Prepared in Accordance With a Financial Reporting Framework Generally Accepted in Another Country

A auditor practicing in the United States may be engaged to report on financial statements that have been prepared in accordance with a financial reporting framework generally accepted in another country that has not been adopted by a body designed by the AICPA to establish generally accepted accounting principles, when such audited financial statements are intended to be used outside the United States.

5.1 Distribution Outside the U.S. Only

Use either the other country's report, the report set out in the ISAs, or a U.S. form report that reflects that the financial statements being reported on have been prepared in accordance with a financial reporting framework generally accepted in another country.

5.2   Distribution Within the U.S.

Use the U.S. form report with an emphasis-of-matter paragraph that identifies the financial reporting framework, refers to the note in the financial statements that describes the framework, and indicates that the framework differs from accounting principles generally accepted in the United States of America.

Question 3	MCQ-09052

Which would most likely determine the appropriate form of audit report when financial statements are prepared in accordance with a financial reporting framework generally accepted in another country?

1. The other country's auditing standards.
2. The geographic location of the company.
3. The expected distribution of the financial statements.
4. The reciprocity agreement between that country and the United States.

1 Government Auditing—Standards and Supplementary Requirements

In performing an audit of government entities, the auditor may be responsible for meeting the requirements of as many as three sources of guidance:

- GAAS
- GAGAS (Generally Accepted Government Auditing Standards, also referred to as the Yellow Book)
- The Single Audit Act (2 CFR 200), which presents supplementary requirements only applicable if the entity spends federal financial assistance in excess of a specific amount.

2 GAAS Requirements for Compliance Audits

2.1 Objectives of Compliance Audits

- Obtain sufficient evidence to form an opinion on whether the entity complied, in all material respects, with the compliance requirements applicable to their programs.
- Report at the level specified in the governmental audit requirement.
- Identify audit and reporting requirements supplementary to GAAS and GAGAS and address those requirements (e.g., Single Audit Act requirements).

2.2 Overall Standards for Compliance Audits

- Perform a risk assessment (audit risk of noncompliance model)
- Design responses to the risk assessment
- Determine if supplementary audit requirements exist
- Obtain written representations from management
- Prepare reports
- Document risk and materiality

2.3 The Audit Risk of Noncompliance Model

The audit risk of noncompliance model adapts the terminology and relationships of the audit risk model. The risk of material noncompliance consists of inherent risk of noncompliance and control risk of noncompliance:

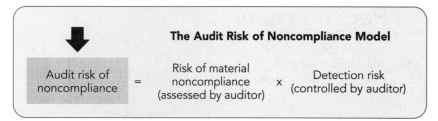

The Audit Risk of Noncompliance Model

Audit risk of noncompliance = Risk of material noncompliance (assessed by auditor) x Detection risk (controlled by auditor)

Risk of Material Noncompliance	Acceptable Level of Detection Risk	Determine "NET" of Testing
High (Bad)	Low	High
Low (Good)	High	Low

2.3.1 Inherent Risk of Noncompliance

The susceptibility of a compliance requirement to noncompliance that could be material assuming that there are no related controls.

- Inherent risk exists independent of the audit.

- The auditor cannot change this risk, but can change his/her assessment of the risk based on evidence gathered during the audit.

2.3.2 Control Risk of Noncompliance

The risk that noncompliance with a compliance requirement that could be material will not be prevented or detected on a timely basis by an entity's internal control over compliance.

- Control risk exists independent of the audit.

- The auditor cannot change this risk, but can change his/her assessment of the risk based on evidence gathered during the audit.

- The stronger the system of controls over compliance, the greater the reliance that may be placed on those controls, and the fewer the tests of details (or the lower the quality) required.

2.3.3   Detection Risk of Noncompliance

The risk that the auditor will not detect noncompliance that exists and that undetected noncompliance could be material.

■ Detection risk relates to the auditor's procedures.

■ The auditor can change this risk by varying the nature, extent, or timing of audit procedures.

■ As the acceptable level of detection risk decreases, the assurance provided from tests of details (including tests of implementation of corrective actions from previous audits) should increase.

2.4   Design Responses to Risk Assessment

■ The auditor should design audit procedures, including tests of details of the entity's compliance with program requirements.

■ The risk assessment, tests of controls, and analytical procedures are not sufficient to address the risk of material noncompliance. Tests of details must be performed.

■ Tests of controls may be required if any one of the following conditions exist:

  • The risk assessment includes an expectation of the operating effectiveness of controls over compliance.

  • Substantive procedures do not provide enough evidence to support a conclusion.

  • Tests of controls are required by the applicable governmental audit requirements.

2.5   Determine if Supplementary Audit Requirements Exist

■ The entity may have audit requirements that go beyond GAAS and GAGAS. The auditor must make that determination.

■ A common example of supplementary audit requirements is the Single Audit requirements related to federal financial assistance described below.

2.6   Obtain a Written Management Representation Letter

Auditors must obtain a written management representation letter that includes statements that management:

■ takes responsibility for compliance.

■ takes responsibility for maintaining controls over compliance.

■ asserts that they have disclosed all programs to the auditor.

■ asserts that they have disclosed any known noncompliance or states that no such noncompliance exists.

2.7 Prepare Reports

The auditor may report in several ways, depending on the audit requirement. Possible reports include a(n):

- Opinion on compliance
- Report on internal control over compliance
- Combined report on compliance and internal control over compliance

2.8 Document Risk and Materiality

The auditor is responsible for documenting the following:

- The assessed risk of material noncompliance
- Responses to the risk assessment
- Materiality levels

3 Government Auditing Standards (GAGAS)

3.1 GAGAS: Source and Content Organization

- GAGAS are contained in the Government Auditing Standards, a publication of the Government Accountability Office (GAO) The publication is sometimes called the Yellow Book.
- Generally Accepted Government Auditing Standards (GAGAS) include ethical principles, general standards, standards for financial audits and attest engagements, and field work and reporting standards for performance audits.

3.2 Ethical Principles

The ethical principles that guide the work of auditors who conduct audits in accordance with GAGAS are:

- serving the public interest;
- integrity;
- objectivity;
- proper use of government information, resources, and positions; and
- professional behavior.

3.3 General Standards

The general standards provide guidance for performing financial audits, attestation engagements, and performance audits under GAGAS. The general standards include:

- independence (of mind and appearance);

- professional judgment;

- competence; and

- quality control and assurance (including maintenance of a quality control system and securing an external peer review at least once every three years).

3.4 Standards for Financial Audits: Additional GAGAS Requirements for Performing Financial Audits

- GAGAS describes a number of standards for financial audits in addition to the GAAS requirements.

- Additional standards include consideration of previous audits and attestation engagements, additional attention to fraud and noncompliance and abuse, development of findings to be reported to the entity and others, and audit documentation that provides evidence of supervision, supports findings, and describes the impact of departures from GAGAS.

3.5 Standards for Financial Audits: Additional GAGAS Requirements for Reporting on Financial Audits

- Auditors should include a statement in the auditor's report that they complied with GAGAS.

- Reporting should include a report on internal control over financial reporting and a report on compliance with provisions of laws, regulations, contracts or grant agreements that have a material effect on the financial statements.

- Auditors must report fraud and noncompliance with laws or regulations that have a material effect on the financial statements, noncompliance with provisions of contracts or grant agreements that have a material effect on the financial statements, and report abuse that is material either quantitatively or qualitatively.

- Auditors should report directly to outside parties when entity management fails to satisfy legal or regulatory requirements to report or when an entity's management fails to take time and appropriate steps to respond to known or likely fraud, noncompliance, or abuse.

- Auditors must report their findings and also solicit and report the views of responsible officials along with any planned corrective actions.

- GAGAS auditors should consider reducing materiality thresholds in response to public accountability issues, various legal and regulatory requirements, and the visibility and sensitivity of government programs.

- GAGAS auditors should consider reporting deficiencies early when the urgency or significance of findings requires faster corrective actions or follow-up or when ongoing noncompliance undetected by management should be stopped.

3.6 Reporting Standards and Requirements

3.6.1 Reporting on Compliance

When reporting on compliance under GAGAS, the report should include the following components:

- A statement that the audit complied with GAAS as well as GAGAS for financial audits.
- A report that states the auditor performed tests of compliance with provisions of laws, regulations, contracts, and grant agreements.
- Identification of noncompliance issues discovered during the audit.

3.6.2 Reporting on Internal Control

When reporting on internal control under GAGAS, the report should include the following components:

- A statement that the audit complied with GAAS as well as GAGAS for financial audits.
- The auditor asserts that internal control over financial reporting was considered as part of planning and performing the audit of the financial statements, but not for the purpose of expressing an opinion on internal control. The internal control reporting requirement under GAGAS differs from the objective of an audit of internal control (as part of an integrated audit).

  (*Note*: An integrated audit is not required for nonissuers under SAS. A nonissuer may engage an auditor to perform a financial statement audit only. In a financial statement audit only under SAS, an auditor will report on internal control only if deficiencies are discovered during the financial statement audit.)

  - An audit of internal control (as part of an integrated audit) requires the auditor to provide a high level of assurance about internal control over financial reporting in the form of an opinion.
  - GAGAS does not require the auditor to render an opinion on the effectiveness of internal control over financial reporting. However, the auditor is not precluded from rendering an opinion on internal control if sufficient procedures have been performed.

- A statement that no opinion is expressed on internal control.
- The definition of deficiency in internal control and material weakness in internal control.
- A description of identified material weakness and significant deficiencies in internal control.
- A statement that no material weaknesses were found if none were found.

3.6.3 Reporting Noncompliance

Material instances of noncompliance should be reported in a separate communication to the entity and should be noted in the auditor's report.

- Material instances are defined as:
  - failure to follow requirements; or
  - violations of rules contained in statutes, regulations, contracts, or grants.
- Reporting illegal acts is required.

Question 1   MCQ-08825

Reporting standards associated with government audits include requirements in addition to those associated with generally accepted auditing standards. A requirement that distinguishes audits performed in accordance with government auditing standards from audits that are not subject to these standards is:

1. An opinion on the financial statements taken as a whole.

2. A written communication of the auditor's work on internal control.

3. An opinion on internal control over financial reporting.

4. No opinion on the financial statements is required.

---

4 Single Audit Act (2 CFR 200) Requirements

4.1 Criteria

- The Single Audit Act applies to entities that receive and spend total financial awards equal to or in excess of $750,000 in a fiscal year.

- The Single Audit Act allows for either a single audit that covers the entire entity, or program specific audits associated with an individual award. Program-specific audits are only available to grant recipients who only have one federal program and who are not required to have a financial statement audit.

4.2 Materiality Determinations

- Materiality of a transaction or other compliance finding is considered separately in relation to each major program, not just in relation to the financial statement as a whole.

- Programs classified as major are generally those that expend $750,000 or more in federal financial assistance. Smaller programs may be classified as major if they are deemed to be high risk.

Question 2   MCQ-09027

The requirements to perform a Single Audit under the provisions of 2 CFR 200 apply to entities that:

1. Receive $500,000 in federal financial assistance in a fiscal year.

2. Receive $750,000 in federal financial assistance in a fiscal year.

3. Receive and expend $500,000 in federal financial assistance in a fiscal year.

4. Receive and expend $750,000 in federal financial assistance in fiscal year.

---

5 GAAS, GAGAS, and SAA: Comparison of Reports

Single Audit Act (2 CFR 200)—

Required reports based on federal programs

1. Compliance (opinion)

2. Internal control over compliance applicable to each major program (report—no opinion)

3. Schedule of findings and questioned costs

GAGAS—

Required reports based on the financial statements

1. Compliance (report—no opinion)

2. Internal control over financial reporting (report—no opinion)

GAAS—

1. Opinion on all financial statements

Question 3   MCQ-04636

A government audit may extend beyond an examination leading to the expression of an opinion on the fairness of financial presentation to include:

	Program Results	Compliance	Economy & Efficiency
1.	Yes	Yes	No
2.	Yes	Yes	Yes
3.	No	Yes	Yes
4.	Yes	No	Yes

1 Special Purpose Frameworks

1.1 Types of Special Purpose Frameworks

Special purpose frameworks include:

- Cash basis.

- Income tax basis.

- Basis required by regulatory agency.

- Basis required by contract.

- Any other basis of accounting that uses a definite set of logical, reasonable criteria that is applied to all material items appearing in the financial statements.

1.2 Report on Special Purpose Frameworks

1.2.1 Report Elements

- Use non-GAAP titles for financial statements.

- Add an emphasis-of-matter paragraph that indicates that the financial statements are prepared using a special purpose framework; states that the basis of presentation is different than GAAP; refers the reader to the related disclosure; and when required, states that the financial statements may not be suitable for any purpose other than the stated purpose.

- Add an other-matter paragraph that restricts the use of the report if the financial statements are prepared using a contractual or regulatory basis, or another basis of accounting that uses a definite set of logical, reasonable criteria, unless the financial statements are regulatory basis financial statements intended for general use.

- If the special purpose financial statements are prepared in accordance with a regulatory basis and intended for general use, the auditor should express an opinion about whether the financial statements are:

  - fairly presented, in all material respects, in accordance with GAAP.

  - prepared in accordance with the special purpose framework.

1.2.2 Sample Auditor's Report on Financial Statements Prepared in Accordance With a Special Purpose Framework (Cash Basis)

Independent Auditor's Report

[*Appropriate Addressee*]

Report on the Audit of Financial Statements

Opinion

We have audited the financial statements of ABC Partnership, which comprise the statement of assets and liabilities arising from cash transactions as of December 31, 20X1, and the related statement of revenue collected and expenses paid for the year then ended, and the related notes to the financial statements.

In our opinion, the accompanying financial statements present fairly, in all material respects, the assets and liabilities arising from cash transactions of ABC Partnership as of December 31, 20X1, and its revenue collected and expenses paid during the year then ended in accordance with the cash basis of accounting described in Note X.

Basis for Opinion

We conducted our audit in accordance with auditing standards generally accepted in the United States of America (GAAS). Our responsibilities under those standards are further described in the Auditor's Responsibilities for the Audit of the Financial Statements section of our report. We are required to be independent of ABC Partnership, and to meet our other ethical responsibilities, in accordance with the relevant ethical requirements relating to our audit. We believe that the audit evidence we have obtained is sufficient and appropriate to provide a basis for our audit opinion.

Emphasis of Matter—Basis of Accounting

We draw attention to Note X of the financial statements, which describes the basis of accounting. The financial statements are prepared on the cash basis of accounting, which is a basis of accounting other than accounting principles generally accepted in the United States of America. Our opinion is not modified with respect to this matter.

Responsibilities of Management for the Financial Statements

Management is responsible for the preparation and fair presentation of the financial statements in accordance with the cash basis of accounting described in Note X, and for determining that the cash basis of accounting is an acceptable basis for the preparation of the financial statements in the circumstances. Management is also responsible for the design, implementation, and maintenance of internal control relevant to the preparation and fair presentation of financial statements that are free from material misstatement, whether due to fraud or error.

Auditor's Responsibilities for the Audit of the Financial Statements

Our objectives are to obtain reasonable assurance about whether the financial statements as a whole are free from material misstatement, whether due to fraud or error, and to issue an auditor's report that includes our opinion. Reasonable assurance is a high level of assurance but is not absolute assurance and therefore is not a guarantee that an audit conducted in accordance with GAAS will always detect a material misstatement when it exists. The risk of not detecting a material misstatement resulting from fraud is higher than for one resulting from error, as fraud may involve collusion, forgery, intentional omissions, misrepresentations, or the override of internal control. Misstatements are considered material if there is a substantial likelihood that, individually or in the aggregate, they would influence the judgment made by a reasonable user based on the financial statements.

(continued on next page)

(continued)

In performing an audit in accordance with GAAS, we:

- Exercise professional judgment and maintain professional skepticism throughout the audit.

- Identify and assess the risks of material misstatement of the financial statements, whether due to fraud or error, and design and perform audit procedures responsive to those risks. Such procedures include examining, on a test basis, evidence regarding the amounts and disclosures in the financial statements.

- Obtain an understanding of internal control relevant to the audit in order to design audit procedures that are appropriate in the circumstances, but not for the purpose of expressing an opinion on the effectiveness of ABC Partnership's internal control. Accordingly, no such opinion is expressed.

- Evaluate the appropriateness of accounting policies used and the reasonableness of significant accounting estimates made by management, as well as evaluate the overall presentation of the financial statements.

- Conclude whether, in our judgment, there are conditions or events, considered in the aggregate, that raise substantial doubt about ABC Partnership's ability to continue as a going concern for a reasonable period of time.

We are required to communicate with those charged with governance regarding, among other matters, the planned scope and timing of the audit, significant audit findings, and certain internal control-related matters that we identified during the audit.

Report on Other Legal and Regulatory Requirements

[*The form and content of this section of the auditor's report would vary depending on the nature of the auditor's other reporting responsibilities.*]

[*Signature of the auditor's firm*]
[*City and state where the auditor's report is issued*]
[*Date of the auditor's report*]

Question 1   MCQ-09779

An auditor's report should include a restricted use paragraph and an alert to readers about the preparation of the financial statements in accordance with a special purpose framework when the financial statements are prepared on the:

1. Cash basis.
2. Contractual basis.
3. IFRS basis.
4. Tax basis.

2 Compliance With Contractual or Regulatory Requirements Related to Audited Financial Statements

2.1 Negative Assurance

The auditor issues negative assurance on compliance in the form of a statement that nothing came to the auditor's attention that caused the auditor to believe that the entity failed to comply with the specified aspects of the contractual agreement or regulatory requirement.

2.2 Report on Compliance

The report on compliance should be in writing and may either be a separate report or provided in one or more paragraphs in the auditor's report on the financial statements.

2.2.1 Separate Report on Compliance

Independent Auditor's Report

[Appropriate Addressee]

We have audited, in accordance with auditing standards generally accepted in the United States of America, the financial statements of XYZ Company, which comprise the balance sheet as of December 31, 20X2, and the related statements of income, changes in stockholders' equity, and cash flows for the year then ended, and the related notes to the financial statements, and have issued our report thereon dated February 16, 20X3.

In connection with our audit, nothing came to our attention that caused us to believe that XYZ Company failed to comply with the terms, covenants, provisions, or conditions of sections XX to YY inclusive, of the Indenture dated July 21, 20X0, with ABC Bank, insofar as they relate to accounting matters. However, our audit was not directed primarily toward obtaining knowledge of such noncompliance. Accordingly, had we performed additional procedures, other matters may have come to our attention regarding the Company's noncompliance with the above-referenced terms, covenants, provisions, or conditions of the Indenture, insofar as they relate to accounting matters.

This report is intended solely for the information and use of the boards of directors and management of XYZ Company and ABC Bank and is not intended to be and should not be used by anyone other than these specified parties.

[Auditor's signature]
[Auditor's city and state]
[Date of the auditor's report]

Question 2 · MCQ-09782

Which of the following reports requires restricted use language in the report?

1. A report on financial statements prepared on the tax basis of accounting.

2. A report on a client's compliance with a contractual agreement, assuming the report is prepared in connection with a financial statement audit of the complete financial statements.

3. A report on the balance sheet only.

4. A report on an examination of a financial forecast.

Class Question Explanations

Auditing Final Review

Topic A

QUESTION 1   MCQ-09795

Choice "4" is correct.

Intentional manipulation of accounting records indicates that management lacks integrity, and as a result, the auditor most likely would conclude that a financial statement audit cannot be performed.

Choice "1" is incorrect. The auditor can accept the engagement even if the auditor does not have experience in the particular industry. However, the auditor should obtain an understanding of the client's business and industry (e.g., by reading appropriate publications) after acceptance of the engagement.

Choice "2" is incorrect. A restriction imposed by circumstances beyond the control of management, such as a hurricane, does not prevent an auditor from accepting an engagement. Additionally, the auditor may be able to perform alternative procedures.

Choice "3" is incorrect. A management-imposed restriction that the auditor believes will result in a qualified opinion does not prevent an auditor from accepting an engagement. However, if the auditor believed the management imposed scope limitation would result in a disclaimer of opinion, then the auditor might conclude that a financial statement audit cannot be performed.

Topic B

QUESTION 1   MCQ-09796

Choice "3" is correct.

A successor auditor's inquiries of the predecessor auditor should include questions regarding communications to management and those charged with governance regarding significant deficiencies (and material weaknesses) in internal control.

Choice "1" is incorrect. The successor auditor generally would not inquire about the number of personnel assigned to the predecessor's engagement.

Choice "2" is incorrect. The successor auditor is responsible for making his or her own judgments regarding the audit, and would not typically inquire regarding the predecessor auditor's judgments with respect to the internal audit function.

Choice "4" is incorrect. The successor auditor generally would not specifically inquire about the response rate for confirmations of accounts receivable. However, the successor auditor would be able to obtain this information when reviewing the predecessor's workpapers.

Auditing I

Topic C

QUESTION 1

Choice "2" is correct.

The engagement letter should include a statement regarding the inherent limitations of the audit. This inherent limitation statement describes the unavoidable risk that some material misstatements may not be detected, even though the audit is properly planned and performed in accordance with GAAS.

Choice "1" is incorrect. The engagement letter generally would not describe the advantages of statistical sampling.

Choice "3" is incorrect. An auditor may not be paid in stock of the entity because this would impair the auditor's independence.

Choice "4" is incorrect. The assessment of risk of material misstatement is not included in the engagement letter. The risk of material misstatement is part of the planning process that occurs after engagement acceptance.

Topic D

QUESTION 1

Choice "4" is correct.

According to PCAOB standards, audit documentation must be retained for seven years.

Choices "1", "2", and "3" are incorrect, per the above explanation.

QUESTION 2

Choice "3" is correct.

Audit documentation should show who performed the work and the date the work was completed.

Choice "1" is incorrect. Audit documentation should be prepared in enough detail so that an experienced auditor, not necessarily a new staff auditor, who has no previous connection with the audit can understand the conclusions reached and any significant judgments made to reach those conclusions.

Choice "2" is incorrect. Audit documentation should enable quality performance reviews and inspections to be performed on the specific audit but does not necessarily by itself "monitor" the effectiveness of the CPA firm's quality control activities. Monitoring is performed at the firm level, not at the individual audit engagement level.

Choice "4" is incorrect. The auditor's understanding of internal control can be documented in a variety of different ways. There is no requirement in professional standards that the design and implementation of internal control must include a flowchart depicting the internal control process.

Topic E

QUESTION 1   MCQ-09062

Choice "2" is correct.

The communication must include material misstatements discovered, even if corrected by management.

Choice "1" is incorrect because while communication to management is allowed, it is not required.

Choice "3" is incorrect because disagreements with management, as well as the other required disclosures, should be communicated in writing when in the auditor's professional judgment, oral communication would be inadequate. Therefore, oral communication of such matters is not entirely precluded.

Choice "4" is incorrect because frequently recurring immaterial misstatements may be communicated if they indicate a particular bias in the preparation of the financial statement.

Topic F

QUESTION 1   MCQ-09061

Choice "2" is correct.

Significant deficiencies and material weaknesses must be communicated in writing to management and those charged with governance. The auditor is required to define and separately identify significant deficiencies and material weaknesses.

Choice "1" is incorrect. Significant deficiencies and material weaknesses must be communicated in writing to management and those charged with governance.

Choice "3" is incorrect. The auditor is not required to obtain a management response to significant deficiencies or material weaknesses.

Choice "4" is incorrect. The auditor is required to define and separately identify significant deficiencies and material weaknesses.

Auditing I

Topic G

QUESTION 1 MCQ-09616

Choice "3" is correct.

Independence is impaired when a close family member of a covered person is employed by the client in an accounting or financial reporting role. Employment in the customer service department is not an accounting or financial reporting role and therefore the wife's employment at Warehouse Company would not impair independence.

Choice "1" is incorrect. Independence is impaired if any covered person, including the lead partner, serves on the client's board of directors.

Choice "2" is incorrect. Independence is impaired if the accounting firm employs a former employee of the audit client and the individual participates in an audit related to the period in which the individual was employed by the client. In this case, the former controller worked for Warehouse during Year 10 and therefore should not participate in the audit of Warehouse's Year 10 financial statements.

Choice "4" is incorrect. Independence is impaired when a former member of the audit engagement team is employed by an issuer client in a financial oversight role during the one-year preceding the commencement of audit procedures. In this case, Smith and Company cannot audit Warehouse's Year 10 financial statements because the former engagement manager was employed by Warehouse as the CFO during Year 10.

QUESTION 2 MCQ-09477

Choice "3" is correct.

Under the Independence Rule of the Code of Conduct, independence is impaired if there is a direct financial interest in an audit client regardless of materiality.

Choices "1", "2", and "4" are incorrect because materiality would be important in considering their effects.

QUESTION 3 MCQ-09589

Choice "2" is correct.

The Sarbanes-Oxley Act of 2002 requires registered firms to maintain audit documentation for seven years, not five years.

Choice "1" is incorrect. The Sarbanes-Oxley Act prohibits auditors from performing certain non-audit services, including internal control outsourcing, for audit clients who are issuers.

Choice "3" is incorrect. The Sarbanes-Oxley Act requires the lead and reviewing partners to rotate off the audit engagement after five years.

Choice "4" is incorrect. The Sarbanes-Oxley Act requires the preapproval of tax services to be provided to audit clients.

QUESTION 4   MCQ-09603

Choice "1" is correct.

Under Department of Labor (DOL) rules, independence is not impaired when an actuary associated with the audit firm provides services to the benefit plan.

Choice "2" is incorrect. Under DOL rules, auditor independence is impaired by direct or material indirect interests in the benefit plan or the plan sponsor.

Choice "3" is incorrect. Under DOL rules, independence is impaired if a member of the audit firm maintains the financial records of the benefit plan.

Choice "4" is incorrect. Under DOL rules, independence is impaired if a member of the engagement team serves on the board of directors of the plan sponsor.

Topic H

QUESTION 1   MCQ-09056

Choice "2" is correct.

A system of quality control should include human resource policies and practices, such as recruitment and hiring, determining capabilities and competencies, assigning personnel to engagements, professional development, and performance evaluation, compensation and advancement.

Choice "1" is incorrect. A CPA firm is required to adopt a system of quality control for its auditing, attestation, and accounting and review services.

Choice "3" is incorrect. A system of quality control should be designed, implemented, and maintained to improve the overall conduct of the firm's professional practice; however, this does not necessarily improve audit efficiency.

Choice "4" is incorrect. While an effective system of quality control is conducive to complying with generally accepted auditing standards, it does not necessarily ensure that such standards are followed on every individual audit engagement.

Auditing II

Topic A

QUESTION 1   MCQ-09804

Choice "3" is correct.

Performing inquiries of outside legal counsel regarding pending litigation would not be performed during the planning stage.

Choice "1" is incorrect. Audit planning includes determining the timing of testing.

Choice "2" is incorrect. During the planning stage, the auditor engages in several information gathering activities to obtain knowledge of the client's business, which may include touring the client's facilities.

Choice "4" is incorrect. During the planning stage, the auditor will determine the effect of information technology on the audit because this will help determine the extent of testing.

QUESTION 2   MCQ-09072

Choice "2" is correct.

In an audit conducted in accordance with GAAS, the auditor must document the audit plan, setting forth in detail the procedures necessary to complete the engagement's objectives.

Choices "1" and "4" are incorrect. Documentation of the auditor's understanding of the client's internal control is required, but may take different forms: a narrative, an internal control questionnaire, a flowchart, or simply a memorandum (for a small client) may be sufficient.

Choice "3" is incorrect. A planning memo, while recommended, is not required under GAAS.

Topic B

QUESTION 1   MCQ-09071

Choice "2" is correct.

A lack of physical controls over the safeguarding of assets implies that internal controls are inadequate. Inherent limitations do not relate to controls that are missing or nonexistent, but rather to reasons why internal controls cannot provide absolute assurance.

Choice "1" is incorrect. A programming error in the design of an automated control is a human error. The fact that we cannot completely eliminate human error is one of the inherent limitations of internal control.

Choice "3" is incorrect. Management override of internal control is an inherent limitation of internal control.

Choice "4" is incorrect. Deliberate circumvention of controls by collusion among two or more people is an inherent limitation of internal control.

QUESTION 2   MCQ-09054

Choice "1" is correct.

While obtaining an understanding of internal control, the auditor is required to obtain an understanding of the design of controls and determine whether they have been implemented. The auditor is not required to evaluate the operating effectiveness of controls, but may choose to do so if it is efficient.

Choice "2" is incorrect. The auditor is not required to evaluate the operating effectiveness of controls while obtaining an understanding of internal control.

Choice "3" is incorrect. The auditor may choose to evaluate the operating effectiveness of controls while obtaining an understanding of internal control, if it is efficient to do so.

Choice "4" is incorrect. While obtaining an understanding of internal control, the auditor is required to obtain an understanding of the design of controls and determine whether they have been implemented.

QUESTION 3   MCQ-08111

Choice "1" is correct.

There are two types of reports on the processing of transactions by service organizations: "reports on controls placed in operation" and "reports on controls placed in operation and tests of operating effectiveness." The former do not include tests of operating effectiveness and, therefore, are not intended to provide the user auditor with a basis for reducing the assessment of control risk below the maximum. Accordingly, such reports should include a disclaimer of opinion regarding the operating effectiveness of the controls.

Choice "2" is incorrect because the report should contain an indication that the controls were suitably designed to achieve specified control objectives, but it does not provide any assurance regarding the achievement of the user organization's (in this case, the retailer's) objectives.

Choice "3" is incorrect because the service auditor (Cook) is not required to identify the service organization's (i.e., PDC's) controls relevant to specific financial statement assertions, because this is not a financial statement audit.

Choice "4" is incorrect because the service auditor (Cook) is not required to disclose the assessed level of control risk for the service organization (PDC).

QUESTION 4   MCQ-04383

Choice "3" is correct.

Test data allows the auditor to determine whether adequate controls exist over data processing. Test data consists of fictitious entries or inputs that are processed through the client's computer system under the control of the auditor. The client's computerized payroll system should have adequate controls to prevent input of invalid employee I.D. numbers.

Choices "1", "2", and "4" are incorrect because these controls do not involve the client's computer system and therefore cannot be tested using test data.

Auditing Final Review

Auditing II

QUESTION 5
MCQ-08126

Choice "2" is correct.

Test data consists of "dummy" data run through the client's computer system. The data should be processed under the auditor's control.

Choice "1" is incorrect because only transactions that the auditor wishes to test must be used.

Choice "3" is incorrect because while the auditor will frequently use many valid and invalid conditions, it is not feasible to test every possible valid and invalid condition using a test data approach.

Choice "4" is incorrect because the objective of the test data approach is to test programs that the client uses to process data. Using different programs defeats the primary purpose of the test.

Topic C

QUESTION 1
MCQ-09030

Choice "3" is correct.

The auditor must obtain reasonable assurance about whether the financial statements are free of material misstatements, whether caused by error or fraud.

Choices "1", "2", and "4" are incorrect, based on the above explanation.

QUESTION 2
MCQ-09037

Choice "2" is correct.

Although the risk of material misstatement due to fraud may be greatest when all three fraud risk factors are observed, the inability to observe any or all of these conditions does not imply that there is no fraud risk.

Choice "1" is incorrect. Fraud risk factors include incentives/pressures, opportunity, and rationalization.

Choice "3" is incorrect. Although the risk of material misstatement due to fraud may be greatest when all three fraud risk factors are observed, the existence of all three risk factors is not an absolute indication of fraud.

Choice "4" is incorrect. It is true that fraud risk factors are often present in circumstances where fraud has occurred.

QUESTION 3
MCQ-09818

Choice "1" is correct.

The auditor provides reasonable, not absolute, assurance that the material misstatements are free from error, whether due to error or fraud.

Choice "2", "3", and "4" are all required documentation regarding the required fraud brainstorming session.

Topic D

QUESTION 1

Choice "1" is correct.

The auditor would initially have planned the audit to achieve a low level of audit risk. If the risk of material misstatement increased, the auditor would need to reduce detection risk to achieve the same low level of audit risk as initially planned.

Choice "2" is incorrect. The increase in the risk of material misstatement results in an increase in overall audit risk. Increasing detection risk would only exacerbate this problem by increasing audit risk even further.

Choice "3" is incorrect. If the auditor does not modify the desired level of detection risk, it is true that the overall level of audit risk will increase, but this is not the most likely situation. An auditor who discovers a higher risk than initially anticipated would need to develop an appropriate response to offset this increase in risk, so that an overall low level of audit risk could still be attained.

Choice "4" is incorrect. Assuming that the auditor had already planned the audit to achieve an appropriately low level of audit risk, the auditor would most likely revise audit procedures in an attempt to achieve the same low level of audit risk as initially planned. Although it is possible that the auditor would reduce detection risk enough to actually lower overall audit risk, this is not the most likely response to the scenario described.

QUESTION 2

Choice "4" is correct.

As the acceptable level of detection risk increases, the assurance that must be provided by substantive tests can decrease. Therefore, the auditor may reduce the sample size.

Choice "1" is incorrect. As the acceptable level of detection risk increases, the level of assurance required from substantive tests decreases. Changing the nature of substantive tests from a less effective to a more effective procedure provides more assurance and is more likely to result from a decrease (not increase) in detection risk.

Choice "2" is incorrect. As the acceptable level of detection risk increases, the assurance that must be provided by substantive tests can decrease. Changing the timing of substantive tests from interim to year-end provides more assurance and is more likely to result from a decrease (not increase) in detection risk.

Choice "3" is incorrect. Although inherent risk affects the level of detection risk, detection risk does not affect the level of inherent risk. Inherent risk exists independently of the audit.

QUESTION 3

Choice "3" is correct.

Analytical procedures used in planning the audit should focus on enhancing the auditor's understanding of the client's business and the transactions and events that have occurred since the last audit date.

Choice "1" is incorrect. Analytical procedures used in planning do not reduce tests of controls or substantive tests.

Choice "2" is incorrect. Analytical procedures used in planning are not designed to identify material misstatements.

Choice "4" is incorrect. Audit evidence has not yet been gathered during the planning process, so its adequacy cannot be assessed.

Auditing II

QUESTION 4

Choice "3" is correct.

The required risk assessment discussion should include consideration of the risk of management override of controls.

Choice "1" is incorrect. The discussion about the susceptibility of the entity's financial statements to material misstatement may be held concurrently from the discussion about the susceptibility of the entity's financial statements to fraud.

Choice "2" is incorrect. The discussion must involve all "key" members who participate on the audit team, including the engagement partner.

Choice "4" is incorrect. The risk assessment discussion is required to occur at the start of the audit, during the planning phase.

Topic E

QUESTION 1

Choice "2" is correct.

The occurrence assertion addresses whether recorded entries are valid. The direction of this test is from the recorded entry in the voucher register to the supporting documents.

Choice "1" is incorrect. Completeness addresses whether all transactions and events are included, and would involve tracing from support for purchases to the recorded entry.

Choices "3" and "4" are incorrect. Tracing from the voucher register to supporting documents provides only limited evidence about allocation and valuation, or about rights and obligations.

QUESTION 2

Choice "1" is correct.

Tracing from source documents (evidence of shipments) to the accounting records (sales journal) provides evidence of completeness. If the auditor finds a shipment that was not recorded, this would indicate a lack of completeness of sales.

Choice "2" is incorrect. Accounts receivable turnover may vary from year to year based on changes in the level of credit sales and receivables. With more than one factor affecting this ratio, however, it is not the most likely means of detecting an understatement in sales.

Choice "3" is incorrect. Using common size analysis, total revenue is set at 100 percent for each company. Comparison of common size financial statements would not be useful in trying to identify understatements in credit sales.

Choice "4" is incorrect. If an audit test starts with a selection of *recorded* sales, unrecorded sales will not be discovered by this test.

QUESTION 3 MCQ-09806

Choice "2" is correct.

The auditor is not required to evaluate operating effectiveness as part of understanding internal control, and therefore, need not document the basis for this decision.

Choice "1" is incorrect. A written audit plan setting forth the procedures necessary to accomplish the audit objectives is required to be documented.

Choice "3" is incorrect. An auditor should document key elements of the understanding of the entity and its environment, including each of the five components of internal control. The five components include the entity's control activities.

Choice "4" is incorrect. The assessment of the risks of material misstatement at both the financial statement and relevant assertion levels are required to be documented.

Topic F

QUESTION 1 MCQ-09865

Choice "4" is correct.

An increase in level of supervision represents an appropriate overall response to an increase in financial statement level risk.

Choice "1" is incorrect. An appropriate overall response to an increase in financial statement level risk is to incorporate a greater level of unpredictability into the audit. Informing management of the specific details of substantive procedures would make the audit more predictable.

Choice "2" is incorrect. Testing of controls in a financial statement audit is performed when the auditor's risk assessment is based on the assumption that the controls are operating effectively or when substantive procedures alone are insufficient.

Choice "3" is incorrect. An auditor most likely would perform tests at period end, rather than interim, because it provides greater assurance.

QUESTION 2 MCQ-08320

Choice "4" is correct.

Using a combined approach involves identifying specific internal controls relevant to specific assertions that are likely to prevent or detect material misstatements in those assertions. If those controls are found to be operating effectively, substantive testing can be reduced.

Choice "1" is incorrect. Using a combined approach would most likely lead to less extensive substantive tests with smaller sample sizes.

Choice "2" is incorrect. A combined approach is based on the relationship between the operating effectiveness of controls and the required level of substantive testing. The level of inherent risk is not part of this evaluation.

Choice "3" is incorrect. Substantive tests performed at year-end would be more consistent with a substantive approach, which would require more competent substantive testing to be performed.

Auditing Final Review **CQ-13**

Auditing II

Topic G

QUESTION 1

Choice "3" is correct.

The client's release of quarterly results before the SEC-prescribed deadline would not result in the auditor reevaluating established materiality levels.

Choice "1" is incorrect. If the materiality level was established initially based on preliminary financial statement amounts and those amounts differ significantly from actual amounts, then this would be a circumstance that would require the auditor to reevaluate the established materiality levels.

Choice "2" is incorrect. A situation that would require reevaluation of established materiality levels include changes in circumstance, such as a major disposition of the entity's business.

Choice "4" is incorrect. A circumstance that would require reevaluation of established materiality levels include significant new contractual arrangements that draw attention to a particular aspect of a client's business that is separately disclosed in the financial statements.

Topic H

QUESTION 1

Choice "4" is correct.

Analytical procedures do not ordinarily provide information about the internal auditor.

Choices "1", "2", and "3" are incorrect. Discussions with management personnel, reviews of the internal auditor's work, and previous experience could all provide information relevant to the evaluation of competence and objectivity.

QUESTION 2

Choice "2" is correct.

An auditor may not divide responsibility with an auditor's specialist. If the auditor decides to express a modified opinion as a result of the work performed by the specialist, then the auditor may refer to the specialist and should indicate that the reference to the specialist does not reduce the auditor's responsibility for the audit opinion.

Choice "1" is incorrect. When an auditor decides to use the work of an auditor's specialist as audit evidence, the auditor should evaluate the competence, capabilities, and objectivity of the specialist. Evaluation of this may be acquired by obtaining knowledge of the specialist's qualifications.

Choice "3" is incorrect. When an auditor decides to use the work of an auditor's specialist as audit evidence, the auditor should evaluate the competence, capabilities, and objectivity of the specialist. Evaluation of this may be acquired by inquiring of the entity and the auditor's specialist about any known interests that the entity has with the auditor's external specialist that may affect that specialist's objectivity.

Choice "4" is incorrect. The external auditor should verify the adequacy of the work of the auditor's specialist. This may include reviewing the working papers of the auditor's specialist.

Topic I

QUESTION 1 MCQ-09074

Choice "3" is correct.

Reviewing confirmations of loans receivable and payable is useful for determining the existence of related party transactions because guarantees are commonly provided by or for related parties.

Choice "1" is incorrect because detection of unreported contingent liabilities is not a procedure that would assist the auditor in identifying related party transactions.

Choice "2" is incorrect because recurring transactions after year-end are a usual business occurrence. Related party transactions would most likely be nonrecurring.

Choice "4" is incorrect because while financial difficulties may be associated with related party transactions, it is unlikely that analytical procedures would assist the auditor in identifying such transactions.

QUESTION 2 MCQ-09822

Choice "4" is correct.

An illegal payment to a foreign official would most likely raise a question concerning possible noncompliance with laws and regulations.

Choice "1" is incorrect. Failure to retire a piece of obsolete equipment is not likely to raise a question about noncompliance with laws and regulations.

Choice "2" is incorrect. Failure to correct material internal control weaknesses may represent a conscious decision by management to accept the degree of risk because of cost or other considerations.

Choice "3" is incorrect. Receipt of governmental financial assistance most likely would not cause the auditor to raise a question about possible noncompliance with laws and regulations.

Topic J

QUESTION 1 MCQ-08121

Choice "3" is correct.

The auditor's overall responsibility is to obtain sufficient competent audit evidence to provide reasonable assurance that fair value measurements and disclosures are in conformity with GAAP.

Choice "1" is incorrect because while it is true that the auditor should determine whether management has the intent and ability to carry out courses of action that may affect fair values, this is just one part of evaluating fair value measurements and not the best description of the auditor's overall responsibility.

Choice "2" is incorrect because while it is true that the auditor should assess the risk of material misstatement of fair value measurements, this is done to determine the nature, timing, and extent of audit procedures. It is not the best representation of the auditor's overall responsibility.

Choice "4" is incorrect because *management* (and not the auditor) should make fair value measurements and disclosures in accordance with GAAP and should identify and support any significant assumptions used.

Auditing II

QUESTION 2

Choice "2" is correct.

The auditor should verify that all material estimates required by GAAP have been developed.

Choice "1" is incorrect. The auditor is responsible for auditing estimated amounts included in the financial statements, to determine that they are reasonable and properly presented and disclosed.

Choice "3" is incorrect. The auditor should focus on assumptions that are *subjective* (not objective), *sensitive* (not insensitive) to variation, and *deviate* from historical patterns, as these types of assumptions are more likely to result in unreasonable estimates.

Choice "4" is incorrect. Management (and not the auditor) bears responsibility for making reasonable estimates and including them in the financial statements.

Topic A

QUESTION 1

Choice "4" is correct.

A misstatement may not be an isolated occurrence. Identification of a misstatement that resulted from an inappropriate valuation method that has been widely applied by the entity may indicate that additional misstatements exist.

Choice "1" is incorrect. Management's enforcement of integrity and ethical values implies a stronger control environment, which may result in fewer misstatements, especially due to fraud.

Choice "2" is incorrect. The inclusion of several large, outstanding checks in the monthly bank reconciliation may be a normal occurrence and is not necessarily indicative of material misstatement.

Choice "3" is incorrect. Sometimes companies will outsource the internal audit function to another CPA firm. The CPA firm hired will perform the internal audit procedures and then report the results to management. Evidence of an internal audit function (outsourced or not) typically results in a reduction of misstatements.

Topic B

QUESTION 1

Choice "4" is correct.

By using statistical sampling, the auditor can quantify sampling risk to assist in limiting it to a level considered acceptable.

Choice "1" is incorrect because statistical sampling does not provide any advantage with respect to converting the test into a dual-purpose test.

Choice "2" is incorrect because statistical sampling still requires judgment to determine sample sizes. The tolerable rate of deviation, the likely rate of deviation, and the allowable risk of assessing control risk too low are all determined by the auditor's professional judgment.

Choice "3" is incorrect because statistical sampling does not afford greater assurance than a nonstatistical sample of the same size. It only provides the auditor with a better measure of the sufficiency of the evidence found, and helps to evaluate the results found.

QUESTION 2

Choice "2" is correct.

Attribute sampling is primarily used to test controls, such as proper approval of purchase orders.

Choice "1" is incorrect. Variables sampling is typically used in substantive testing, such as confirming accounts receivable balances.

Choice "3" is incorrect. Variables sampling is typically used in substantive testing, such as verifying proper extensions and footings of invoices.

Choice "4" is incorrect. Variables sampling is typically used in substantive testing, such as testing that cash receipts are appropriately credited to customer accounts.

Auditing III

QUESTION 3

Choice "1" is correct.

The risk of incorrect rejection and the risk of assessing control risk too high relate to the efficiency of the audit. These two errors generally result in an auditor performing unnecessary additional procedures.

Choice "2" is incorrect because the application of additional procedures will ordinarily still lead the auditor to the appropriate conclusion.

Choice "3" is incorrect because these risks do not relate directly to selection of the items included in the sample.

Choice "4" is incorrect because these risks do not relate directly to quality controls.

QUESTION 4

Choice "4" is correct.

All else being equal, the sample size required to achieve the auditor's objective increases as the auditor's assessment of tolerable misstatement for the balance or class decreases.

Choice "1" is incorrect because a greater reliance on internal control will lead to a smaller sample size in a substantive test of details.

Choice "2" is incorrect because greater reliance upon analytical procedures will reduce the need for reliance on substantive tests of details, which in turn will result in a smaller sample size.

Choice "3" is incorrect because as fewer errors are expected, a smaller sample size would be used.

QUESTION 5

Choice "4" is correct.

The auditor will reduce reliance on a control if the upper deviation rate exceeds the tolerable rate. The upper deviation rate consists of the sample deviation rate plus an allowance for sampling risk. Therefore, if the sample deviation rate plus the allowance for sampling risk exceeds the tolerable rate, that is equivalent to the upper deviation rate exceeding the tolerable rate.

Choice "1" is incorrect because if the sample deviation rate plus the allowance for sampling risk equals the tolerable rate, the auditor may still place the planned amount of reliance on the control.

Choice "2" is incorrect because whether the actual sample deviation rate is less than the expected deviation rate is irrelevant for making decisions about planned reliance levels.

Choice "3" is incorrect because if the tolerable rate less the allowance for sampling risk exceeds the sample rate of deviation, then the upper deviation rate is less than the tolerable rate. This situation supports the planned reliance, and no reduction in planned reliance would be necessary.

Topic C

QUESTION 1

Choice "3" is correct.

Confirmation of accounts receivable is a substantive test, not a test of controls.

Choice "1" is incorrect. Records documenting the usage of computer programs may indicate whether access is appropriately controlled.

Choice "2" is incorrect. Examination of canceled supporting documents helps the auditor determine whether this control is being appropriately applied.

Choice "4" is incorrect. Signatures on authorization forms help the auditor determine whether or not required authorizations are received.

Topic D

QUESTION 1

Choice "2" is correct.

Interest costs related to construction of a fixed asset by a company may be capitalized to the asset being constructed. This bests explains the reason for the increase in debt outstanding (acquisition of new debt) and interest expense staying approximately the same (the additional interest expense from the construction loan is being capitalized to the construction of the building).

Choice "1" is incorrect. If the company paid off a significant portion of debt, then the overall debt outstanding probably would decrease, not increase.

Choice "3" is incorrect. The company only invests in debt that has a fixed interest rate; therefore, a decrease in the Federal Reserve rate probably would not affect their interest expense.

Choice "4" is incorrect. Acquiring a new loan at midyear would increase the debt outstanding, but would not explain why interest expense stayed approximately the same.

QUESTION 2

Choice "4" is correct.

Accounts receivable turnover is calculated as net sales divided by average receivables. Allowing a grace period for customer payments is likely to increase the average receivable balance, thus decreasing accounts receivable turnover.

Choice "1" is incorrect. Accounts receivable turnover is calculated as net sales divided by average receivables. Early payment incentives are likely to reduce average receivables, thus increasing accounts receivable turnover.

Choice "2" is incorrect. Accounts receivable turnover is calculated as net sales divided by average receivables. If credit policy is tightened, there are less likely to be delinquent customers and the average receivable balance should decline, thus increasing accounts receivable turnover.

Choice "3" is incorrect. Accounts receivable turnover is calculated as net sales divided by average receivables. Implementation of more aggressive collection policies will tend to result in a decrease in average receivables, thus increasing accounts receivable turnover.

Auditing III

Topic E

QUESTION 1   MCQ-08112

Choice "3" is correct.

Expenses for the current year are not complete if an expense occurring in one year is not recorded until the following year.

Choice "1" is incorrect. Accuracy relates to recording at an appropriate amount.

Choice "2" is incorrect. Classification relates to recording in the proper accounts.

Choice "4" is incorrect. Occurrence relates to recording only events that have occurred during the given year.

QUESTION 2   MCQ-09839

Choice "4" is correct.

Examining open vouchers as part of the search for *unrecorded liabilities* is a substantive procedure.

Choice "1" is incorrect. Verifying that the vouchers payable package is properly approved is a test of controls, not a substantive procedure.

Choice "2" is incorrect. Observation of the payroll distribution on an unannounced basis is a test of controls, which involves verifying that all personnel being paid are actually employed by the company.

Choice "3" is incorrect. Observing the preparation of the accounts receivable aging schedule is a test of controls, not a substantive procedure.

Topic F

QUESTION 1   MCQ-09833

Choice "3" is correct.

An acceptable alternative procedure is to examine the applicable sales order, shipping document, and subsequent cash receipts.

Choice "1" is incorrect. Generally, an auditor would not visit the client's customer and review documents in their possession. An appropriate alternative procedure is to review the specific subsequent cash receipts, shipping documentation, and invoice to verify the existence of the receivable.

Choice "2" is incorrect. Obtaining an aging of accounts receivable and tracing it to the general ledger control account would provide evidence about the completeness, not existence, assertion.

Choice "4" is incorrect. Examining subsequent cash disbursements and related receiving reports would be an appropriate alternative procedure when testing accounts payable for completeness when the accounts payable confirmations are not received.

QUESTION 2

Choice "2" is correct.

Lapping best describes the employee fraud scheme. Lapping occurs when current receipts of cash are withheld and not recorded. Subsequent receipts are applied to prior accounts.

Choice "1" is incorrect. This scheme does not describe kiting. Kiting occurs when a check drawn on one bank is deposited in another bank and no record is made of the disbursement.

Choice "3" is incorrect. This scheme most likely is not identity theft. Identity theft occurs when someone uses a person's personal information for financial gain (e.g., makes purchases).

Choice "4" is incorrect. Fraudulent financial reporting involves intentional misstatements or omissions of amounts designed to deceive financial statement users. It does not appear that the employee is trying to deceive financial statement users. Lapping is more likely to be categorized as a misappropriation of assets, which involves theft of an entity's financial assets.

Topic G

QUESTION 1

Choice "1" is correct.

The daily sales summary will include all "billed" sales for a particular day. Comparing this summary to the postings to the accounts receivable ledger will provide evidence regarding whether billed sales are correctly posted.

Choice "2" is incorrect. Comparing sales invoices to shipping documents provides evidence that invoiced sales have been shipped.

Choice "3" is incorrect. Reconciling the accounts receivable ledger to the control account will not provide assurance that all billed sales were posted. The receivable ledger and the control account may both have omitted the sales.

Choice "4" is incorrect. Comparing shipments with sales invoices provides evidence regarding whether all shipments have been invoiced, not whether billed sales are correctly posted to accounts receivable.

QUESTION 2

Choice "2" is correct.

Tracing shipments to sales invoices would provide evidence that shipments to customers were properly invoiced.

Choice "1" is incorrect. Tracing from invoices to shipping documents would provide evidence that sales billed to customers were actually shipped.

Choice "3" is incorrect. Tracing from invoices to shipping documents would provide evidence that shipments to customers were invoiced, but does not necessarily indicate that invoices were recorded as sales.

Choice "4" is incorrect. The auditor would compare the signed purchase order to shipping documents to determine if all goods ordered by the customer were shipped.

Auditing III

QUESTION 3 MCQ-09849

Choice "4" is correct.

An auditor most likely would compare subsequent bank statements (specifically looking for cash payments made after the balance sheet date) with the accounts payable listing in searching for unrecorded payables. The auditor is looking for payables that should have been recorded as of the balance sheet date, but were not.

Choice "1" is incorrect. Obtaining a sample of vendor statements and recalculating the invoice amount would provide evidence about the accuracy of the invoice amount.

Choice "2" is incorrect. Obtaining the accounts payable listing and agreeing to subsequent cash payments provides evidence about existence, not completeness.

Choice "3" is incorrect. Comparing cash disbursements made before year-end with vendor invoices would not help the auditor search for unrecorded payables. Cash payments made before year-end for vendor invoices should result in the payable being eliminated.

QUESTION 4 MCQ-08325

Choice "4" is correct.

Companies sometimes erroneously expense property and equipment acquisitions rather than capitalizing them as assets. An analysis of repair and maintenance accounts may reveal such errors.

Choice "1" is incorrect because while auditors will want to determine that noncapitalizable expenses for repairs and maintenance have been recorded in the proper period, analyzing only the recorded entries is an incomplete test. The auditor would also need to look at payments that were not recorded in the current period, in case they should have been.

Choice "2" is incorrect because expenditures for property and equipment would not be included in repair and maintenance accounts.

Choice "3" is incorrect because analyzing items already included in the repair and maintenance account would not identify noncapitalizable expenditures that have been erroneously capitalized.

QUESTION 5 MCQ-08124

Choice "1" is correct.

Payroll is generally determined in a fairly objective manner and is easily tested by the auditor. As such, specific representations with respect to payroll are not often requested.

Choice "2" is incorrect. Segregation of duties is a key control within the payroll cycle. The auditor should verify that the functions of authorization, record keeping, and custody are appropriately segregated.

Choice "3" is incorrect. Year-end payroll accruals are fairly easy to recalculate, and such recalculation provides good audit evidence supporting financial statement amounts.

Choice "4" is incorrect. Payroll is fairly predictable and thus is often compared with standards and budgets.

QUESTION 6   MCQ-08868

Choice "3" is correct.

The legality of a dividend depends in part on whether it has been properly authorized. Thus, the auditor must determine that proper authorization exists, as both cash and stock dividends affect retained earnings.

Choice "1" is incorrect because only a memo entry is required for a stock split.

Choice "2" is incorrect because the write-down of an account receivable will not, in general, be recorded in retained earnings.

Choice "4" is incorrect because gains from the disposition of treasury shares are recorded in paid-in capital accounts.

Topic H

QUESTION 1   MCQ-09830

Choice "3" is correct.

During a tour of the manufacturing plant or production facility, the auditor should be alert for items that appear to be old, obsolete, or defective.

Choice "1" is incorrect. Testing the mathematical accuracy of the inventory report would determine that the numerical amounts are computed correctly, but would not provide evidence about whether the inventory is slow-moving, defective, or obsolete after manufacture.

Choice "2" is incorrect. Inquiry of management about pledged or assigned inventory would provide evidence about the rights and obligation of the inventory, but would not inform the auditor about slow-moving, defective, or obsolete inventory.

Choice "4" is incorrect. Testing the computation of standard overhead rates relates to the accumulation of costs during the manufacturing process, and not to whether the inventory is slow-moving, defective, or obsolete after manufacture.

QUESTION 2   MCQ-08905

Choice "1" is correct.

A custodial statement provides valid and relevant external evidence regarding the existence of securities.

Choice "2" is incorrect. The client's securities ledger is internal evidence, and as such it is not as valid as a custodial statement.

Choice "3" is incorrect. Broker's advices regarding purchases and sales provide valid external evidence about transactions occurring during the year, but a custodial statement provides more direct evidence about the existence of securities as of the year-end date.

Choice "4" is incorrect. A year-end listing of market prices is not relevant to the existence of marketable securities, although it would provide evidence about the valuation of such securities.

Auditing III

Topic I

QUESTION 1 MCQ-09851

Choice "2" is correct.

The attorney's refusal to respond when the attorney has given substantial attention to the matter would represent a scope limitation. Depending on materiality, this may result in a qualified opinion or disclaimer of opinion.

Choice "1" is incorrect. A refusal to permit inquiry will generally result in a disclaimer of opinion or withdrawal from the audit.

Choice "3" is incorrect. If the auditor is satisfied that financial statement disclosure is adequate, no modification to the opinion would be required.

Choice "4" is incorrect. Lawyers may limit their replies to matters to which they have given substantial attention.

QUESTION 2 MCQ-09047

Choice "3" is correct.

The primary purpose of an external inquiry of the client's attorney is to obtain corroboration of information provided by management regarding litigation, claims, and assessments.

Choices "1" and "2" are incorrect. The auditor's external inquiry of the client's attorney provides information about litigation, claims, and assessments, such as the nature of the matter, the progress of the case, the degree of likelihood of an unfavorable outcome, and an estimate of potential loss. It does not provide information about the client's controls with respect to recognizing the financial statement impact of such matters.

Choice "4" is incorrect. The client's attorney provides information such as the nature of the matter, the progress of the case, the degree of likelihood of an unfavorable outcome, and an estimate of potential loss, but does not comment or provide advice regarding the fair presentation of such matters in the financial statements.

Topic J

QUESTION 1

Choice "3" is correct.

Calibro should issue an unmodified opinion and add a separate section to the auditor's report with the heading "Substantial Doubt About the Company's Ability to Continue as a Going Concern" describing the situation.

Choice "1" is incorrect. In situations in which there is substantial doubt about the entity's ability to continue as a going concern, the auditor generally should add a separate section to the auditor's report with the heading "Substantial Doubt About the Company's Ability to Continue as a Going Concern" (not other-matter paragraph) to the unmodified opinion.

Choice "2" is incorrect. In situations in which there is substantial doubt about the entity's ability to continue as a going concern, the auditor generally should add a separate section to the auditor's report with the heading "Substantial Doubt About the Company's Ability to Continue as a Going Concern" with an unmodified opinion. There is no need to qualify the opinion.

Choice "4" is incorrect. In situations in which there is substantial doubt about the entity's ability to continue as a going concern, the auditor generally should add a separate section to the auditor's report with the heading "Substantial Doubt About the Company's Ability to Continue as a Going Concern" with an unmodified opinion. As long as the auditor adds the appropriate language to the auditor's report, there would be no need to withdraw from the engagement.

QUESTION 2

Choice "4" is correct.

Management's ability to negotiate reductions of required dividends will decrease required cash outflows, and thereby increase the likelihood that the entity will be able to continue as a going concern.

Choices "1", "2", and "3" are incorrect because they involve spending cash, rather than reducing outflows of cash.

Topic K

QUESTION 1

Choice "3" is correct.

Significant deficiencies in the design or operation of internal control are control weaknesses that are important enough to merit attention by those charged with governance.

Choice "1" is incorrect because information that significantly contradicts the auditor's going concern assumption is not considered a significant deficiency.

Choice "2" is incorrect because fraud perpetrated by high-level managers should be reported to the audit committee (i.e. those charged with governance). However, it does not necessarily represent a significant deficiency in internal control.

Choice "4" is incorrect because fraud should be reported to an appropriate level of management, and sometimes to the audit committee (i.e. those charged with governance). However, it does not necessarily represent a significant deficiency in internal control.

Auditing III

Topic L

QUESTION 1

Choice "2" is correct.

U.S. GAAS require the date of the written representations to be the date of the auditor's report.

Choice "1" is incorrect. According to ISAs, not U.S. GAAS, the management representation letter should be dated as near as possible to, but not after, the date of the auditor's report.

Choice "3" is incorrect. U.S. GAAS require the date of the written representations to be the date of the auditor's report. The auditor will complete the audit after the date of the financial statements.

Choice "4" is incorrect. U.S. GAAS require the date of the written representations to be the date of the auditor's report. The auditor will complete the audit after the date of the financial statements.

Topic M

QUESTION 1

Choice "3" is correct.

The acquisition provided evidence of a condition which came into existence after year-end [a "Type 2" (nonrecognized) subsequent event] and therefore the proper accounting approach would be note disclosure rather than adjustment.

Choice "1" is incorrect because adjustments are only appropriate for subsequent events which provide evidence that the condition was in existence at year-end ["Type 1" (recognized) events].

Choice "2" is incorrect because the auditor does not issue financial statements for the client.

Choice "4" is incorrect because the opinion paragraph of the report need not be modified. The auditor might choose to add an explanatory paragraph emphasizing the matter, but is not required to do so.

QUESTION 2

Choice "3" is correct.

The auditor has an active responsibility to investigate subsequent events between the date of the financial statements and the date of the auditor's report, and must also consider the effect of any events occurring after the date of the auditor's report that come to his/her attention.

Choice "1" is incorrect. The auditor has no active responsibility to investigate events occurring after the date of the auditor's report, unless such events come to his or her attention.

Choice "2" is incorrect. The auditor has an active responsibility to investigate the 2/1/Year 2 event, but also may have some level of responsibility with respect to the 3/1/Year 2 event. Despite the fact that it occurred after the date of the auditor's report, if the event comes to the auditor's attention, it cannot be ignored.

Choice "4" is incorrect. The auditor has an active responsibility to investigate subsequent events between the date of the financial statements and the date of the auditor's report, and must also consider the effect of any events occurring after the date of the auditor's report that come to his/her attention.

Topic N

QUESTION 1   MCQ-09775

Choice "4" is correct.

The question addresses subsequent discovery of facts that may have existed at the balance sheet date that the auditor should have known about during the audit. Discovery of information related to a material *unrecorded* expense that occurred during the year under audit most likely would result in the auditor making further inquiries about the previously issued financial statements.

Choice "1" is incorrect. The issuance of a bond for a material amount is an example of a subsequent event occurring after the date of the auditor's report that the auditor has no obligation to investigate. The issuance of the bond does not provide additional information about the previously issued financial statements, nor did the issuance exist at the date of the audit report.

Choice "2" is incorrect. The loss of a plant is an example of a subsequent event occurring after the date of the auditor's report that the auditor has no obligation to investigate. The loss of the plant does not provide additional information about the previously issued financial statements, nor did the loss of the plant exist at the date of the audit report.

Choice "3" is incorrect. The purchase of a business is an example of a subsequent event occurring after the date of the auditor's report that the auditor has no obligation to investigate. The purchase of the business does not provide additional information about the previously issued financial statements audit. In addition, the purchase of the business occurred after the date of the auditor's report.

Topic O

QUESTION 1   MCQ-14941

Choice "2" is correct.

Audit data analytics alone cannot provide absolute assurance over every account balance because inherent risks still exist.

Choice "1" is incorrect. Audit data analytics will allow the auditor to enhance fraud detection through advanced analytical procedures.

Choice "3" is incorrect. Audit data analytics will allow the auditor to better understand the client and its operations.

Choice "4" is incorrect. Audit data analytics will allow the auditor to better communicate findings with data visualizations.

Auditing III

QUESTION 2 MCQ-14942

Choice "3" is correct.

Predictive analytics provide expected or predicted outcomes based on historical data. This analytic is using past transactions to create a model that would predict whether current transactions should have been approved or rejected.

Choice "1" is incorrect because descriptive analytics describe what happened within the data. This analytic is predicting an outcome as opposed to describing it.

Choice "2" is incorrect because prescriptive analytics prescribe or recommend actions to be taken based on advanced analytics to reach a desired goal. This analytic is only predicting an outcome as opposed to prescribing an action.

Choice "4" is incorrect because diagnostic analytics explain why something happened. This analytic is predicting an outcome as opposed to explaining the drivers or underlying causes of the value of the output.

Topic A

QUESTION 1

Choice "4" is correct.

Determining the type of work to be performed on the components is not required when the group auditor decides to make reference to the component auditor. The group auditor should determine the type of work to be performed on the financial information of the components when assuming responsibility for the work of the component auditor.

Choice "1" is incorrect. The group auditor should be satisfied with the independence of the component auditor even when the group auditor references the component auditor in the report.

Choice "2" is incorrect. One of the requirements to reference the component auditor in the group auditor's report is that the component auditor's report is not restricted.

Choice "3" is incorrect. The group auditor should be satisfied with the competence of the component auditor even when the group auditor references the component auditor in the report.

QUESTION 2

Choice "3" is correct.

Financial statements that are prepared in accordance with a special purpose framework require the use of an emphasis-of-matter paragraph in the auditor's report.

Choice "1" is incorrect. An other-matter paragraph is required when there is an alert in the audit report that restricts the use of the audit report.

Choice "2" is incorrect. A separate section of the auditor's report with the heading "Other Information" is required when prior to the audit report date, the auditor identifies a material inconsistency in other information that is included in the document containing audited financial statements that management refuses to revise. A description of the material misstatement should be included.

Choice "4" is incorrect. A separate section of the auditor's report with the heading "Supplementary Information" is required when the auditor chooses to report on supplementary information presented with the financial statements in the auditor's report, rather than in a separate report.

QUESTION 3

Choice "4" is correct.

Inadequate disclosure of a material item or event results in a qualified or adverse opinion.

Choice "1" is incorrect. Although the general rule in adequately disclosed going concern cases is to add an emphasis-of-matter paragraph to an unmodified opinion, the auditor is not prohibited from choosing to disclaim an opinion due to a going concern uncertainty

Choice "2" is incorrect. Management's refusal to permit inquiry of the attorneys generally will result in a disclaimer of opinion or withdrawal from the audit.

Choice "3" is incorrect. When the auditor is not independent but is required by law or regulation to report on the financial statements, the auditor should disclaim an opinion and should specifically state that the auditor is not independent.

Auditing IV

QUESTION 4

Choice "2" is correct.

Randall may revise the prior opinion, but must include an emphasis-of-matter or other-matter paragraph describing the situation and including the date and type of the previous opinion, the reason for the previous opinion, the changes that have occurred, and a statement that the new opinion differs from the old.

Choice "1" is incorrect. Randall may revise the prior opinion if the situation warrants such revision.

Choice "3" is incorrect. Randall may revise the prior opinion if the situation warrants such revision, and is not prohibited from issuing a report on the comparative financial statements.

Choice "4" is incorrect. Randall may revise the prior opinion, but must include an emphasis-of-matter or other-matter paragraph describing the situation and including the date and type of the previous opinion, the reason for the previous opinion, the changes that have occurred, and a statement that the new opinion differs from the old.

Topic B

QUESTION 1

Choice "2" is correct.

Entity-level controls are high-level controls that have a pervasive effect on the company's internal control. Entity-level controls include controls related to the period-end financial reporting process, such as management's procedures used to initiate, authorize, and record journal entries into the general ledger.

Choice "1" is incorrect. An entity-level control exists at the client and is independent of the audit. Therefore, the auditor's adherence to a system of quality control would not be considered an entity-level control.

Choice "3" is incorrect. Entity-level controls are high-level controls that have a pervasive effect on the company's internal control. Examples of entity-level controls include controls related to control environment, monitoring the results of operations, centralized processing, period-end financial reporting process and the company's risk assessment process. Preparation of an aging schedule relates to the revenue cycle and is a control at the assertion level.

Choice "4" is incorrect. Entity-level controls are high-level controls that that have a pervasive effect on the company's internal control. Creating a duplicate listing of checks after receipt of a customer check by mail is a control related to the revenue cycle and is a control at the assertion level.

Topic C

QUESTION 1

Choice "1" is correct.

The auditor of a nonissuer may be engaged to express an opinion on the design and/or operating effectiveness of the entity's internal control. This is considered an audit engagement. Note that an audit of internal control should be integrated with an audit of the financial statements.

Choice "2" is incorrect. The auditor of a nonissuer may not express an opinion as a result of a financial statement audit, but may report on significant deficiencies or material weaknesses noted during the audit. The report on control deficiencies noted should specifically state that the auditor is not expressing an opinion on the effectiveness of internal control.

Choice "3" is incorrect. A financial statement audit includes consideration of internal control as a basis for designing audit procedures, not as a basis for expressing an opinion. An auditor of a nonissuer may report on significant deficiencies or material weaknesses noted during the audit, but is prohibited from expressing an opinion based solely on the audit.

Choice "4" is incorrect. While an auditor of a nonissuer is required to communicate significant deficiencies or material weaknesses to management and those charged with governance, this type of report does not provide an opinion on the operating effectiveness of the entity's internal control.

QUESTION 2

Choice "3" is correct.

A material weakness in internal control, which is a control deficiency, or a combination of control deficiencies in internal control such that there is a reasonable possibility that a material misstatement of the entity's financial statements will not be prevented, or detected and corrected on a timely basis, requires the auditor to issue an adverse opinion.

Choice "1" is incorrect. A material weakness would result in an adverse, not unmodified, opinion.

Choice "2" is incorrect. A material weakness would result in an adverse, not qualified, opinion.

Choice "4" is incorrect. A disclaimer of opinion is rendered when there is a scope limitation.

Auditing IV

Topic D

QUESTION 1

Choice "2" is correct.

An engagement for agreed-upon procedures provides no assurance, which means that a disclaimer of opinion is rendered on the subject matter. Specifically, the report should state that "We do not express an opinion," which is a disclaimer of opinion.

Choice "1" is incorrect. The procedures do not need to be comparable to those performed in a compilation. The procedures that the practitioner and specified parties agree upon may be as limited or as extensive as the specified parties desire.

Choice "3" is incorrect. The report includes a listing of procedures performed and the related findings, but does not provide any assurance on these items.

Choice "4" is incorrect. The sufficiency of procedures is solely the responsibility of the client, not the practitioner.

QUESTION 2

Choice "4" is correct.

Financial forecasts are considered prospective financial statements, and they are appropriate for general use.

Choice "1" is incorrect because financial projections are only appropriate for the party responsible for preparing them or for third parties with whom the responsible party is negotiating directly.

Choices "2" and "3" are incorrect because partial presentations and pro forma financial statements are not considered prospective financial statements.

Topic E

QUESTION 1

Choice "3" is correct.

Statements on Standards for Accounting and Review Services do not apply to preparing a working trial balance or to preparing standard monthly journal entries. Accordingly, no compilation or review report needs to be issued when these services are provided.

Choices "1", "2", and "4" are incorrect, based on the above explanation.

QUESTION 2   MCQ-09051

Choice "1" is correct.

Before issuing a compilation report, an accountant should read the compiled financial statements and consider whether they are appropriate in form and free from obvious material errors.

Choice "2" is incorrect. Inquiry and analytical review procedures are performed as part of a review engagement, not as part of a compilation engagement.

Choice "3" is incorrect. A representation letter is obtained in audit and review engagements, but is not required for compilation engagements.

Choice "4" is incorrect. Accounts receivable confirmations would be sent during an audit, but not during a compilation engagement.

QUESTION 3   MCQ-09789

Choice "3" is correct.

A change in client requirements represents an acceptable reason for a change in engagement.

Choice "1" is incorrect. Generally, refusal to provide a signed representation letter is considered an unacceptable reason for the change. In addition, the auditor would not be able to issue a review report without a representation letter.

Choice "2" is incorrect. The client's refusal to allow correspondence with legal counsel is not an acceptable reason for the change.

Choice "4" is incorrect. The client's attempt to create deceptive financial statements is not an acceptable reason for the change.

QUESTION 4   MCQ-09788

Choice "2" is correct.

The predecessor accountant is not required to obtain a letter of representation from management before reissuing a compilation report. This procedure is required when an audit, not compilation, report is reissued.

Choice "1" is incorrect. The predecessor accountant is required to read the financial statements and the report of the current period before reissuing a compilation report.

Choice "3" is incorrect. The predecessor accountant is required to compare the prior period financial statements with those issued previously and currently before reissuing a compilation report.

Choice "4" is incorrect. The predecessor accountant is required to obtain a letter from the successor accountants before reissuing a compilation report.

     Auditing Final Review

Auditing IV

Topic F

QUESTION 1 MCQ-14950

Choice "3" is correct.

A review report states that a review includes primarily applying analytical procedures to management's financial data and making inquiries of company management.

Choice "1" is incorrect because the review report does not state or express an opinion on the financial statements. The report states that the accountant does not express an opinion because the procedures are substantially less in scope than an audit.

Choice "2" is incorrect because an audit report, not a review report, refers to "examining on a test basis." A compilation report, not a review report, refers to "information that is the representation of management."

Choice "4" is incorrect because although a review does not contemplate obtaining corroborating evidential matter or applying certain other procedures ordinarily performed during an audit, this is not stated in the report. The review report simply states that a review is substantially less in scope than an audit.

Topic G

QUESTION 1 MCQ-14953

Choice "4" is correct.

The auditor should read the letter to the shareholders (considered other information) and verify the information is materially consistent with the information presented in the audited financial statements.

Choice "1" is incorrect. The audited financial statements may be contained in a document that contains additional financial information that is outside the audited financial statements. In addition, the auditor's opinion is on the basic financial statements, not the entire document that the financial statements may accompany.

Choice "2" is incorrect. The auditor is required to reference the other information in the auditor's report, but such reference should be made in a separate section of the auditor's report with the heading "Other Information" rather than in an emphasis-of-matter paragraph.

Choice "3" is incorrect. The auditor should inquire of management regarding the purpose of the supplementary information and the criteria used to prepare the information when engaged to report on the supplementary information. The auditor is not engaged to examine this information, so the auditor is not required to perform those inquiries.

QUESTION 2 MCQ-09044

Choice "4" is correct.

With respect to the supplementary information, Jorge should perform limited procedures in order to determine whether required supplementary information is included and is presented in conformity with GAAP requirements.

Choice "1" is incorrect. Jorge may accept this engagement, but must perform limited procedures in order to determine whether required supplementary information is included and is presented in conformity with GAAP requirements.

Choice "2" is incorrect. Jorge must perform limited procedures in order to determine whether required supplementary information is included and is presented in conformity with GAAP requirements.

Choice "3" is incorrect. Jorge may accept this engagement and should perform limited procedures with respect to the required supplementary information. There is no requirement that an attest engagement be performed.

QUESTION 3   MCQ-09052

Choice "3" is correct.

The appropriate form of audit report is dependent upon the expected distribution of the financial statements. If distribution is to occur outside the United States only, the auditor may use either the other country's audit report, the report set out in the ISAs, or a U.S. form with reference to the other country's standards. If there is to be distribution within the U.S., a U.S. form report with an emphasis-of-matter paragraph is required.

Choice "1" is incorrect. The other country's auditing standards do not determine the appropriate form of audit report for financial statements prepared in accordance with a financial reporting framework generally accepted in another country.

Choice "2" is incorrect. The geographic location of the company does not determine the appropriate form of audit report for financial statements prepared in accordance with a financial reporting framework generally accepted in another country.

Choice "4" is incorrect. Countries generally do not have reciprocity agreements with respect to the appropriate form of audit report.

Topic H

QUESTION 1   MCQ-08825

Choice "2" is correct.

Audits performed in accordance with government auditing standards require a written communication regarding the auditor's work on internal control. Generally accepted auditing standards only require written communication about internal control when significant deficiencies are noted.

Choice "1" is incorrect. Both GAAS and GAGAS require an opinion on the financial statements taken as a whole.

Choice "3" is incorrect. Neither GAAS nor GAGAS audits require an opinion on internal control over financial reporting.

Choice "4" is incorrect. An opinion on the financial statements taken as a whole *is* required by both GAAS and GAGAS.

QUESTION 2   MCQ-09027

Choice "4" is correct.

The provisions of the Single Audit Act apply to entities that receive and expend federal financial awards equal to or in excess of $750,000.

Choice "1" is incorrect. Pure receipt of federal financial assistance does not mandate application of the provisions of the Single Audit Act to an entity's financial statements. Federal financial assistance must be expended by an entity in an amount equal to or in excess of $750,000 to result in an audit subject to 2 CFR 200 single audit requirements.

Choice "2" is incorrect. Pure receipt of federal financial assistance does not mandate application of the provisions of the Single Audit Act to an entity's financial statements. Federal financial assistance must be expended by an entity in an amount equal to or in excess of $750,000 to result in an audit subject to 2 CFR 200 single audit requirements.

Choice "3" is incorrect. The provisions of the Single Audit Act apply to entities that receive and expend federal financial awards equal to or in excess of $750,000.

Auditing IV

QUESTION 3   MCQ-04636

Choice "2" is correct.

The requirement is to determine the proper scope of a government audit. The Government Accountability Office's Yellow Book suggests that in addition to financial statements, such an audit may include consideration of (1) program results; (2) compliance with laws and regulations; and (3) economy and efficiency.

Choice "1" is incorrect because government audits may involve expression of an opinion on economy and efficiency.

Choice "3" is incorrect because government audits may involve expression of an opinion on program results.

Choice "4" is incorrect because government audits may involve expression of an opinion on compliance.

Topic I

QUESTION 1   MCQ-09779

Choice "2" is correct.

An auditor's report should include a restricted use paragraph and an alert to readers about the preparation of the financial statements in accordance with a special purpose framework when the financial statements are prepared on the contractual basis of accounting.

Choice "1" is incorrect. An auditor's report should include an alert to readers about the preparation of the financial statements in accordance with a special purpose framework when the financial statements are prepared on the cash basis of accounting. There is no requirement that the auditor's report must be restricted for this type of framework.

Choice "3" is incorrect. Financial statements prepared using IFRS do not require a restricted use paragraph in the auditor's report. In addition, IFRS is not considered a special purpose framework.

Choice "4" is incorrect. An auditor's report should include an alert to readers about the preparation of the financial statements in accordance with a special purpose framework when the financial statements are prepared on the tax basis of accounting. There is no requirement that the auditor's report must be restricted for this type of framework.

QUESTION 2   MCQ-09782

Choice "2" is correct.

A report on a client's compliance with a contractual agreement, assuming the report is prepared in connection with a financial statement audit of the complete financial statements should include a restriction as to the use of the report.

Choice "1" is incorrect. A report on financial statements prepared on the tax basis of accounting does not require a restriction as to the use of the report.

Choice "3" is incorrect. Reports on a single financial statement do not require restriction as to the use of the report.

Choice "4" is incorrect. A report on the examination of a financial forecast does not require a restriction on the use of the report.